Recite in the Name
of the Red Rose

Studies in Comparative Religion
Frederick M. Denny, Series Editor

Recite in the Name of the Red Rose

POETIC SACRED MAKING IN TWENTIETH-CENTURY IRAN

Fatemeh Keshavarz

UNIVERSITY OF SOUTH CAROLINA PRESS

© 2006 University of South Carolina

Published by the University of South Carolina Press
Columbia, South Carolina 29208

www.sc.edu/uscpress

Manufactured in the United States of America

15 14 13 12 11 10 09 08 07 06   10 9 8 7 6 5 4 3 2 1

Library of Congress Cataloging-in-Publication Data

Keshavarz, Fatemeh, 1952–
   Recite in the name of the red rose : poetic sacred making in twentieth-century Iran /
Fatemeh Keshavarz.
     p. cm. — (Studies in comparative religion)
   Includes bibliographical references and index.
   ISBN-13: 978-1-57003-622-4 (cloth : alk. paper)
   ISBN-10: 1-57003-622-5 (cloth : alk. paper)
   1. Persian poetry—20th century—History and criticism. 2. Holy, The, in literature.
I. Title. II. Studies in comparative religion (Columbia, S.C.)
   PK6420.H64K47 2006
   891'.5509382—dc22

                                       2005035535

Chapters 1 and 3 quote one stanza from Ahmad Shamlu's poem "The Tablet," translated
by Ahmad Karimi-Hakkak, which originally appeared in *An Anthology of Modern Persian
Poetry* (Boulder, Colo.: Westview Press, 1978). Chapters 3 and 4 quote Forough Far-
rokhzad's poems "The One I Love," "I Pity the Garden," "Union," "The Sun Coming
Up," "In Night's Cold Street," "The Lagoon," "To Ali His Mother One Day Said," "In
an Eternity of Setting Sun," "Mechanical Doll," "Summer's Green Waters," and "Frontier
Walls," translated by Jascha Kessler with Amin Banani, which originally appeared in *Bride
of Acacias: Selected Poems of Forugh Farrokhzad* (New York: Caravan Books, 1982).

For *baba*
My first and best teacher of poetry

Contents

Series Editor's Preface

Since this book series was launched twenty years ago, the academic study of religion has continued to extend, invent, diversify, and enrich its theoretical and methodological approaches and resources. One area of significant innovation has been in the use of literary studies as a central component not only in interpreting and understanding religious consciousness and experience in contemporary life, but indeed in discerning them in the first place.

Fatemeh Keshavarz published her pathbreaking *Reading Mystical Lyric: The Case of Jalāl al-Dīn Rumi* in 1998 in this series. That book did not focus on the iconic Persian Sufi poet so much as on his actual literary creation utilizing contemporary theory and method. The results of her probing and refreshing discourse have inspired a new understanding of that great Muslim poet and his craft; his verse is the world's most widely read in English translation.

With *Recite in the Name of the Red Rose: Poetic Sacred Making in Twentieth-Century Iran,* Fatemeh Keshavarz has applied literary studies to discerning and understanding new ways in which modern Iranian poets have endeavored to address what it means to be human. She calls this process "sacred making," and it extends well beyond what we are accustomed to expect in the too often reified and bifocal notions of religion and secularity opposing each other in Iranian culture during the past century. To signify cultural and artistic expressions as either religious or secular is to miss the actually widely shared, "expanding, merging, and mingling" worlds of poetic creativity and sacred making in Iran in the modern era. If modern Iranian poetry is read from the perspective of an imagined traditional Islamic or Persian literary correctness, it may be dismissed by many as secular, erotically transgressive, godless, and heretical. The author shows that sacred making is not a new development in the history of Iranian poetry, but that bold innovation and invention have been central to the great steps that the poetic craft has made throughout its history in discerning, defining, affirming, and celebrating nature and the human condition.

A Note on Translation, Transliteration, and Dates

I have used a slightly modified version of the Library of Congress transliteration system throughout the book. The minor modifications include omitting the dot from under the letters *s* and *z*. For dates, I have used the Christian calendar alone in the body of the book to avoid cluttering a text that contains Persian terms. However, in the notes I provide the Christian as well as the Persian/Islamic solar calendar publication dates for the sources. All translations in this volume are mine except for the brief quote from the poem *Tablet* by Ahmad Shamlu in chapter 1 and several of the excerpts from the poetry of Forugh Farrokhzad appearing in chapters 3 and 4. As footnotes in these instances indicate, I have benefited from Karimi-Hakkak's translation of *Tablet* and Amin Banani / Jascha Kessler's renderings of Farrokhzad's poetry, which I find to be of excellent quality.

*Recite in the Name
of the Red Rose*

Prologue

"So Shone the Mountain That God
Was Manifest"—Poetic Reflections of the Sacred

This is a study of the literary evolution, diversity, and resilience of the concept of the sacred in its poetic environment. The poetry is from twentieth-century Iran. There are several reasons for choosing the twentieth century. First, the era has not been recognized for its outstanding contribution to Persian poetry, which is usually valued for its premodern achievements. Second, the period is associated with the flowering of Iranian modernity, which is thought to be incompatible with a healthy and thriving sacred. A case is put forth here for revising both these notions.

Various literary genres may provide the opportunity to examine the ways in which the sacred is perceived and/or expressed. While one may argue that poetry is only one of these genres, the focus of the present study on poetry is a deliberate response to specific conditions. The English speaking reader, who has little access to the complex and boldly expressive poetry from twentieth-century Iran, may assume that the inquisitive iconoclastic tendencies in Persian poetry came to an end with Omar Khayyám or Jalāl ad-Dīn Rūmī. In the rare instances that samples of modern Persian poetry are translated and/or discussed, they are often parts of exclusively literary debates rather than interdisciplinary discussions. As a result, this poetry is absent from attempts to bring Near Eastern / Islamic literatures into significant global debates on the humanities.

I have specifically methodological arguments for the choice of poetry here. Its concise form allows examination of numerous examples in a single chapter. At the same time, in freeing itself of old traditions, poetry is a great ally to hermeneutics because it has a strong tendency to create and appreciate new ways of acting and speaking. While not denying the significance of other genres, I foreground the special affinity between poetic creativity on the one hand and the act of "sacred making" on the other. I return to this point in the epilogue.

Rigidity, persistence, and seeking control are among the popular attributes of the sacred. "Believers" are often perceived to be a homogeneous group prohibited, if not paralyzed, by this unalterable force. The expression "sacred making" in the title will, therefore, come to some as a surprise. The use of the phrase is a deliberate attempt to underline the centrality of human agency in the process of imagining, and reimagining, the sacred. The act itself—as evidenced by the poems examined here—entails a complicated, often unconventional, and highly creative process, which involves perceiving (and expressing) a vast and malleable entity. Whether we believe or disbelieve in the divine origins of this entity, uttering it in language is part of a constant human struggle to make sense of it and to articulate it. In this study, I argue that the poetic grappling with the sacred, documented here, is not just descriptive but constitutive in nature. How else can one understand the challenge that these poems present to rigid institutional definitions of the sacred, and the ways in which they reimagine and rearticulate the concept? And so the goal of this study is not only to point to the malleability of the sacred itself in human perception, but at the same time, to develop a new perspective on the poetic tradition of the period. What results is a new appreciation for the complexity and diversity of the tradition.

Many Persian poets and critics discussed here are completely or relatively new to the reader. I try to introduce these new figures without cluttering the text with too many unfamiliar details. Comparatively less central figures are introduced generally with short descriptive statement such as "poet and literary critic," "political commentator," "translator," and the like. Published works, and their translations, are listed in the notes when available. For frequently quoted poets larger amounts of biographical data are provided in the relevant sections of the work.

The works of three major poets are used to document paradigmatic change in the poetic expressions of the sacred. Forugh Farrokhzad (1935–67), who is the focus of chapter 4, is best known to the American reader. Farrokhzad grew up in Tehran in a middle-class family with creative, artistic, and unconventional siblings. She wrote poetry from an early age and went through a short, unhappy marriage. She never attended college and yet was recognized as an influential literary figure in her midtwenties. Her attempts at filmmaking and her extramarital relationship with the writer Ibrahim Golestan added to her reputation as an avant-garde and daring intellectual. Despite her frank expression of her sexuality, Farrokhzad's poetry remained popular through the Islamic Revolution of 1979. Suhrab Sepehri (1928–81), quoted extensively in chapter 5, was born in the city of Kāshān. His middle-class family appreciated music, calligraphy, and poetry, and Sepehri received his college education from the School of Fine Arts in Tehran University. Although he did not try as many artistic media as Farrokhzad, Sepehri committed himself to painting in a serious and sustained manner. His desire to see paintings and organize exhibitions of his own work motivated him to travel as far as China in the East and the United States in the West despite suffering from a chronic illness. He received genuine recognition as a poet and a painter in his lifetime. Ahmad Shamlu (1925–2000), whose poetry is the focus of the closing chapter, is arguably the most influential poet of modern Iran. An activist intellectual and an avid searcher for new literary media, Shamlu experimented with many genres. He translated fiction from French and collected folk literature side by side with writing his own poetry. Along with his political commitment, he worked with young activist writers while editing artistic and literary journals such as *Kitab-i kuchih* and *Kitab-i jum'ah*. Shamlu remained a controversial political figure throughout his life.

I have to introduce one more poet here, Muhammad Riza Shafi'i-Kadkani (1939–). Shafi'i-Kadkani is the author of the well-known poem "Recite in the Name of the Red Rose," which has inspired the title of the present study. While discussions of his poetry do not occupy an entire chapter, they provide opportunity for numerous readings in this study. His reputation as a poet peaked in Iran around the time of the 1979 Islamic Revolution, when his revolutionary poetry echoing Qur'anic rhythms found widespread recognition. Shafi'i-Kadkani holds a Ph.D. in Persian language and literature from Tehran University. Alongside being a noteworthy poet of this century, he has established himself as a first-class literary critic and historian of Persian literature in the past few decades. He has traveled widely and taught Persian literature in the United States, Britain, and Japan.

Many prominent poets from twentieth-century Iran have not been mentioned because their work does not focus on issues particularly relevant to the specific concerns of the present study. Some, such as Mehdi Akhavan-Saless (1928–98), discussed briefly in the third chapter, deserve more attention in any study of twentieth-century Persian poetry if judged by the impact of their poetry. A political activist, and a native of Khorāsān, Akhavan-Saless demonstrated mastery of poetic tradition and devoted his energy and vision to a revival of pre-Islamic Zoroastrian ideals. In an attempt to stay within the scope of this study, I had to forego attention to Akhavan-Saless and some others like him.

Finally, many hazy concepts such as the sacred, the secular, and the mystical are talked about in the following pages. A straightforward glossary of such terms in this epilogue could have made matters appear clearer. In the pages that follow, I discuss in length the reasons for not providing such a glossary at the outset. The sacred, the secular, the mystical, and the like are not static concepts, and a major goal of this study is to emphasize that the attempt to define them is itself a process. Every concept is therefore subjected to extensive scrutiny and subsequently defined in the course of the debate. The ultimate goal of the study, if one can decide on an ultimate goal, is to demonstrate the artistry, boldness, and originality with which poetry from twentieth-century Iran has tackled the complex and controversial question of the sacred. These poetic documentations of the resilience of the sacred in the face of a suspecting modernity should be brought into larger debates in the humanities. I hope this study will be a step in that direction.

The completion of this project would not have been possible without loving support from family, friends, and my colleagues at Washington University. I am most indebted to my husband, Ahmet T. Karamustafa (Washington University), whose gift of love and intellectual companionship remains vital. My dear friend and colleague Jack Reuard (St. Louis University) has read and commented on the first draft of this book. Finally, I am thankful to Ms. Kathleen Foody for a thorough proofreading of the galley.

1

>-I-‹›-○-‹›-I-‹

The "Imaginative Struggle with Language"
A Story Told in the Thickness of Oil

THE SHIFTING SHAPES OF THE SACRED IN POETIC INTERACTION

Though manifested in texts, monuments, or rituals that seem reified, God / the sacred (henceforth referred to as the sacred when appropriate) is a vibrant essence evolving in time. New things, persons, and concepts are sanctified continuously, while others lose their sanctity. The process of sanctification itself is in flux. Nowhere is this evolutionary process better assisted, understood, and articulated than in poetry. Poetry is the site of the emergence of the self and the sacred, as well as their interaction, in the human "imaginative struggle with language."[1] In this work I examine the evolutionary journey of the sacred, its construction and reconstruction, in twentieth-century Persian poetry in ways described later in this chapter. Sifting through poets' life events and writings, I provide a systematic and unprecedented study in pursuit of the newly sanctified. As the sacred's nature and role evolve, so do the poetic modes of expression in which they are embedded. The result is a dazzling array of religious/spiritual expressions, which has escaped the standard critical tradition dividing twentieth-century Iranian culture between a literalist religious revolution and a handful of secular intellectuals.

The discussion can be hampered with ambiguity. Virtually all categories used in the following chapters from religion and the sacred to spirituality, mysticism, secularism, and the like have multiple faces requiring clear delineation. That thinking the sacred is easier than speaking it with clarity is not a discovery of modern literary theory. However, time-tested solutions have their disadvantages. For example, providing a short glossary seems a logical methodological start. While it will prevent chaos, it will also fly in the face of the main objective of the work, which is to discover the shifting shapes of the sacred in poetic interaction. No easy solutions are available. I use, here, a combination of partial definitions, hyphenated constructions, and footnote clarifications when ambiguity is likely. At the same time, I navigate through the poetry allowing for new concepts and definitions to emerge. Let us start with a few general methodological observations.

THINKING THE SACRED, SPEAKING THE THOUGHT

The playing field of human critical pursuit has become unsafe for thinking and talking about the sacred. There is still the believing thinker/scholar, to be sure. But the interaction with the sacred, often, remains limited to historical investigation or a worshipful hope for grace and inspiration. While these are legitimate modes of inquiry and feeling, what Robert Detweiler calls an "imaginative struggle," which can in this case result in remolding the sacred itself, is typically absent from the interaction. The unbelieving mind, on the other hand, operates at the other extreme. Either it does not engage the subject in any serious manner or grants it the scholarly legitimacy of the kind granted to mythology, examining the human behavior of the pre-enlightenment era concerning truths that are less than palpable. The subtext is that only if "scientific" methodology of distance and detachment are implemented, the genealogy and the context of the phenomenon are worth sifting through. There is of course the option of carrying on the conversation behind the closed disciplinary doors in fields as clearly allotted to the sacred as theology. The resulting polarization, true for modern Near Eastern thought and elsewhere, has left the very notion of the sacred narrow, neglected, and undernourished.

In purely scholarly terms, therefore, the study of the human search for an ultimate purpose is now at a critical point. On the one hand, making sense of the human sacred impulse remains at the core of the struggle for understanding the self. On the other, the depth, scope, and legitimacy of speaking about this struggle have turned into highly contested domains. Even a simple broaching of the subject matter has to be carried out with sensitivity and through disciplinary conduits that have earned intellectual legitimacy. Still, any expression of emotion for religious practice can mar that legitimacy. A proper display of theoretical orientation, on the other hand, bolsters authority. On the whole, if believing of any kind is suspected, the sophistication and rational credibility of the scholarly voice will—at best—remain open to question.[2]

For those of us who are in the business of exploring literary meaning, however, this uncertain state of affairs is not necessarily bad news. Ideally, we are equipped to thrive in domains lacking in well-defined borderlines. We look forward to hesitation, ambiguity, and chaos, even crisis. Ideally, our poetic logic is persuasive, our creative use of language can invest a text with entirely fresh values, our symbols speak chapters, and our interpretive tools transform. We have all the freedom we need for engaging in the "imaginative struggle" that Detweiler suggested as a solution to yielding to "uncompromising categories." In other words, what may be a source of anxiety in many disciplines for us can turn into a fountain of creativity and play. True, even Detweiler agrees that much remains shrouded in mystery when he observes, "How we interpret and what we believe are fatefully entangled, and the best one can do is to become self-conscious about the intricacy."[3] Yet, according to him, our ultimate hermeneutic concern is to transform, hence reading is an existential exercise. This is a good place to touch on the overall goal of the literary critical journey I have started. I hope the present work to be an example of the above mentioned existential exercise, an in-depth hermeneutic exploration of the poetic process that transforms the displaced premodern sacred and relocates it in the inner and outer universe of the twenti-eth-century Iranian poet.

To bring clarity to this highly abstract debate, and in the spirit of play, let me pose a few randomly selected "simple" questions. Is one who, passing by a tem-ple, feels the urge to step inside—for a silent encounter with whatever permeates that space—a religious individual? Is what resides in that space somehow other-worldly? Is one who responds to the pull of the otherworldly less rational? More specifically from twentieth-century Iran, is the poet who wishes to pray "in the direction of a red rose" after "the wind has recited its call to prayer from the cypress tree" expressing a Muslim sentiment?[4] Is he simply nostalgic or does he evoke the sentiment deliberately to highlight it? Perhaps he wishes to radically reconstruct the notion in the process of poetically engaging it. If the desire for reconstruction is the main motive, what does it tell us? Does the poet find some-thing inherently valuable in the worshipful sentiment animating the construct, which motivates him to renew and preserve it? Perhaps he is just a secular poet making use of resonant religious imagery? What does "secular" mean? Is it not one of the "uncompromising categories" we impose on people and ideas when it is difficult to say something more meaningful about them? Besides, there are equally resonant secular images in every culture. Why does our poet not use those? Perhaps the ritual offers him a special tool for enhancing meaning gener-ation. Should we, then, opt for a less committing term and call the poet spiritual instead of religious? To be sure, that will protect him against general accusations of irrationality and dogmatism often associated with religion. In its place, "spiri-tuality" will allow for the assumption of a faint and unclear tie between him and the equally faint and unclear notion of secularism. The use of these categories has not brought us closer to understanding our poet's yearning for the sacred. Nor has it added to our insight into the ways his generation may have transformed the experience culturally. We do not understand his artistic impulse any better. His particular preference for the ritual of prayer, as opposed to any other ritual, remains equally beyond our grasp.

Once the complexities of a cross-cultural perspective are added to the above setting, the questions become even harder to deal with. The recent debates in the field of religious studies surrounding the very notion of religion are often rooted in, and enlivened by, the same complexity. From a cross-cultural perspec-tive, the very concept of religion, as a coherent category of analysis, is challenged effectively. According to some, such as Timothy Fitzgerald, religious studies must examine its own purpose, boundaries, and subject of inquiry instead of perpetuating "attempts to construct a decontextualized, ahistorical phenomenon and divorce it from questions of power." As Fitzgerald notes "one pervasive assumption is that religions are defined by a common faith in the transcendent or the divine—belief in superhuman agencies, or preferably in one Supreme Being who gives meaning and purpose to human history." Examining the ethnic beliefs of Japan and India, the author works to demonstrate that the word "religion" is analytically redundant and even misleading in the context of these two cultures. The rationale behind the broader implication of Fitzgerald's claim that religion "cannot reasonably be taken to be a valid category" is that "it does not pick out any distinctive cross-cultural aspect of human life."[5]

Once again literary studies can help introduce fresh perspectives precisely because literature embodies the missing component, the "distinctive cross-cultural aspect of human life," among other things. In fact, in the search for context-specific details and historicized moments that enable us to see the culturally infused colors of each sacred, literature—and poetry in particular—plays a unique role. This is not only because the way we interpret and what we believe are "fatefully connected," and poetry opens a window to the very specific, very private, and very personal, but also because, despite its specificity, poetry is capable of reflecting, at the same time, the broader public currents that animate bigger cultural moves marking decisive historical moments. In other words, poetry rises above the sweeping social and political discourses that leave no room for fears, desires, and doubts of the individual. And yet, it captures with precision the fine details that would otherwise be washed over by these masking currents resulting in the use of general decontextualized categories such as religion, mysticism, and so forth. The poetic process performs what might be described as a dual role. It empowers the personal voice—enriched with historical specificity—to expand and embody the general and the public without losing its historicity. No wonder the move toward the evolution of religion and literature as a new field of inquiry has been steady. Let us overlook the limitations of both conventional categories for now and examine their disciplinary union in greater detail.

We are beginning to witness the full-fledged emergence of religion and literature acknowledged as a distinct discipline, as Greg Salyer describes in his short and lucid essay on the subject. The slow shaping of the borderlines of the discipline, as he observes, is no cause for complaint. As scholars from English (and other literary traditions), theology, philosophy, and other fields come together to write on the subject, they bring an outsider status to the field. While this outsider status could result in neglect in some instances, in others it means freedom from disciplinary limitations and "a kind of healthy play that permeates writing in religion and literature."[6] In short, the time is ripe for attempts to strengthen the arc between the two forms of human expression—religion and literature—that participate prominently in the construction of meaning for individuals, societies, and cultures. The time is ripe for working with these two powerful generators of meaning and the hardships and rewards that come with it. There may be instances of falling into the trap of "trivialization or pontification," as Salyer predicts. By the same token, there will be discovery and the joy of keeping literary texts alive by engaging them in repeated readings "even as we as individuals and cultures change."[7] I demonstrate through the present study that these texts, particularly in the broad genre of poetry, have much to offer in voicing the sacred as it evolves in its historical context.

A Story Told in the Thickness of Oil

The specifics of the methodology need further clarification. I have suggested that literary texts are a significant cultural site for human struggle to make sense of the sacred, for constructing and reconstructing its meaning, and for expressing it. The larger question is what does one do exactly to unlock the doors and unearth the riches that bring these texts to life? Here I wish to borrow momentarily the conceptual frameworks applied with remarkable results by an art historian. Naturally, I suggest a partial adoption rather than a wholesale application to poetry of a methodology that has been constructed to make sense of visual devices in painting. In his fascinating study of oil paintings titled *What Painting Is,* James Elkins writes:

> Neither alchemy nor painting is done with clean hands. Book-learning is a weak substitute for the stench and frustration of the laboratory, just as art history is a meager reading of pictures unless it's based on actual work in the studio. To a nonpainter, oil paint is uninteresting and faintly unpleasant. To a painter, it is the life's blood: a substance so utterly entrancing, infuriating, and ravishingly beautiful that it makes it worthwhile to go back into the studio every morning, year after year, for an entire lifetime. As the decades go by, a painter's life becomes a life lived with oil paint, a story told in the thicknesses of oil.[8]

In the present study, I suggest a close examination of a wide range of concepts, themes, and ideas by twentieth-century Iranian poets within a framework that constructs an argument similar to Elkins's for thinking about poetry. I hope to demonstrate step-by-step that a real way to observe and understand the transformation of the sacred into its modern guise is to get into the poet's studio and watch the literary processes that result in the finished designs, colors, and textures. Engaged closely in this "imaginative struggle with language" sharing the dusty and chaotic workspace of the poet, we see how s/he breaks the familiar poetic structures, the substance of his/her art form, into workable pieces and invests them with fresh values. Like Elkins's ideal art historian, we shall not maintain clean hands for long. We will, however, see for ourselves how the dulled is polished, the scratched is sandpapered and glazed over, while the unusable is melted for a complete remold.

As things stand currently in criticism of poetry, particularly in its Near Eastern version, we have followed many avenues that parallel what Elkins terms "bookish studies." Literary influences, intertextual transmissions, socioeconomic factors, deconstructionist approaches, and patterns of semiotic behavior have been explored. Some valuable opportunities have been exploited and some missed, some lessons have been learned and many are waiting to be learned. This is as good a time as any to roll up our sleeves, step into the studio, and pick the pieces of the many stories of the sacred told in the thickness of the poetic substance. What are the materials that our modern poets work with? How do they powder the colorful stony building blocks of images and personae? What thickness do they chose for oil of life they mix with the powdery substance—slippery and muddled as it is in its unfinished form—to give it the right thickness? After all, it has to stick to their paintbrush and be carried back to the poetic landscape shaping on the canvas. Otherwise the reconstruction process, the blood life of poetry, will come to a halt. Other significant choices have to be made at conscious and subconscious levels. For example, not all rhythmic structures of the past are discarded. What is it that makes some resilient and reusable? Do these old structures stay on the margins and frame, literally, the new works? Or do they run invisible through the landscapes keeping the winds blowing and the streams running? When do these rhythmic devices need repair and reshaping to house fresher, perhaps one can say more modern, melodies? Deeper ontological mysteries find room to surface as well. What are the sources of the poetic, in this case sacred/poetic, and creative energy? What is God made of in this reconstructed landscape? Is s/he made of green natural beauty, white ethical cleanliness, red political action, or the old heavenly blue illusive and unreachable? Perhaps the heavenly blue is not quite as unreachable if we stay mindful of the poetic transformation. How distinct, important, and familiar are the broad compositional lines in the newly painted landscapes? How central are the fine constituent details that may stay invisible if we focused solely on the broader compositional structures? Questions are numerous and may be posed with emphasis on what is considered relevant and significant at the time of their formation.

The answers will be as varied as the questions and colored, to the finest detail, by the thinking underlying the questions. Throughout the work, I argue that a real and concrete feel for the evolution of the sacred in this landscape will develop only by attention to details on every inch of the canvas. First, let us look at the basic events and debates behind the formation of major visual themes in this landscape.

MODERNITY AND RELIGIOUS/SPIRITUAL EXPRESSION

Poetry is often examined in search of a deeper insight into the human religious/ spiritual experience.[9] I expand this into a two-way road, an exchange. Perhaps "exchange" is not the most appropriate term as it implies a separation between the spiritual and the poetic impulses rather than emphasize their comingling. More precisely, I look for poems that enrich our understanding of the modern Iranian poet's yearning for the sacred, what might be termed the spiritual impulse. At the same time, I remain mindful of the ways in which the religious/spiritual experience, in the works of these poets, in turn, informs structures of poetic expression. Sifting through the colorful contributions of a relatively small number of influential writers in twentieth-century Iran, I identify paradigmatic ways in which their encounter/struggle with the divine has informed the specific strategies that they use to encode poetic messages. While the main aim here is to recover poetic paradigms rather than to evaluate individual contributions, I welcome the opportunity to celebrate these modern Iranian poets whose works remain relatively understudied.[10]

As I describe in some detail later, around the turn of the nineteenth century, Iran experienced a constitutional revolution in which the intellectuals and reformers demanded change in the country's social and political system.[11] The architects of these events demanded a revitalization of the Iranian poetic system of signification and communication. They viewed the sociopolitical reform intrinsically bound with "freeing" poetry from what they considered a "pathological obsession with an idealized sense of beauty" and stylized expression to prepare the society for arrival of modernity.[12] These nineteenth-century intellectuals were followed by twentieth-century counterparts prior to the 1979 revolution, among them such towering figures as Ahmad Shamlu (1925–2000), Forugh Farrokhzad (1935–67), and Suhrab Sepehri (1928–81), who dissociated themselves from institutionalized religion. The elitist unwelcoming attitude toward Islam, coupled with the exaggerated literalist disposition of the 1979 Islamic Revolution, has led to generalized and erroneous assumptions concerning the intellectual elite and the populace in modern Iranian culture. In its extreme version, this view describes the twentieth-century Iranian society as schizophrenic. According to historian Nikki Keddie, in this society the elite are "secular" and completely out of touch with the populace whose folk culture and popular art forms are replete with Shiite religious themes and images.[13]

I challenge the bifocal view of the modern Iranian culture on many grounds. On the one hand, through close examination of the writings of the above authors, and their strong ties with the past, I demonstrate the narrowness and artificiality of applying designations such as "secular" to these poets. On the other, I will draw attention to the wide distribution of the works of these poets, which in itself testifies to the strong ties between these writers and their popular readership of a diverse background.[14] I argue that the above misperception is based, at least in part, on a lack of close attention to details on every inch of the poetic canvas. Heedless of the presence of a new and transformed sacred in the works of these writers, we have noted the absence of traditional patterns of pious expression such as Qur'anic quotations and argued for their secular nature. However, the absence of traditional religious patterns often proves to be compensated with alternative poetic strategies of celebrating the new sacred. Upon close examination, these alternative strategies, with varying degrees of currency, are constructed predominantly with familiar pieces stretched, bent, broken, and eventually remolded into new shapes.

Another erroneous assumption concerning these twentieth-century writers is that since they all belong to a secular class, they wish to distance themselves from their spiritually committed forefathers, such as 'Attār (d. 1220) and Rūmī (d. 1273). This assumption is reinforced, in part, by the refusal of the modern writer to make use of premodern generic forms, such as the ruba'i or the ghazel. The refusal, as will become clear in the course of this work, is part of an overall rebellious posturing, toward a towering tradition, by a young movement celebrating its own coming of age. It is a rebellion that needs to be placed in the broader context of modernity and appreciated for its constructive components. A close examination of the building materials and re-creation strategies used by these modern poets reveals a deep longing for a spiritual identity beneath the seditious posture of their poetry. It also uncovers a strong desire on their part to remain connected to the premodern literary tradition. Their need to be heard—and respected—by the "religious" populace at large is equally evident. Still, to discard the imagined notion of discontinuity between the premodern and modern Iranian poetic tradition is not easy. By mid–twentieth century, the absence of familiar literary/religious paradigms has left a tangible vacuum. The obsolete paradigms are not limited to old generic forms or Qur'anic quotations either. The premodern literary tradition has been resilient and extensive. So is the range of what needs to be discarded or re-envisioned. Homiletic poetry and biographies of the saints, for example, are among the disappearing genres that further enhance the illusion of discontinuity with their absence. In the present work, I attempt to construct a substantive understanding of the evolutionary journey of the sacred, in this dynamic milieu, into its new poetic environment. This will be achieved through examining a wide range of poems.[15]

Naturally, Iranian poetic modernity does not evolve in isolation. Neither do the unnuanced perceptions portrayed by some of its critics. These perspectives are rooted in the ongoing intellectual developments on the world scene. Confusion with change reflected in the discourse of Persian modernity, in other words, is a reflection of the changes in a confused world at large. So is the view that religion is a phenomenon of the premodern world unsuited to play a role in the formation of modern artistic traditions. Indeed, this latter may be the most universal oversight characterizing the twentieth century as a whole. It reflects decades of struggle between the human intellectual and spiritual tendencies that come increasingly to be viewed as opposing forces. The result is a total displacement of the sacred. Here, I suggest a momentary shift in our current literary debate to take a glance at the depth and the breath of this displacement. The universal struggle to define, situate, modify, or completely discard the notion of the sacred unfolds in various disciplinary domains. To the educated intellectual poets in twentieth-century Iran, this struggle on the world scene forms the backdrop to their debate on the function and purpose of poetry.

Disciplines and the Religious/Spiritual Quest

By mid–twentieth century, it is clear that modernity has not nullified the human need for religion, which has not been rendered obsolete by the modern notion of the supremacy of reason. On the other hand, the fear of irrationality and the need for empirical certitude continue to challenge faith. Various disciplines have had to acknowledge the presence of religion as the catalyst for social moves, a mode of perceiving reality, a means of communicating with "higher truths," or a category of analysis pertinent to exploring the subjective domain. Historians of religion confirm that religious experience can no longer be dismissed as a series of "illusions departing from the scene as rational education and technological advances make their impact on human lives." The global presence and impact of religion are obvious and require exploration.[16]

   Iranian intellectuals of the twentieth century share this ambivalence. A considerable majority attempt to rechart the past to foreground the Iranian (as opposed to Islamic) characteristics of their cultural heritage in the encounter with modernity. Language, and specifically poetry with its highly personalized discourse, plays a crucial role in providing the semantic tools for the process of dissociating Iran from its Muslim past and introducing a newly forged national identity.[17] Language remains at the heart of the yearning for modernity not just as a tool for recording the events, but rather as a formative element. So does the need for redefining institutional religion to make it suitable for the modern era.[18] A persistent search for tangible substantive proof continues to dominate various modes of inquiry. Is there any substance to a "higher truth" or is all faith based on misapprehension? This is the question, and a relatively unnuanced one at that.

Searching for Truth-Value

The skeptics are large in number and eager to push the illusion of transcendence out of the way of scientific inquiry. Although most of their studies of the religious/spiritual phenomenon respond, like Ulrich's rats, to the positivist hunger for certainty rather than issues central to human spiritual concern, the skeptic camp is by no means devoid of color and nuance.[19] The anxiety of giving in to unfounded certainty concerning transcendental truths makes its way into the religious camp as well. Max Horkheimer's definition of religion as "longing" rather than "certainty" is but one modern example. In a warm and engaging appraisal of religious experience, Horkheimer presents the philosopher's longing as a rearticulation of the mystic's age-old quest for inner fulfillment. He, then, incorporates the concept into his caring and socially oriented worldview. Rooting spirituality in temporal experience, Horkheimer rescues religion as an expression of humanity's unappeasable longing for justice and the tool for liberation of reason from its present positivist limitations.[20] Following his example, many children of modernity translate religion into metaphoric yearning to avoid the discomfort of living with a mystery. Robert Penn Warren, America's first official poet laureate, commenting on religious conversion describes himself as a "yearner." He, then, further defines the "yearner" as a person with a "religious temperament" and a "scientific background." Although Warren does not elaborate on how his "temperament" and "background" remain unaffected by one another, a routine explanation may be that the former belongs to the domain of feelings whereas the latter to that of reason and rationality.[21]

The Iranian poetic/intellectual milieu of the time is occupied with similar issues. The conviction that poetry should be rooted in the rational and the real to be worthy of the name is a running theme in Farrokhzad's interview with Hasan Hunarmandi. A more politically colored version of this devotion to reality is championed by Shamlu in his manifesto of modern poetry, *Shi'ri ki zindagist* (Poetry That Is Life). The Cartesian duality, epitomized by Warren in yearning temperament versus scientific dexterity, appears in Shamlu's dispute between the reformist and the traditionalist view in the form of extended and overstated metaphors. While the poet of the times past, epitomizing irrational behavior, is captive in the ludicrous snare of the imaginary beloved's curls, the realistic and courageous poet of today is rooted practically in the forest of the masses, using poetry as an effective weapon to improve the conditions of life.[22]

Warren and Farrokhzad could have lived, as some of us have, to find the above categorization proven to be unscientific. Scientists now dismiss, on empirical grounds, the Cartesian mind/body duality and the myth that our feelings are any less rooted in the cognitive endeavors of the brain than what is commonly considered rational behavior. In a fascinating study called *Descartes' Error*, the prominent neurologist Antonio Damasio describes the brain as "body's captive audience" and expresses amazement at the intricate mechanisms that make the magic of feelings possible. He considers degrading the emotions such as anguish or explaining away the elation of love as erroneous. Instead, he thinks, we should have a sense of deep wonder for these and similar feelings that form the "base for what humans have described for millennia as the human soul or spirit." A more recent neurophysiological mapping of the complex intersections between the several human brains confirms Damasio's view. This study by Joseph LeDoux demonstrates that the amygdala (a small almond-shaped brain located at the base of the cortex responding to emotions, particularly those resulting from fear) exercises a powerful influence on the prefrontal cortex that controls the more sophisticated and refined cognitive functions.[23] Whether our souls can be found concretely rooted in our neurophysiology is, here, less significant than the fact that a discipline squarely devoted to the empirical method finds the question legitimate enough to make it subject of comprehensive studies.[24] In this light, Warren and Horkheimer's "yearning" or "longing" are as much a legitimate brain function as is any verifiable objective act. Dismissing or degrading it is as irrational as leaving a hungry stomach unnourished.

SEARCHING THE SUBJECTIVE DOMAIN

From a subjective vantage point, the emergent landscape is more varied and complicated. Regardless of objective analysis, the personal need to interact with, and make sense of, a sacred inner or outer reality remains central to human struggle. The sacred may have been displaced, but it cannot be discarded easily. Its presence is as indispensable for defining the boundaries of the self as its function is practical for making sense of a rapidly changing world. Ironically, the age of marketing and economic competition has intensified the need for the transcendental. This is, in part, because the transcendental resists quantification and consequently commodification. Furthermore, it can transcend Otherness and competition because it is, by nature, conducive to sharing. Here it would help to borrow the Freudian vantage point for a moment. From his perspective, the search for the transcendental can be viewed as an expression of the social need to overcome the "collective anxiety neurosis."[25] One may choose to disagree with the proponent of early childhood sexuality attributing the need to a mechanism of infantile repression. Indeed one may search for other culprits such as the brutality of constant competition with Others, or even believe in a supernatural force external to human psyche. Regardless of the source, the outcome is worthy of attention. As long as the need for a God / higher truth / the sacred is felt within, the phenomenon deserves acknowledgment and exploration. In the discourse of modernity, held in reputable academic circles, the standard response to this need for exploration is vague if not confused.

The confusion concerning the sacred is in part connected to the need for retooling ourselves to ask the appropriate questions. In other words, if the transcendental is not about to leave the intellectual scene, what are we doing to understand it better? What do we know of the ways in which it informs our intellectual needs, including the need for scientific certitude? How does it shape, or reshape, our evolving artistic ability for expression? To what extent does it fuel our creative impulse? The discourse of modernity, with its hard and fast devotion to rationality, appears unwilling or ill-equipped to furnish the due attention. Under the illusion of having dismantled the very notion of irrational faith, it continues to look the other way.[26] There is almost a hope that by not granting the issue scientific legitimacy it can be made to vanish. Disciplines other than theology, the appointed playground for the exercise of irrational temperaments and the legitimate place where religion can be studied for what it is worth, need to concentrate on their appropriate subject matters and remain alert to religious "illusions" that may lure them away from their objective endeavors. "Rational" blows dealt to the foundation of "irrational" faith in the twentieth-century crusade for the supremacy of reason are a reminder that antireligious sentiments can become as disruptive as religious ones. They need to be considered as much a hindrance to the study of the topic as any exaggerated emotional devotion can be. Still, the discourse of modernity has had its positive methodological contributions to the study of the sacred as well. It has valued and propagated characteristics such as curiosity, energy, and the promise involved in reaching the "transnational epoch" and the "age of the globe," to use Smart's terminology.[27] Searching for global perspectives does underline the importance of distinctive motifs and richness of the beliefs and values in the global civilizations. From a global perspective, overlooking the energy generated by the inner need of the world's diverse population is even more of a wasteful neglect. The varied global interactions with the sacred are to be acknowledged and responded to with a natural curiosity about the ways in which they inform various cross-cultural expressions of creativity.

Theology will no doubt continue to house discussions of normative issues within belief systems. The human religious/spiritual experience has, however, evolved beyond doctrinal boundaries. To be able to handle it in its varied disciplinary colors and shapes, we are in need of new paradigms. Thomas S. Kuhn has demonstrated the need for paradigms in finding meaningful relationships and anticipating their developments.[28] The existing theological paradigms focus frequently on fundamental, specific practices, as well as on specialized doctrinal issues such as the genealogy of God, the mission of the prophets, the origins of religion, and so on. These issues may continue to be central to the discipline of theology. Further afield, however, there is need for changing structures of inquiry to allow the process of "paradigm shift."[29]

One may argue that a paradigm shift is here meaningless since the study of religion/spirituality is still in a preparadigmatic state. Kuhn, it can be argued, defines the success of a paradigm in eliminating competition whereas there are ongoing competitions between incommensurable approaches to the study of the above topic. The concern is well placed in so far as it points to a lesser degree of clarity here, compared to the kind attainable in the study of natural sciences. One should, however, take into account the philosophical discussions in this century, which point to clear advantages in the variability of human experience. Philosophers such as Hans-Georg Gadamer have argued that these experiences are never identical even when the outer conditions that lead to them are exactly the same.[30] But far from being a shortcoming, they have noted rightly, this characteristic results in a "radical transformative" quality of human experience. The competing, even conflicting, approaches that inform the study of religion/spirituality can, therefore, be understood not as an imprecision but a reflection of the subjective nature of human experience, the unpredictability that motivates—and enriches —these studies.

INTERDISCIPLINARY CONTRIBUTIONS

The rich subjective nature of the human experience calls for equally rich methodologies not limited to single disciplinary horizons. Indeed rich competing approaches have emerged from within disciplines other than theology intent on probing the sacred or religious/spiritual phenomenon from within their disciplinary domains. Operating from such vantage points, Emile Durkheim and Sigmund Freud, to use two celebrated examples, demonstrate the relevance of the sociological and psychological perspectives on the topic. Durkheim and Freud are both searching for the fountainhead of faith in the human psyche. And they both look for systems of natural causes unrecognized by the conscious intentions of the believers themselves. The forces they identify as generating the belief are, therefore, different from what the believers themselves would acknowledge.[31] Their contribution, however, lies not in accepting or rejecting the divine origin of these beliefs but rather in recognizing their complexity and in dismissing the notion of their illusory nature. Durkheim, who defines religion as a reality interlocked with society itself, considers it an essential postulate of sociology that a long-lasting human institution cannot rest on mere errors and lies. In *The Elementary Forms of Religious Life* he notes, "It is inadmissible that systems of ideas like religion, which have held such a considerable place in history, and to which, in all times, men [and women] have come to receive the energy which they must have to live, should be made up of a tissue of illusions."[32] Freud's contribution to the debate is equally significant. It deserves special attention particularly because Freud's reputation as an adversary of faith has led to gross oversimplifications of his approach to the topic. For this reason, his presence, except in a destructive role, remains unrecognized. It seems in the first instance that Freud is reducing humanity to a bundle of "instinctual predispositions the ultimate course of which is determined by the experience of childhood." The prototype for God in this simplified approach is none but the figure who protected the infant against the danger and its anxiety: "the primal father."[33] It is easy to assume that this is all that Freud has to offer: the story of a childlike humanity and the way it invented a protective spiritual father, God. In truth, Freud is saying much more that merits attention. He speaks of the inner conflict the individual feels with the imperfect cultural forms s/he has to conform to and the mechanism of internalization of cultural values, which makes conforming possible. In the process, he describes "religious ideas" as "the most important part of the psychical inventory of culture" even "the most precious possession of a culture."[34] Freud realizes that protection against immediate danger cannot be the sole motivating force behind religious longing and, in this vein, acknowledges deeper more fundamental issues such as the impenetrability of the "riddle of death." Spirituality as a strategy of immortalizing the self through uniting with a higher reality is also recognized by Freud. While he does not accept that spiritual doctrines contain such immortalizing realities, he does acknowledge that they extend beyond personal discoveries.[35] The most inexplicable reaction on Freud's part is his innocent expectation, which comes as a surprise considering his impressive analysis of the complexity of religion. Upon discovering the unscientific basis for religious belief, Freud seems to hope humanity will abandon faith in God as a grown child would lose interest in "fairy tales" once aware of their legendary nature. That a thinker of his caliber should underestimate the attraction, or function, of fairy tales despite their fictive nature is almost as bad as his failure to recognize that the effectivity of faith's boundless reservoir of inspiration is not rooted in being subject to laboratory verification. Much to his credit, however, Freud acknowledges the depth of the desire behind the human need for spiritual attainment. In this way, he too defines religion as longing when he describes it as wish fulfillment. His reference to religion as an "illusion" should, therefore, not be understood as emphasizing dishonesty or falsehood but as placing the wish in the quest above its attainability. Furthermore, these "religious ideas," according to Freud, are not ordinary "illusions" but the "fulfillments of the oldest, strongest and most insistent wishes of humankind." His following statement leaves no doubt about the centrality of these wishes in human life: "the secret of their [humans] strength is the strength of these wishes."[36]

The closest interdisciplinary effort to that of Freud—in twentieth-century Iran—is a study of the psychological type of Shams (d. 1247), the teacher of the medieval poet/mystic Rūmī (d. 1273). The work, which quickly topped the bestselling list in Iran, is called *Khatt-i sivvum* (The Third Script). The title is borrowed from Shams's self-descriptive remarks intended to deepen the mystery of his identity as an enigmatic script not decodable even by the divine scribe:

> That Scribe wrote three kinds of scripts:
> One, He could read not others
> One, He could read as well as others
> One, neither could He read nor anyone other than Him
> I am that [third script].[37]

The author, Nasir al-Din Sahibzamani, is a psychoanalyst with many best-selling titles famed for success with the lay readership and popularizing the field. In *Khatt-i sivvum,* after laying out the historical context in some detail, Sahibzamani analyzes Shams and classifies him as the shy introverted type. Members of this type, according to our psychoanalyst, display "arrogant iconoclastic traits," which counter and complement their "isolationist tendencies." They are restless, torn between conflicting feelings, and are *nashinas-i darun-i khvish* (strangers) even to their "inner" selves. The detailed descriptions fit the little we know of the historical Shams perfectly.[38] Sahibzamani demonstrates an impressive control over his premodern mystical/literary/historical sources, which he uses to demystify the master/disciple relationship into a modern objective educational exchange. Extended discussions of scientific psychological concepts aim to unravel the riddle of Shams's monumental spiritual power over Rūmī and the broader congregation. We are to understand that the definitive purpose of authentic Iranian mysticism was the "objective reality" of producing "exemplary" human beings capable of educating those in need. Through analyzing his type, and examining the corruption of his premodern environment, we are to make sense of Shams's charisma as well as his spiritual conviction. According to this reading, Shams used his relation with Rūmī and others to enable them (and now us) to see that the universe is centered around the personality and actions of the *insan-i kamil* (the perfect human being) who is his/her own true creator.[39] The discussion of the *Khatt-i sivvum* should not be closed without pointing to its very prominent subtext. Shams, the third script, the one indecipherable even to God, has been unraveled and explained to us through the insights of modern psychology. The very writing of the book is a statement, a symbolic celebration if you will, of the human triumph through modernity.

Interestingly, the *Khatt-i sivvum* displays a trait typical of the twentieth-century interdisciplinary attempts by Iranian authors to make sense of the sacred or those who expound it. It overlooks entirely the literary dimensions of the utterances of Shams and the role they might play in understanding his purpose and his personality. Even though Shams is at times tremendously lyrical in his sayings, and despite the fact that he inspired Rūmī in composing *Divan-i Shams,* the largest and most colorful body of lyrical poetry in Persian literature, *Khatt-i sivvum* does not make use of literary analysis nor does it show awareness of the need.[40] This reflects the broader disregard for literature as the arena for human struggle, growth, and change.

What is it that prevents Sahibzamani from paying attention to the way his "perfect human being" expresses himself or, as Detweiler put it, handles the "imaginative struggle with language"? Being a psychoanalyst, and one clearly well versed in literature, why does he not treat the words of Shams, these products of his creative impulse, as keys to his inner treasure? He treats them, instead, as a mere repository of religious/historical facts. I suggest, while moving at this point beyond the *Khatt-i sivvum,* to stay just a moment longer with the issue of literature as the neglected treasure house of nuanced human expression. Attention to these nuances is our only protective measure against full surrender to uncompromising categories such as religious, secular, and the like. That is why it is absolutely essential for literary studies to join other interdisciplinary attempts to make sense of the sacred. In the literary domain, where rational discourse is empowered through cohabitation with paradox, and poetry provides the tool for the deepest subjective self-exploration, questions can be formulated in manners very different to those posed in objective methods. The processes of defining the self, the divine, and the relation between the two fall naturally in this domain. In a sense, all poetry tells the story of searching for the divine even when it is not thematizing it directly. It does so by its very existence, through its struggle to make sense of life, of itself, and of the specific poetic strategy that unfolds in its encoded message.

When it comes to modern Persian poetry, heir to a strong spiritual tradition, there are more compelling reasons to look for the developments as well as mutations of the sacred. There is of course the 1979 religious revolution often misunderstood and presented as a literalist monolithic expression of modern Iranian search for higher truths. However, the poetic encounter with the sacred in twentieth-century Iran includes decades of robust artistic expression prior to 1979. Such strong nonrevolutionary currents continue to flow alongside the revolution and survive to this day. These valuable accounts of the sacred will fall through the cracks if we continue to define as secular all who do not embrace a traditional Muslim way of life. Our perception of the sacred will remain narrow just as this lively body of modern literature will be denied its spiritual richness and depth.

The simplistic reading of the 1979 revolution, as well as the simple division of the Iranian culture into religious and secular, are themselves symptoms rather than causes. They are partially the result of the fear to offend secular sensibilities if a strong and sympathetic interrelation was to be imagined between the poetry of this period and the sacred. An even greater handicap is the one-sidedness of the modern critical apparatus, which has deprived us of a deeper insight into the human inner developments by succumbing to uncompromising categories such as the secular.[41] I will not, here, dwell on the losses that have resulted from this narrowness of vision. Instead, I will take a moment to examine the loosely constructed rubric "secular," which concerns us most, as it is applied frequently and indiscriminately to modern Persian poets discussed in the present work. Put into perspective, the concept proves ill-fitted to these contemporary Iranian writers including such rebellious figures as Shamlu, who prefaces his collection *Hava-yi tazah* (Fresh Air) with "*Isyan-i buzurg-i khilqatam ra shaytan danad khuda namidanad*" (the grand mutiny of my creation is known to the Devil, not to God).

Other "uncompromising categories" (i.e., mysticism) will be scrutinized as we move forward.[42]

REFASHIONING THE SECULAR

The contemporary German philosopher Hans-Georg Gadamer reminds us that as observers of historical events and concepts we can never attain an omniscient perspective. Our task remains infinite and our knowledge forever incomplete. This partiality of knowledge reflects the fact that in our glance at what we try to comprehend, we are not dealing with "disinterested, theoretical knowledge of objects" but rather the active engagement of historical agents. An extensive discussion of the Gadamerian perspective on historical knowledge is not necessary here. Nevertheless, it is helpful to remember his warning that the meaning of events, actions, and concepts are correlated with particular perspectives and therefore they themselves are "historically situated, perspectival, and partial." It is in this sense that he describes all understanding as being "rooted in prejudice." Gadamer concludes that this "prejudice" influences our "aesthetic understanding" as well as our "social and psychological self-understanding."[43] Even if we disagree with certain aspects of the Gadamerian scheme of defining understanding, his insight into the perspectival and ever-changing nature of concepts is particularly relevant and enlightening here. The key postulate I wish to focus on is that all concepts are in need of constant refashioning to make sense in specific times and contexts. This is specifically the case with basic, loosely used, and all-encompassing concepts such as the secular, which appear to be known to all and are particularly susceptible to being removed from context. They need to be refashioned even within the context in which they originally generated. The critic William Connolly corroborates this need in an interesting and engaging essay, which has inspired the title of this section.[44] The essay focuses on what the secular modus vivendi ignores or devalues and why the concept needs to be refashioned for some of these inadequacies to be readjusted.

Connolly makes use of concrete examples, many of which can be applied safely to poets in twentieth-century Iran. He reminds us at the outset that Bertrand Russell and Nietzsche were both atheists, but they diverged dramatically in their orientations to ethics, justice, and morality. Hence the inadequacy of the adjective "secular," which we may use to describe both and which fails to capture these significant distinctions. The core argument here may be extended to almost any two secular poetic figures in twentieth-century Iran. Farrokhzad and Sepehri, featuring prominently in chapters 4 and 5, are very good examples particularly with respect to their common choice of images and concepts borrowed from nature. Generally speaking, they both remove the sacred from a distant unfriendly sky and place it in a nearby garden. Their intense involvement with nature goes beyond the luxurious need for beautification of the background, even beyond artistic devotion to lavish description. They have locked themselves out of mosques, put away books of *fiqh* (religious law), and refused to be excited by the mystery and freshness of rituals such as early morning prayers. Nature seems to be the only space left worthy and pure in which to reinvent the sacred and give it proper poetic articulation. Whether we choose to view the process as sacralization of nature or naturalization of the sacred, we have to admit that these poets' ethics of relating to nature, their personal proximity to it, and their general use of natural elements is entirely different. For Sepehri, whom we found earlier venerating a red rose, nature is distant and holy. It is practically the temple or the mosque from which the call to prayer, recited on cypress trees, spreads out:

> I am a Muslim
> Praying in the direction of a red rose . . .
> I say my prayers
> When the wind has recited its call to prayer
> From the cypress tree.[45]

One is always drawn to Sepehri's musical and magnetic nature but the prospect of reaching it is remote. Once there, however, one is transformed, even sanctified to become worthy of being completely "absorbed into the music of the night."[46] For Farrokhzad, on the other hand, nature is nearby. It is messy, mischievous, and humanlike. There is a price to be paid: one can be lost in this nature, injured, or even devoured by the death prowling in its undiscovered corners. On the bright side is the fact that this accessible nature knows the human habits well because it shares their humanity. Not only does Farrokhzad unite passionately with the spring in which she bathes, she plants her hands in the garden certain of the fact that she will grow.

> My share is to stroll quietly in the garden of memories
> And to die remembering the sad voice that says:
> "I love your hands."
> I plant my hands in the garden
> I will grow, I know, I know, I know
> And the sparrows will lay their eggs
> In the hollow of my ink-stained fingers.[47]

The realistic process of cutting and grafting complete with mud, blood, and ink stains is almost unthinkable in Sepehri's pure and spotless universe. If there are any stains there, they are too far to be detected with the naked eye. In a way, Sepehri has lifted nature in its entirety to the sky where the holy resides, whereas Farrokhzad has pulled it to herself and endowed it with flesh and blood, as well as the ability to sin.

More examples of ethical or political significance can be cited for the difference between the above writers, and for the incongruence of what has to be fit under the rubric secular if we choose to apply the label to them both. However,

Connolly does more than highlight the limitations of the concept by way of practical application. He looks at the origins of the idea of the secular in the Kantian struggle to give universal philosophy primacy over ecclesiastical Christian theology. The aim of this struggle, that according to him is still very much at the heart of the secularist move, is to cleanse the university and public life of the adverse effects of sectarianism. This is to be accomplished by elevating universal philosophy, also known as Rational Religion, to the authoritative position previously reserved for Christian theology. Connolly criticizes the Kantian view as responsible for creating new dogma out of reason and universal philosophy in an attempt to curb dogmatic Christianity. The problems he detects in the current definition of secularism are relevant to our discussion. In the standard current understanding of the term, Connelly sees an exaggerated need to dredge out of public life as much cultural density and depth as possible so that muddy metaphysical and religious differences do not flow into the pure water of public reason, procedure, and justice. He also makes the excellent point that in distinguishing secularism from religion we seem to treat the word "religion" as if it were a universal term, as if it could be always "distilled from a variety of cultures in a variety of times" rather than representing a specific fashioning of the spiritual life "engendered by the secular public space carved out of Christendom."[48]

The major contribution of the essay is its observation that drawing a sharp line between presecular and secular understandings is an exaggeration. Connolly backs the observation with the argument that public discourses do operate within "dense linguistic fields that specify how beliefs are to be articulated and tested." Ethical claims, he points out, are redeemed in the same way. Under these circumstances, repetitions, defenses of these articulations also write "scripts upon prerepresentational sites of appraisal." In other words, although secular presentations of public reason and moral discourse remain tone deaf to "the registers of intersubjectivity," they are nonetheless immersed in it and depend on it.[49] Depending completely on these dense, intertwined linguistic fields for self-understanding and self-articulation, we cannot sift the religious from the secular unaffected by one another. Connolly's last point will be corroborated fully in the course of the present work. Examples quoted throughout demonstrate that twentieth-century Iranian poets do not sift the religious from the secular either. They make use of personae, formal structures, patterns of expression, and strategies of encoding poetic messages that cross the border between the two. A fitting example is the often quoted political poem *Hallaj* by Shafi'i-Kadkani. In this poem, Shafi'i-Kadkani revives the ninth-century mystic killed for expressing oneness with deity to voice his social criticism.[50] In so doing, the poet makes full use of vibrant spiritual pathos to expose the oppressive Pahlavi regime. Hallāj is a higher being, his image reflected in a mirror, a common metaphor for the pure heart. His hair flies in the wind, as if he were suspended in midair or standing on a high pedestal.

The mystic, the political activist in the poem, protests the social injustice with the "surud-i surkh-i ana al-Haqq" (the red song of I am the truth).[51] Shafi'i-Kadkani is a believing Muslim himself, but the religious figure he empowers in his poetry transforms into a revolutionary over a short period of time and serves the oppositional forces of every persuasion throughout the 1979 revolution. If Shafi'i-Kadkani's use of personalities such as Hallāj may be viewed as a result of his sympathy with Islam, Shamlu, for whom creation begins with the human mutiny inspired by the devil, can hardly be placed in the sympathetic camp. Still, the poet of rebellion has an equally hard time to stay away from traditional/religious structures of poetic expression embedded in what Connolly calls the "dense, intertwined linguist fields for self-understanding." For example, Shamlu devotes an entire poem to the crucifixion of Jesus entitled *Marg-i Nasiri* (The Death of the Nazarene).[52] Shamlu's poem captures the last moments in the life of Jesus without lingering on details. There is no mention here of the triumphant life-giving 'Isa celebrated throughout classical Persian literature. The prophet is, here, used to expose the ignorance of the crowd who cooperate with his murderers. 'Isa, the miracle worker of Persian ghazel, is refashioned into a dying sufferer and referred to only as Nasiri (the Nazarene). The epithet is familiar enough to identify Jesus but not associated with triumphant miracles. We soon realize that the poem is about the stifling censorship at the time of the poet and the masses co-opted by the regime, an observation confirmed in the concluding phrase of the last stanza: "avaz-i ruy dar khamushi-i rahm" (the dying voice of mercy). An even more revealing example of Shamlu's surrender to the subjectively acquired linguistic patterns of expression is his direct critique of religion embodied in the paradoxical antireligious prophet in a poem called *Lawh* (The Tablet). In "The Tablet" Shamlu reverses history and borrows the mantel of Moses to preach freedom from the old religious myths of a crucified Christ. To the crowd, who desires another "Gospel" and seek the "horrid truth in legends," Shamlu offers his personal commandments and comments "today every woman is another Mary, and every Mary has a Jesus upon the Cross."

> Then I held up the clay tablet crying unto them:
> "This is all there is, and sealed
> It is an old inscription, aged and worn, lo! Behold!
> However tainted with the blood of many a wound
> Mercy it preaches, friendship and honesty."[53]

Connolly's excellent observation concerning our dependency on dense, intertwined linguistic fields for self-understanding, and our inability to sift the religious from the secular unaffected by one another, deserves further attention. This is particularly the case in less obvious instances. Religious personae such as Hallāj, Jesus, and Moses stand out easily to be seen. All linguistically embedded patterns of expression are not that simply conspicuous. One example is the adoption of formal communicative patterns. For example, poetry may borrow the structural rhythm of a certain event, activity, mode of experience, or text that has normative quality for the era or for what needs to be expressed. The pattern should be effortlessly resonant with the reader for reasons such as historical significance, aesthetic attraction, or ethical/emotional value. The scriptures of many belief systems possess such communicative patterns with these and similar qualities. Let us look briefly at two such instances of using communicative patterns, which in this case I term "scriptural structures." In *Ayah'ha-yi zamini* (The Earthly Scriptures), Farrokhzad evokes the scriptural structures even in the title she chooses for her work. The poem itself opens in the fashion that the book of Genesis does. Needless to say, the poet subtly expands and redefines the structure to serve the poem's specific purpose. For instance, she turns the pattern against itself by, ironically, reversing the narrative line. In Genesis first there is darkness and God commands the light to be; Farrokhzad's earthly scriptures open as the sun dies and all life perishes on earth:

> Then,
> The sun went cold,
> and prosperity left all lands.
> And grass withered on the fields,
> And fish perished in the sea.
> And from then on
> the dead were not taken in by the earth.[54]

The Bible is not the only text used for such poetic purposes. Scriptural structures more resonant with Persian Muslim readers resurface in the writings of others such as Sepehri. This is mostly in the form of rhythm borrowed from the Qur'an. In *Surah-yi tamasha* (The Chapter of Sight), as with Farrokhzad's poem, the resonance begins with the title evoking the scripture. The poem continues to echo the Qur'anic patterns of communication in numerous and concurrent ways. For example, it replicates the Qur'anic condemnation of human forgetfulness, which leads to the severance of the primordial covenant with God. What the poet truly mourns, however, is the loss of the mythical memory connecting human beings to nature:

> I swear by sight!
> And by beginning of speech
> And by the banishing of the pigeons from memory
> What is in the cage is merely a word![55]

As the Qur'an offers *dhikr* (remembrance of God) to remedy the forgetfulness, the poem encourages the unremitting quest for the jewel hidden in the closed palm of the earth to revive the bond with nature. The Qur'an promises its followers a happy life and afterlife; Sepehri guarantees unperturbed peace to the one who makes friends with the birds in the air and sees the green garden living in the memory of every piece of wood. Toward the end of the poem, the poet echoes the Qur'anic challenge put before the believer, to produce evidence sounder than the scripture. The poet picks a leaf from a willow tree challenging those present to remain unconvinced of the miracles manifested in nature.[56]

Examples quoted from these twentieth-century Persian poets confirm Connolly's argument that in our complex linguistically embedded process of understanding and meaning generation, the line between secular and religious is too blurred to allow a simple classification according to subject matter. Connolly concludes by stating that the distinction between the two concepts of "religious" and "secular" comes into sharp relief not in the public discourse as a whole but in its political sphere. American courts, he reminds us, would rule "legitimately" on issues of abortion, homosexuality, and the right to die, in ways that disenfranchises a large majority of the religious American public. This in his view is the result of giving in to an "austere post metaphysical partisanship that places itself above the fray." The political/nonpolitical dichotomy highlighted here can serve the critique dealing with twentieth-century Persian poetry as well. The conflict between the "religious" as defined in the politically sanctioned public dialogue and that articulated in the privately and poetically expressed discourse is easily detectable in the Iranian situation. What is often not acknowledged is that all the privately expressed oppositional discourse may not, by virtue of its conflict with the public version, be labeled as secular.

Connolly concludes by offering an attractive solution to the problem, working toward understanding and acknowledging the pluralistic nature of secularism. Such a secularism will be able to "pursue the ethos of engagement in public life between plurality of controversial metaphysical perspectives, including for starters, Christian, other monotheistic perspectives, secular thoughts, and refashioned secular perspectives." Feeling confined by the limitations of the existing notion of secularism, despite its claim to scientific foundation, the author is working to expand the concept into the pluralistic ground for the engagement between multiple cultural worlds to honor a variety of moral sources and metaphysical constituencies.[57]

I would like to epilogue Connolly's argument by adding one reason why we need to reconstruct our all-purpose unsophisticated understanding of secularism. Connolly highlights the blindness of the construct to global cultural differences and to what religion means to different constituencies. I would add that the concept is equally insensitive to the changes that faith itself undergoes, not only in its journey from culture to culture, but in the space of one individual's life. Religion does not come prepackaged; neither does it remain static. The conviction is a constant process of making and breaking. In short, religion is that which the individuals make it to be in varying stages of their lives. Within the boundaries of practice there are numerous variations on the traditional themes, which are worth studying for their particular religious/spiritual nuance rather than dismissed as deviations (or as secular tendencies for that matter).

That the concept of the secular is in serious need of refashioning even within the cultural context in which it was created is clear. There is no justification for exporting it to modern Persian literature and authorizing it to represent the entire corpus of the colorful, complicated, and individualized poetic expressions reflecting encounters with the self and the sacred. The hasty borrowing would amount to what Anouar Majid describes as "collapsing differences" into a universalism that according to him is a dictate of capitalism. Whatever is the source of this collapsing of differences, Majid has a point in warning that this kind of universalism would obliterate the promise of non-Western systems to struggle for cultural plurality. Acknowledging a similar right for the West to benefit from this plurality, he sees in this hazy universalism the danger of depriving the world of the alternatives born in old and complex traditions that have had a long history of bridging the past and the present, the new and the familiar, the continuous and the changing.[58] Labeling the multifaceted and highly developed poetic voice in twentieth-century Iran as secular would rub it off of its contrapuntal nature and reduce it to a vague shapeless mass highlighted *not for what it has to offer* but for an *absence* of spirituality. The approach is a negative assertion that closes potential avenues of investigation. Furthermore, the claim of absence itself is open to serious debate.

Here, I propose a complete shift of perspectives to investigate the art of sacred making by the poetic voices in modern Iran. I suggest abandoning the conventional search for Qur'anic quotations, allusions to prophetic hadith, and standard ethical instructions. These time-honored, but outmoded, paradigms will no longer help to make sense of the literature in question. Indeed, in some cases, these paradigms have been discarded completely. Religious/ethical instruction and quotation of prophetic hadith fall into this category. But the absence of these quotations does not signal an absence of prophetic figures. A more common development is not to discard the paradigms but to refashion and infuse them with new life for further use. Replacing direct Qur'anic quotations with an adoption of the scriptural rhythm discussed earlier is but one example. Another instance is the refashioning of Sufi themes and images into poetic constructs that are open to views compatible with modernity. Following the journey of traditional religious symbols into their "modern" environments leads to observing hitherto unstudied poetic transformations. This involves breaking new grounds, which is always signposted by prominent elements from the old assisting in the construction of the new pathways. The search for totally unconventional spiritual images and concepts in works of poets who do not conform to institutional religion at all is the hardest. Sanctification of sexuality in Farrokhzad's poetry is an example discussed in chapter 4. Here, we are on completely new grounds facing the question "what defines the spiritual significance of a paradigm?" The main problem is to negotiate the borders of the paradigm. If too loosely defined, anything will slip through the blurred lines, and if too restrictive, much that deserves inclusion will be left out. The context of the poems needs to be examined carefully, and the conventions of the genres understood. Still, there will be times when the line between quick dismissal and hasty generalization will be unclear. The attempt, however, cannot be delayed for the fear of error. Breaking new grounds will always be laden with the unexpected, but the unexpected may also characterize the rewards at the end of the exploration. Remarkable among such rewards is the emergence of rich fresh poetic patterns of sacred making not detected and acknowledged before.

There is a prerequisite to all of this. To begin the search for the poetic art of sacred making requires the acknowledgment that poetry is more than a podium for expression, or a loudspeaker for premade inner sentiments. It is instead, the complex/combined public/private space in which the re-envisioning of the self as well as the conditions for this remaking are perpetually negotiated. Where texts end and the processes of remaking begin is another shifting border. Literature cannot be completely and permanently defined as it is not static or constant. Rather, it alters its role, its actions, and its forms of practice as the environment of which it is a part evolves. Despite the changing nature of this role, the significance of literature for social stability and personal understanding of the truth remains crucial.[59] This significance is explained variously by various philosophers. For some the central and transformative nature of poetry is a result of its "claim to truth," a claim that is often differentiated from any authorial intention or access to such truth. Neither does the process depend solely on the reader's experience and perception. A review of the manner in which contemporary theoreticians have dealt with the matter is not necessary. The wide range of views includes the formalist complete reliance on the text to exaggerated trust of the reader response school on what the reader brings to the text. Hans-Georg Gadamer, the German philosopher discussed earlier in this chapter, bridges the divided camp with insightful observations. According to him, the process of "understanding the meaning" of a text, is a complex aesthetic experience, in which a common language is "constructed" to mediate the meaning. He calls this process "a fusion of horizons."[60] Gadamer, a believer in the transforming quality of works of art, attributes the quality to a phenomenon he defines as "recognition." According to him, in our encounter with texts, or works of art, we see more of that object than we have previously understood. In this sense, we experience looking at things in a new way. Yet, at the same time, we recognize something familiar in what is brought to our attention. In the process of Gadamerian recognition, there is a joy that is caused by knowing "more than only the known." Here, what we already know "emerges" as if by "illumination" from all the contingency and variability of circumstances that condition it. Then, it is grasped in its "essence." Gadamer is by no means the first philosopher who highlights the enigmatic ways in which encounter with poetry (and art in general) can lead to a collapse of the customary and ultimately to the transformative experience that enables the experiencer to confront and change his/her life.[61] His special attention to understanding texts, however, makes his work specially pertinent to literary studies.[62] It is in this regard that one can envision the full complexity of creating poetry entailing the configuration of a strategy of expression not just descriptive of events but constitutive of the process of growth and remaking. Once again, in this deep ontological sense, defining poetry as "secular" or "religious" is meaningless in that it reduces the complexity of the art form to its immediate thematic specifications.

I would like to end with emphasis on the descriptive/constitutive nature of every poetic interaction with the sacred. There are numerous ways in which the poet and the sacred touch each other, and ways in which the poet and the sacred are remade upon each poetic exchange. This mutual reshaping can take place in a vast variety of poetic spaces from the green temple constructed for mother earth to the red battleground of oppositional discourse built to emancipate the socially oppressed. Sometimes, it is a simple reinvention of a reachable and meaningful God.

In mapping the modern poetic interactions with the sacred, I have emphasized the need for acknowledging continuity and connection with the past. The ways in which poets of premodern Iran defined and negotiated the process is key to understanding the current thinking. While a full landscaping of the sacred in the classical era is beyond the scope of this work, looking at outstanding patterns is possible and necessary. What did the sacred look like before the modern voice rearticulated it?

2

⊱━◂◆▸━◉━◂◆▸━⊰

"The Primordial Mysteries,
Neither You Understand nor I"

The Changing Sacred in Premodern Persian Poetry

It is a pattern among skeptics to stay fascinated, even preoccupied, with God /
the sacred, the object of their denouncement. Despite repeated denial, expressed
with force and clarity, the anxiety of error seems to persist. It is easy for us to view
this rearticulation of opposition, particularly when occurring in premodern
times, as a sign of the speaker's frustration with the overwhelmingly God-fearing
majority. Closer examination reveals an equally strong purpose: the need to arrive
at a persuasive final position and a sense of closure. Yet, comfort seems to remain
elusive. In the case of the twelfth-century Iranian skeptic poet and mathemati-
cian Omar Khayyám (d. 1122), he clearly needed to convince himself before con-
sidering the reaction of the readers:

> The bridge between infidelity and belief is a fleeting moment
> The road from doubt to certitude is one breath, one instant
> Enjoy the precious moment, the one breath left to live
> For all you shall take with you is that fleeting moment.[1]

I will discuss Khayyám's stormy relationship with creation's "master potter" in
some detail later in this chapter.[2] On the Persian premodern literary scene, his
kind of painful outcry of doubt and denial stands out against the calm and rev-
erent norm of praising the divine glory. These resemble a few red tulips punctu-
ating an open green field. Yet, as examples in this chapter demonstrate, doubting
and probing the sacred are present and indigenous to the premodern poetic envi-
ronment. The red tulips exist and the green is far from uninterrupted long before
echoes of European enlightenment or results of encounter with modernity are
felt. Furthermore, the imaginary uniformity that we tend to attribute to the
notion of the Qur'anic God as perceived by medieval Muslims is subjected to
serious questioning even with the small selection of poems quoted here. The
sacred emerging from these poems is changing and pluralistic in nature. The plu-
rality is sustained throughout different poems and generic forms I sift to uncover
the many faces of the sacred.

However, the purpose of this study is to appreciate the diversity of the sacred in its modern poetic environment in Iran. The significance of the past here is not because it documents fully the evolution of the sacred but rather in its "perspectival" multiplicity, to revive a Gadamerian concept from chapter 1.[3] I strive to keep the twentieth century in the foreground at all times in order for the continuity between the modern and the premodern not to be masked from view. No doubt, on the modern world scene the preponderance of red and green have changed, but the loud cries of denial and the anxiety of error have not. The twentieth century panorama of denouncements ranges from positivist/empirical rejections of the sacred to subjective philosophical repudiations touched on in chapter 1. The Iranian poetic/intellectual environment is not wholly different. The need to come to terms with the concept of the sacred itself and, above all, the challenge that its elusive nature presents to all humanity, modern as well as premodern, continues to attract the greatest of minds.

CAPTURING THE ELUSIVENESS OF THE CONSTRUCT

To present a panorama of the elusive faces of the sacred in premodern Persian poetry, I need a working model outlining at least some seminal characteristics of the sacred. I will construct the model with the help of a few contemporary thinkers starting with a basic question. With that model in mind, I then begin the survey of the premodern literature. The basic questions I have selected are the following: What is in the elusive construct known as the sacred that makes it the subject of the most intricate theological discussions as well as the most accessible, commonsense dimension of everyday life in any culture? Should it be considered a universal phenomenon? If so, what can be done with all the regional differences, conflicting interpretations, even outright incompatibilities surfacing in any cross-cultural examination? If, on the other hand, the sacred is to be treated in relative terms using particularistic methodologies, what is to be done with the unmistakably universal sentiments it generates across cultures? The horror, awe, delight, and ecstasy associated with the sacred is not the property of any particular culture. Perhaps reconciling the two dimensions (particularity versus universality) is not as important as recognizing that the tension between these dimensions is a constructive one. Indeed, it is the propelling force generating many colorful exploratory journeys shared by contrasting positions. Below, I cite a few models resulting from such journeys.

Early in the twentieth century, there is great admiration for Mircea Eliade's groundbreaking phenomenological approach treating the sacred as an ontological category, a subjective human awareness of the presence of numen. Although a historian of religion, Eliade blends the primitive, premodern and modern, elements benefiting selectively from philosophy and psychology to construct a model for universal subjective human rootedness in the sacred. However, his monumental work *The Sacred and the Profane: The Nature of Religion,* first hailed as original, is soon denounced as ahistorical.[4] In a lucid discussion of the sacred, Veikok Anttonen describes the concerns of the philosophers and anthropologists who criticize the phenomenological approach foregrounding the emotion and other introspection in the study of human interaction with the sacred.[5] Quoting Richard Comstock's essay *Behavioral Approach to the Sacred*, for example, Anttonen reminds us of the artificiality of the distinction between feelings and behavior. Not only can human behavior not be treated as detached from feelings, there is no justification for the treatment of the sacred as a solely subjective category independent of the social matrix in which all human experience takes place. Comstock's objection to subjective approaches to the study of the sacred is an indication of a broader paradigm shift acknowledging the significance of patterns in human behavior. Thoughts are still crucial, particularly in the way they impact the processing of information, but only as reflected in behavioral patterns. Claude Lévi-Strauss further affirms the significance of behavioral and social dimensions of thought. According to him, culture is a system of communication in which thoughts are carried back and forth across real, symbolic, and imaginary levels by means of language. Symbolic bridges are needed to carry information back and forth between these levels. In Lévi-Strauss's complex model, we turn things, animals, persons, times, and spaces into sacred by means of ritual, myth, epic, and fiction, thereby letting them function as these bridges. The significance of this approach is in its emphasis on the social function of the process of creation and re-creation of the sacred. We fear, Lévi-Strauss tells us, the violation of certain categories central to our social stability, such as marriage, justice, purity, and national boundaries. Through sacralizing such categories, we hope to ensure their inviolability.[6] In other words, we enter God(s) into the picture to guard our values against our own human aggression.

Anttonen, writing decades after Lévi-Strauss, takes the debate into the poststructural space in anthropology arguing for the interrelation of cognitive psychology, linguistics, philosophy, and the study of religion where the borders between cognitive and cultural are given attention. Anttonen reminds us that socially transmitted concepts such as religious ones, and other culture-specific knowledge structures, which in turn shape human behavior, do not float in the air as abstract entities. They are inseparably connected to corporeality and the territoriality of human beings.[7] In this approach, the sacred is a clear result of human capacity to make judgments about ideal norms and boundaries defining and transforming the taxonomical status of persons, animals, and objects. The purpose is to define and access the cultural significance of these beings and objects.

The urge to avoid universal generalization and to acknowledge culture-specific patterns gains vigor and persistence in the last decades of the twentieth century, threatening, at times, to deconstruct the most generally unquestioned categories of analysis such as the secular. Timothy Fitzgerald's fascinating study *The Ideology of Religious Studies*, mentioned earlier, is another example.[8] Our capitalist perspective on cultures, Fitzgerald argues, irons out cultural particularity and blinds us to differences that transform the understanding and practice of a religion from region to region. Considering that such regional reconfigurations entail fundamental structural idiosyncrasies, he expresses serious doubts concerning the usefulness of the universal application of such social constructs as religion or spirituality as useful categories of analysis.[9]

Fitzgerald's warning is a symbolic attempt to be taken seriously if not accepted in every detail. It leads to a self-questioning outlook, which I use here as a concluding note to our brief excursion into the nature of the sacred. Constant renovation of models and reconfiguration of key concepts within any discipline are the alternative to carrying the dead weight of obsolete and dysfunctional paradigms. Unconditioned loyalty to outdated models is a result of misunderstanding their temporal significance and contextual relevance. Working models are important but not in and of themselves. Rather they become meaningful within specific time frames in which the need for them as paradigms is felt. As important as recognizing the significance of paradigmatic details and their developments is to understand that the application of any specific model will entail, by necessity, a gradual dismantling or transformation of the model itself. The shift is by necessity in favor of a reconfiguration that can meet the demands of updated articulations of the problem. In other words, any model is constructed only in order to begin to be dismantled and reconstructed from the first instance of application. The reconstruction is part of the function of the model rather than a sign of flaws in its structure. Key concepts and models are subject to constant renovation because it is impossible to make them in such a way as to remain compatible to dramatically varying cultural circumstances and sociohistorical conditions.

I hope with this brief tour of the twentieth century, I have prepared us for a similar journey into earlier times. Premodern Persian poets were in the business of building and dismantling their models of the sacred as well. Even within the interconnected cultural space of medieval Persian poetry, norms and concepts did not remain uniform and unchanging. God / the sacred and its relationship with the creation were in constant flux even within relatively interconnected universes. The sacred remained a lively, dynamic, and rather floating idea, as did membership in the community of the believers. To use an organic parallel, the believers acted similar to the way the joints do in the human body. They work together as a floating assemblage of bones interacting through flexible joints. They depend on one another closely, while not connected to each other as rigid unbending extensions in a single bone.

How to Define the Sacred?

Although our excursion into the premodern times will be methodologically exploratory, with a deliberate openness to the floating nature of concepts and processes that constitute the sacred, we need a working definition. To that end, I here outline the outstanding characteristics that will govern our search in these writings. These characteristics are open to modifications suggested by the literature under examination.

To stay inclusive, I opt for the model based on the patterns identified in a wide range of cultural practices brought together by Anttonen in his lucid summary.[10] The "set-apartness" is one such recurring pattern. In most belief systems, God / the sacred is symbolically, or literally, in heavens. Buildings that house the sacred are built in such a way as to stand out from miles away. When inside, the use of space and the decoration work as a constant reminder that the worshiper is not in a private home or ordinary public space. Not only beings and spaces but also sacred times are set apart. Christians celebrating Christmas or Shiites celebrating the month of Muharram carry the markers of set-apartness in their personal clothing, the decoration of their personal space in a certain manner, or in eating special food. The details may change in time and across geographical localities but the overall patterns remain the same.

Another defining characteristic of our model of God / the sacred is its connection with growth. The sacred is often viewed as having an intrinsic life-giving quality and as such is considered to be a fountain, a source for the generation or the process of growth, in realistic or symbolic ways. Objects or life forms that are chosen to bear the sacred value in rituals often embody/represent growth in form or function. Heavenly bodies such as the moon, for example, display visual growth in their monthly cycle while at the same time are believed to facilitate the growth of plants and other life forms on earth. Trees, closely associated with the sacred in many traditions, show even more tangible signs of growth and preservation of life.

Last but not least, the sacred characteristically involves rituals, regardless of its varying cultural context. These rituals perform multiple functions, which go beyond mere manifestations of the sacred. Each ritual is a highly complex culture-specific edifice of thought and action, which can be a means of transforming and redefining its own boundaries. Such a transformation is made possible through creating new symbolic spaces within which a familiar object, space, or act may be thoroughly reconfigured or replaced with newly sacralized ones.

Specifically related to our discussion, the highly ritualistic literary space is ideal for generation or alteration of the sacred. This space is easily set apart with generic norms and conventions. It is a symbolic space similar to that of a ritual, in which to act out feelings and articulate themes and concepts verbally. The result is not just expression but rather transformation of these themes and concepts. Putting it differently, language production is an act. Literature, particularly poetry, is the moment in which the act acquires highly dramatic yet concrete dimensions. Producing literature is a daring ritualistic act of acknowledging one's subjective personal experience in a highly public manner. Instead of allowing the subjective forces to draw him/her into seclusion, the poet makes a candid move to give voice to the inner self and to the inner selves of the readers not able to step out of their subjective seclusions to speak. This daring public act of self-display is rewarded with an empowerment possible only within poetry's ritualistic space. The reward is substantial, for in this space the poet redefines concepts, expands semantic fields, breaks the modality of words, and crosses the border between seemingly paradoxical spaces. Empowered to authorize unusual cohabitations, the poet mingles the public and the private, the magical and the real, the silent and the voiced, and finally the sacred and the profane. Poets have boasted of this miraculous empowerment in terms of a prophetic privilege from time immemorial.[11]

With these points in mind, I now turn to medieval Persian poets and observe them in the ritualistic act of sacred making in their poetic space. At the outset, I should remind you of two points. First, this is a random, and highly selective, exploration of the premodern landscape in search of the changing faces of God / the sacred. A systematic study would have been beyond the scope of the present work. Second, of the three characteristics of the sacred described by Anttonen, the set-apartness, and the life-giving qualities are more readily detectable in these examples. The third, the involvement of the sacred with rituals, is less perceptible due to the brevity of these examples. This quality is more evident in the longer poems by twentieth-century poets quoted in later chapters. In the epilogue, I revisit the three characteristics proposed by Anttonen to observe the ways in which modern Iranian poets may have expanded or redefined them.

"The Illuminator of the Moon, the Venus, and the Sun"

The twelfth and the thirteen centuries are seminal historical moments for the poetic acts of sacred making in Persian literature. Around this time, which in part coincides with the Mongol invasion of Iran, Sufi rituals and concepts begin to infuse the process of encoding poetic messages and transform the literary tropes. In the early Islamic era, God / the sacred has a powerful but relatively simple presence devoted to protection of order, justice, and goodness. In their passage from textual adolescence to maturity, the Sufi writings provide us with colorful and creative configurations of the sacred that exceed the above practical functions. In the process the sacred acquires an ontological as well as epistemological presence, which endows it with concurrent remoteness and attainability. In one sense it is the sublime bordering on the unimaginable; in another it mirrors human physical love in its powerfully concrete pleasure. Lyric poetry, mostly *ruba'i* (quatrains) and ghazel (odes; in its earlier version often called *taghazzul*), is the domain in which this transformation becomes most visible. A brief survey of these premodern literary expressions of the sacred provides a view of what looms on the distant horizons of tradition, resonating (and of course continuously changing) through centuries, as the later poets write. Sufi writings appropriate the sacred and rearticulate it as a complex subjectively explorable literary construct and a loud display of action.

The mass flourishing of Sufi writings in the twelfth and thirteenth centuries has its roots in earlier times when single figures such as the poet of Hamadān, Bābā Tāher, called ʿOryān (the naked), appear (d. 1055). At the same time, the sacred leads a confident but relatively simple and uneventful existence in the writings of many non-Sufi poets prior to the Mongol invasion. This simplicity, as I demonstrate with the next few examples, does not mean a lack of spiritual force or intellectual complexity. The God depicted in these works rules from the center of his universe emanating love and wrath as the occasion might demand and remains beyond the reach of the individuals. Khorāsān's poet par excellence, the epic writer, and the embodiment of the revived Iranian identity in the modern era, Firdawsī (d. 1020) is an example. Author of the *Shāh-nāmeh* (*The Book of Kings*), Firdawsī is a towering presence in the Persian-speaking world and an interesting example to look at. Invisible, and intellectually impenetrable, Firdawsī's *afrinandah* (the creator) is there mostly to assist humanity through its struggle for survival. It owns all life and wisdom, all objects and places, gives sustenance and guidance, and keeps the heavens illuminated with the moon, Venus, and the sun.[12] The creator loves humanity and gives it a special place in his universe. The poet informs us of this favor explicitly: "tu ra az du giti bar avardahand" (you are given superiority over creatures of the two worlds). Yet, there is no talk of an intimate love affair between God and his human creation let alone any ambitions of annihilation in the sacred. The worshipers can hope to perform their duty within the boundaries of their human abilities. They must seek knowledge, follow the manner of worship that wisdom (*khirad*) deems appropriate, and show respect for the commands (*bi-farmanʾha zharf kardan nigah*).[13] Twentieth-century Iranian nationalists idealize Firdawsī as devoted to preservation of Iranian values "uncontaminated" by blind obedience to the Arab/Muslim deity controlling the minds and hearts of the defeated people. Whatever the extent of the Iranianness of Firdawsī's sentiments, his devotion to God and the Prophet of Islam imbues the spiritual impulse pervading the 160 opening verses of the *Shāh-nāmeh.* These verses that revere the divine and his loving creation of the world provide only occasional Qurʾanic and hadith allusions, perhaps a sign of Firdawsī's lack of interest in technical religious details.

Besides clear allusions to the divine in opening verses, Firdawsī remains conscious of the presence of the sacred in the lives of the mythical figures, which he describes to us in affectionate detail. In the account of the founding of the *sadih* celebrations marking the discovery of fire by King Hushang, the rumor of the worship of fire by Zoroastrians is refuted in explicit terms. At the same time, a conciliatory note is introduced through connecting the Zoroastrian holy fire—possible to be made by rubbing two pieces of stone together—with stones as an

essential component in the construction of the *mihrab* marking the direction of
Mecca in a mosque:

> [Hushang's] ancestors had their religion, their spiritual practice.
> Worshipping Izad [God] was the way they pursued.
> At that time, fire with its beautiful color [was to them]
> What stone in the mihrab is now to Arabs [Muslims].
> Fire was placed in the heart of stones in order for
> [Divine] light to spread from *it* throughout the world.

The pronoun "it" in the last verse may refer to stone or fire simultaneously,
thereby affirming their parallel sacred status. At the same time, we learn that nei-
ther Muslims nor Hushang's ancestors worship the object of their reverence itself,
but see in it the divine light that has liberated the world from darkness. The dis-
covery of fire occurs when King Hushang attempts to kill a black serpent with a
stone that misses the swift prey and hits another stone instead. The friction leads
to the appearance of the divine light *furugh-i Izadi,* which continues to banish
darkness in numerous ways. It keeps the nights illuminated and marks the begin-
ning of the sadih celebrations, but above all endows Hushang with divine wisdom
and glory *farr u jah.* It is with this wisdom that he teaches his people to separate
domestic animals from the wild and benefit from them for survival.[14] In Fir-
dawsī's work, divine grace and glory pervading the world does, when necessary,
find more active manifestations that avert evil. It appears, in a later anecdote, in
human form as a *surush* (messenger from the unseen) to assist Faridun in his strug-
gle against the tyrant Zahhak, who feeds the snakes grown on his shoulders with
human brains. In a nocturnal encounter, the surush gives the young Prince Faridun,
intent on eliminating Zahhak, the secret that opens all the doors of the palace.[15]

All the master poets of this period may not be covered here. A glance at the
immediate contemporaries and successors of Firdawsī, however, will provide the
broader context for the later mass emergence of Sufi writings. Fairly similar pat-
terns surface in the poetry of Rūdakī of Samarqand (d. 941), who writes in the
genres of *qasidah* (the panegyric mode) and *taghazzul* (lyrical pieces of varying
length). Rūdakī has occasional strong devotional sentiments expressed in verses
such as "come, let us submit heart and soul to God and have no concern for the
wealth of this world."[16] Yet, sifting through his work for allusions to the Qur'an
or to the traditions of the prophet proves to be fairly unproductive. Allusions to a
sacred presence or rituals related to worship are equally rare. When such allusions
occur, their spiritual significance is subordinated completely to the aesthetic/lit-
erary role they fulfill in the poem. The following verses are a good example in
which praising the beloved Rūdakī contrasts the imagery of *payambar* (prophet)
with that of the *afaridgar* (creator). The parallel depicts the autumn as a messen-
ger and connects the creativity of the spring with that of the creator:

To wisdom's green pasture, you are the autumn,
to love's garden, the spring.
If you are a messenger from the divine where love is concerned,
to beauty you are the creator [himself].[17]

In a rare reference to religious practice in a taghazzul, he is critical of superficial and hypocritical conformation to rules of pious behavior:

What is the benefit in facing the mihrab [to pray]
When your heart is in Bukhara occupied with the beauties of Taraz.
The temptation to fall in love is more acceptable
to our God than praying [with an absent heart].[18]

Sporadic use of religious imagery in a detached and subdued manner, to serve the poem's overall purpose, is a trend present in works of Rūdakī's non-Sufi contemporaries. As late as the mid–twelfth century, lyric poetry maintains the subcurrent of lyricism detached from spirituality in the works of some mainstream figures. ʿAbd al-Vasiʿ Jabali (d. 1160) occasionally employs such prophetic figures as Jacob, Job, and David to evoke sadness, wakefulness, and love. Contrasting stock characters such as *kafir* (the infidel) and *ahl-i din* (the follower of religion), he provides exaggerated personifications of the beloved's cruelty toward the lover.[19] While touching reverently on the theme of the sacred in these verses, ʿAbd al-Vasiʿ leaves no doubt that the theme of profane love is central and the reference to the sacred a poetic accident. The work is not consciously oriented toward teaching, propagating, even analyzing the spiritual impulse that it employs in a momentary encounter with the sacred. Still, like other twelfth-century poets, compared to Rūdakī, such references are more frequent as well as elaborate in his work.

Amir Muʿizzi (d. 1125), a contemporary of ʿAbd al-Vasiʿ, makes wider use of key Islamic concepts such as *bihisht* (paradise), *taubah* (repentance), *nadhr* (alms giving), *kufr* (infidelity), *haram* (forbidden), *halal* (permissible), *tasbih* (rosary), *namaz* (prayer), *qiblah* (the place toward which the prayer is performed).[20] Though sporadic, and still subordinate to the poems' larger agenda, Amir Muʿizzi demonstrates a more developed awareness of textual religious knowledge by employing Qurʾanic quotations.[21] What is absent in the non-Sufi strata is a sense of interdependence, or organic connection, between the lyrical and the spiritual impulse. Love is a rather straightforward, profane longing for the presence of the earthly beloved and his/her beauty. The beauty is perceived to have been created by the divine but not solely as a manifestation or embodiment of the sacred. The God/beloved continuum is not yet envisioned, so longing in the works of these poets retains its clear sensual aroma.[22] Religious imagery is borrowed if it can help express that longing better, just as nature imagery or any other element from the poet's universe may be borrowed to serve that purpose. Institutionalized, superficially

observed religion is at times evoked to contrast/highlight the sincerity and inten-
sity of "true" devotion embodied in love. But even that contrast is not sufficiently
developed and charged with emotion to serve the kind of lively oppositional
encounter taking place frequently, later in the poetry of Ḥāfez (d. 1388?), for
example. In all the poets mentioned thus far, the instances of religious/spiritual
allusion can be taken away without creating a substantial vacuum in the work. A
similar hypothetical extraction of such themes from the works of later Sufi poets
such as Ḥāfez or Rūmī (d. 1273) would prove literally impossible, due not just
to the frequency of occurrence but to the seminal role that these elements play in
making the poetic expression possible.

The Temperamental Master Potter: A New Perspective on the Sacred

Before pursuing further the development of sacred-making themes in later ghazel
writers such as Ḥāfez, Saʿdī (d. 1292), and Rūmī, I look at the genre of *rubaʿi*.
No discussion of encounter with the sacred in Persian poetry would be complete
without a reference to Omar Khayyám (d. 1122), the mathematician poet of
Neyshābūr and the skeptic par excellence in premodern Persian poetry. I will first
make a quick observation on Khayyám's popularity with the Iranian readership.
This is not the place for an in-depth assessment of Khayyám's place in premod-
ern literature, yet his frank encounters with the sacred make the point relevant to
the present discussion. These encounters have long motivated historians of Per-
sian literature to assume that devout Iranian Muslims did not care for Khayyám's
poetry due to the skeptical orientation of the poems. The proponents of this view
argue that the poet remained obscure until the immense popularity of Edward
FitzGerald's translation of the quatrains into English in the eighteenth century
revived worldwide interest in his poetry, attracting the attention of the Iranian
readership in the process.[23] While FitzGerald's role in universalizing the quatrains
should be acknowledged, there are indications that the quatrains were popular
earlier. The celebrated Sufi thinker of the thirteenth century Najm al-Din Razi
felt it necessary to refute Khayyám's denial of the afterlife quoting two of the
quatrains that were obviously known at the time. On a different front, the large
volume of existing manuscripts of the quatrains throughout the centuries demon-
strates that the poet's rare appearance in manuals of prosody does not indicate
anonymity among readers. Even though a large number of poems in these collec-
tions are of doubtful authorship, the very desire to attribute them to Khayyám
testifies to his popular recognition.[24]

The Quest for the Primordial Mysteries

Are Khayyám's configuration of the sacred and his conflicting relationship with
faith what make him a controversial figure? Does he deny God's existence? Does
he incite fellow human beings to rebel against the divine ordinance? Does he feel

empowered by his human nature? Does he fight the prevalent predeterministic ideologies of his time that curb the human will to action? Is his work free from the shadow of an omnipotent God? Interestingly enough the answer to all these questions is no. Two things need to be stated at the outset. First, there is hardly any other Persian poet quite as obsessed with the creator and his relation with the world. Second, Khayyám's articulations of his conflicting feelings concerning this creator are varied and nuanced. The rubrics "rebellious" or "skeptical," often used to describe the poet, do not begin to capture the panoramic nature or the depth of these expressions. If one defining label were to be selected for the poems, the poet's frustration with his own limits would be a more suitable one. The frustration begins with inability to understand the riddle of existence:

> The primordial mysteries, neither you understand nor I
> This veiled language, neither you read nor I
> Behind the curtain, there is talk of me and you
> When the curtain is removed, neither you remain nor I.[25]

The riddle is all the more difficult to unravel because humanity is not given the chance to stay on earth long enough to learn to deal with it. The truth be told, we are denied even the chance that a simple blade of grass has:

> Would that this place be a place of rest,
> Or, this long journey would lead to some destination someplace.
> Would that after thousands of years from the depths of the earth
> We could grow back as do the simple blades of grass.[26]

Not only do we not grow back after being deposited in the earth, we do not make much of a difference to anything even when we are in this world. We look ridiculous indeed carrying the load of an inflated ego and behaving arrogantly when we are but a "drop in a vast ocean," a "speck of dust," or worse still, a "fly that appears on the horizon for a fraction of an instant." We do not even have the assurance that our feeble existence may be of any use to the creation at large. How happy can we be, then, with the gift of life for which we are expected to be deeply grateful?[27]

The frustration with the riddle of life leads to numerous angry exchanges with the creator in the quatrains. While in these quatrains the response of the sacred is not heard, the heated nature of the assertions assumes the presence of an accused party. The master potter is considered present and commanding full agency. Indeed, if divine agency were not held responsible for the marginality of the human cosmic role, anger would be meaningless. There are instances in which Khayyám's direct, dramatic, and sarcastic tone is not addressed to the sacred presence directly. Even in these instances, such a presence—near enough to overhear the conversation—is implied:

When the owner [of things] prepared the synthesis that is our nature,
Why did He leave out important ingredients now and then?
If the outcome was good, what is the purpose of breaking [us]?
And if it is not, who is to blame for the faulty creation?[28]

It is not death or shortness of life, but rather their enigmatic nature that leaves
the poet frustrated. In other poems, he objects to not knowing why he was
brought into this world as much as he detests ignorance about death. And he is
not alone in his protest; the entire universe—even simple seemingly incognizant
objects—share the frustration:

I hit the ceramic jar on stone and broke it
I was drunk acting foolish and clumsy.
The jar spoke to me in its own silent way
"I was like you, you would someday be like me."[29]

The most striking feature of this quatrain is not that humanity is equated to a
clay jar that is made to carry wine, or that objects surrounding us are equally frus-
trated with their captive and imperfect existence. It is not even the fact that the
poetic presence degenerates into drunken unruly behavior. The most striking fea-
ture of this poem is the close and clear parallel drawn between the creator and the
drunken master potter acting without control and propriety. In other variations
on the same theme, God's destruction of his created artifact is not excused with
the influence of wine. It is a result of his indecisiveness and lack of direction. The
"primordial painter" simply does not know why he paints the "tulip" face and the
"cypress" figure that represent humanity in his beautiful earthly garden.[30]

The demotion of God to human status is not all negative. Beneath the frus-
tration and anger, the loneliness, and the feeling of being shut out of the divine
space, there is a deep nostalgic desire for closeness with the creator. There are even
moments of fantasy. If only God changed his stubborn ways and allowed the poet
a creative share in formation of the cosmos, then everything would be remade in
a way that the wise and the free-spirited would lead a fulfilled existence. What
harm could come of such a simple cooperation? This plea for cooperation with
the sacred presence does not extend beyond combining creative impulses. It is not
motivated by the anxiety of separation from God, nor does it desire any broader
romantic union with the divine beloved, let alone the self-effacing annihilation
of the mystical kind prevalent among the Sufis. I shall shortly turn to this latter,
which introduces a new dimension into the God/humanity dialogue. To conclude
the discussion of our skeptic mathematician/poet in need of a cosmic refashion-
ing opportunity, two final points have to be made. First, the fallouts resulting
from frustration with God's inaction are more than simple rejections. In their dis-
tinct childlike screaming, stomping of the feet, and pointing a blasphemous finger

at the divine, they are but tantrums in the hope of breaking the celestial silence and getting attention:

> They say Paradise with *huris* [heavenly beauties] in it is to be desired
> I say, drink wine when you still have the chance.
> Take what is yours now, abandon hope in the promised
> The sound of the drum is good only from a distance.[31]

Finally, Khayyám's daring and critical exchange with God endow him with a heroic dimension that comes handy in the late-nineteenth- early-twentieth-century Iran. To the modern Iranian critic at this time, the puzzle of our "backwardness" is too painful if not too complicated to be dealt with in detail or with frankness. A strong and confident premodern Iran has reached the threshold of modernity completely unprepared. The exact reasons why we got into the mess will have to do with factors imposed from outside rather than with our Iranian incompetence. The omnipotent, omnipresent, paralyzing God of Islam imposing predestination and causing paralysis must have a lot do with it. That our post-Islamic existence may indeed be a subtle and gradual progression of the pre-Islamic one, and not entirely different from it, is hard if not impossible to accept. Opting for this nuanced perspective requires facing the fact that our current difficulties in the encounter with modernity and change may be the result of longer sociohistorical processes. Ironically, the courageous and opposing voice of Khayyám helps such complicated debates to be avoided. It confirms the popularly embraced vision of Islam as superstition among ignorant masses. What better proofs than the presence of free thinkers such as Omar Khayyám demonstrating as early as the twelfth century that Iranian intellectuals would have wished to break out of the Islamic captivity and reconfigure a new self-awareness. The most prominent Iranian novelist, short-story writer, and folklorist of this century, Sādeq Hedāyat (1903–51), idealizes the poet for this very reason. In his introduction to a selection from the quatrains, which gains as much fame as the poems themselves, Hedāyat writes a detailed introduction that portrays Khayyám as the embodiment of courage and rational thinking suppressed by the harshness of Arab-Islamic indoctrination. Using the popularity of FitzGerald's translations, Hedāyat then situates the poet at the heart of world literature:

> The influence of Khayyam on English and American literatures, and in general on today's civilized world, testifies to the distinction of his work from other [Persian poets]. . . . Khayyam represents the strangulated and tortured spirit, he is an articulation of the complaints, the mutiny of the grand, glorious and prosperous Iran in pre-modern times getting gradually poisoned and destroyed under the pressure of Arab dominance and the weight of unrefined Semitic thinking.[32]

In other words, had we pursued Khayyám's vision, we would have earned ourselves the centrality we rightfully deserve in world civilization!

"I Carry Your Beauty in the Palm of My Hands": The Sacred Comes of Age

Long before Khayyám voiced his criticism of God's single-handed and self-centered handling of the creation, other more divine-friendly visions of the cosmos had developed through the genre of mystical *ruba'i*, or quatrains. The genre of *ruba'i* is found in the writings of the earliest Persian poets such as Shahid in the early Samanid period, Rūdakī, and Abu Shakur of Balkh (ca. tenth century). A large number of Sufi writers adopt the genre and refine it for expression of mystical themes. This panorama of mystical expression and exchange with the divine range from the playful writings of intoxicated figures such as Bābā Tāher ʿOryān (The Naked), the poet of Hamadān (d. 1055), to sober doctrinal discussions of self-development in the works of such influential figures as Abd Allah Ansari (d. 1088) and Abu Saʾid Abu al-Khayr (d. 1174).[33] Of the diverse and colorful group, Abu Saʾid Abu al-Khayr may be the most suitable for the present discussion. This is not just because he is closer to Khayyám in time, but because his spiritual/poetic temperament may be situated in between the two extremes mentioned above. Abu Saʾid's writings contain flashes of Bābā Tāher's intoxication as well as instances of thoughtfulness and sobriety.

Abu Saʾid was a respected Sufi sheikh in Mayhana. As an exemplary believer and wayfarer on the mystical path, his self-perception and relation to God may be expected to be something of an opposite to that of Khayyám.[34] In line with this celebrated public office, he observes a degree of surrender and reverence to the divine, which is not shared by Khayyám. Abiding by rules of propriety (*adab*) during the mystical journey is of foremost significance among the Sufis. These are the same rules of conduct that Hāfez evokes humorously in a celebrated verse close to two centuries later:

> Though avoiding sins was not an option, Oh Hafiz!
> Keep your good manners and call them "my sins."[35]

As predecessors to Hāfez, Abu Saʾid and fellow Sufi poets had played a significant role in setting the boundaries of that which Hāfez refers to as "good manners." Whether this poetic decorum may be viewed as a mirror image to that of a figure as oppositional as Omar Khayyám is open to debate. What is certain is that Sufi reverence does not result in uncritical surrender, silence, or lack of self-exploration. The writings of Abu Saʾid, and other Sufi poets, are replete with attempts to understand the sacred, its interactions with the creation, and ways in which humanity may observe and comprehend the process. Although the dialogue is mostly with the divine and the desire to eliminate the distance, the poetic self-awareness is substantial and complicated. This is particularly the case in comparison to the *Mathnavi, Qasidah,* and *Taghazzul* writings of Rūdakī, Firdawsī, and their counterparts in the ninth and tenth centuries. The world is imbued with the divine in complex and paradoxical manners. The presence of the sacred is so apparent that it is rendered invisible except to those able to unravel the riddle of love. God is free from space and yet all space is taken over by him.[36] Humanity faces this world of riddles and paradoxes with an intellect unequipped to solve the complications. Inevitably, suffering results. Though not desirable in itself, suffering can become productive once its contribution to human growth and its transforming quality are utilized. Through this secret suffering, "the burning without smoke," which is perceived only by other lovers, the "selves" develop to the point of becoming worthy of union with the divine.[37] Preventing the ego from self-worship is a key matter. The burning in secret, for instance, remains so in order to protect the individual from a loud display of suffering and from the temptation of projecting a pious public image. Again, the suffering is not rooted in an idealization of weakness, just as it does not endorse a passive and timid relationship with the divine. Indeed, Abu Sa'id, like many of his counterparts, is not shier than Omar Khayyám in his scrutiny of the creation and the divine responsibility in fashioning personalities:

> I am the one whom you have raised from dust
> Then fashioned and designed according to your wish
> Since you have taken my affairs in your own hands
> I grow in accordance with the way you planted the seed.[38]

Sufis should not be treated as if they were a monolithic voice. Yet it would be fair to consider it emblematic of their various branches to emphasize the significance of worship beyond a superficial display of piety and a mere protection against the fire of hell. Abu Sa'id, too, in his wayfaring is looking at horizons beyond the practical considerations of reward and punishment. Neither is his understanding of heaven and hell as simple as the standard modern expectation of a premodern traditional sheikh would project:

> I am slain by love, this world is none other than the slaughterhouse
> I am not here to eat and drink but to be cooked in this fire
> I don't entertain any fancy dreams of paradise
> Paradise, improved a hundred fold, is still a torment compared to
>   what I want.[39]

Abu Sa'id and his Sufi/poet counterparts render an invaluable service to the Persian speaking parts of the Muslim world: simple poetic codification of immensely intricate concepts. It is their conviction that mysteries of creation need not be made further complicated by adopting inaccessible philosophical methodology.

Why ramble on the difficulty of seeing the sacred in the world of multiplicity when everyone can understand the concept by imagining the difficulty of noticing the water in a pond overcrowded with fish. Those who are happy with the surface visual message will stay at that level, and those capable of taking the metaphor further will understand that purity and flow come from the water, as does the sustenance of all life forms in the pond.[40] Abu Sa'id's major achievement in this regard is transforming the harshness of judgment through a loving and intimate fusion of the lover and the beloved. The rules of propriety that could curb the will to action and rebellion dissolve in the heat of longing, devotion, and intimacy:

> Tomorrow when men and women gather for judgment
> Fear of being held accountable written on faces
> I carry your beauty in the palm of my hands and say:
> "This is the explanation for all that I have done!"[41]

As in all allegorical expression, there is a more accessible surface meaning: your seductive beauty is responsible for my complete surrender to love and deviation from the right path. The less obvious allusion, however, is to the transformation of the lover into an extension of the beloved. S/he rises from the grave having preserved enough of the *husn* (beauty) of the beloved to carry it to the scene of judgment and pass the test. The journey of transformation itself is a hazardous one despite frequent appeals to the divine goodwill. Indeed the spiral nature of the progress and frequency of setbacks often result in frustrations not unlike those described in Khayyám's struggles with human limitations. Thus, Abu Sa'id reminds us of Omar Khayyám:

> My heart traversed this wasteland time and again
> Splitting hair, but left without a grain of knowledge.
> A thousand suns rose from the horizons of my heart
> None shed light on the perfection in a small speck of dust.[42]

What distinguishes Abu Sa'id's frustration from that of Khayyám is the fact that, to our Sufi poet, the dead end is itself the door to a higher stage. It is the propelling force, the magnet that pulls to the divine. To him losing hope is the worst of all sins, for susceptibility to sin itself is another divinely installed mechanism designed to activate his will to forgive, his tenderness for human childish misbehavior. Captive of the little boat built out of ignorance and mischief, human beings do not realize that they are carried forward ultimately by waves from the sea of sacred mercy and not by their meager attempt to navigate the ocean.[43] Remaining unaware of this closeness, forgetting the nature of the connection to the sacred, is the real sin in disguise. Had humanity understood the imaginary nature of this distance, there would be no need for the sins to be transformed, for humanity would—in that case—inhabit paradise, where it is impossible to commit sin:

> I moved away, blood dripping on the road from my heart
> Hells full of blazing fire in every one of my sad sighs
> I returned to the garden of being eager to be with you
> Flowers bloomed from my sins, my every foolish act.[44]

The perception of love—and intimacy with the divine—as universal and transforming provides the additional possibility of opening the gates of the sacred space on all humanity. If the condition for materializing the potential paradise given to every individual is to overcome the illusion of separation, rather than conformity to certain institutionalized rules of pious behavior, no specific faith will have the ultimate claim to salvation. The purpose of worship is to disclose the universal tricks of the stubborn ego, which sustains the illusion of separation from the sacred to divide and rule. Breaking away from this imagined prison is the purpose, and means of achieving it are many:

> Walking to you is a pleasure, whatever the style
> Seeking union with you is bliss, whatever the reason
> Your countenance is beautiful, whoever the onlooker
> Your name is delightful to the tongue, whatever the language.[45]

Mutiny in the Wine House: Grappling with the Sacred

It is the legacy of poets such as Abu Sa'id that enables the Sufi successors to Firdawsī, Rūdakī, and Amir Mu'izzi to reconfigure the sacred and utilize it for purposes concurrently, and inseparably, poetic and spiritual. The works of Saʿdī and Ḥāfez are often viewed as the culminations of this poetic integration and singled out for their "diamond-like" finished perfection.[46] Complexity and verbal perfection are the most distinct contributions of these two poets in preserving and enhancing the legacy of Abu Sa'id. ʿAttār and Rūmī, on the other hand, are often viewed as the carriers of the message of intoxication and rapture in the above *rubaʿis*. Moving from the concise genre of rubaʿi to the realm of ghazel, these poets (and their counterparts) bring new depths to the poetic expression of spirituality. Rūmī in particular, producing over 35,000 lyric verses, plays a significant role in redefining the horizons of the genre. Not only does he break structural conventions of rhyme and meter, but refashions thoroughly the thematic possibilities that could become conventional straitjackets if defined in narrow terms. In these ghazels that linguistically act out the human participation in the universal whirling of love, the sacred shifts, as does the poetic voice, from the conventional God and the divine scripture to the most unlikely candidates. In this universe, equally sacralized and empowered with divine love, donkeys, cows, and whales are as sacred and as poetic as the dawn chorus praising the Lord. Mosquitoes are "restless lovers," flies symbolize complete devotion in their "homelessness," and grasshoppers do what love does to the "plantation of the lover's existence."[47] This friendly universe is not divided into base and sublime. The equal distribution of the sacred makes it a place of learning and growth for all. The readers follow the poet's eventful journey from complete dependency to the point of empowering others:

> I became blood gushing forth in the vein of love.
> I became tears in the eyes of His lovers.
> Sometimes, like Jesus, I became all tongue.
> Sometimes, like Mary, I remained a silent heart.
> Hear the voice of the eternal flute from me,
> though I am bent like the back of the harp.[48]

Saʿdī, Hāfez, and Rūmī are tips of the iceberg. Their contributions are monumental beyond doubt. But the master narrative of Persian literary history has portrayed them as sole players overlooking many a significant contribution and formative current. The premodern poetic landscape is vibrant with the longing to make sense of the sacred. So is the voice of the large number of poets who rise to the challenge with striking originality, vigor, and artistic excellence. They often earn the praise of literary biographers who testify to the currency of their work and their acceptance by the elite readership. Yet, overshadowed by megastars, they mostly fall through the cracks in the historiographical process that outlines the poetic canon in highly selective patterns to hand down to later generations.

Instead of focusing only on the stars, I would like to use the opportunity here to present the lyrics of one such unacknowledged master poet whose artistic skill and originality of mind are as striking as is his spontaneous poetic access to moments of intoxication. Fakhr al-Dīn ʿIrāqī (d. 1288) lived a controversial life notorious for acts of pious conformity as well as transgression and misconduct. The only biographical account left about him describes him as having perfected his education in all existing fields by the age seventeen. This standard exaggerated description testifies to ʿIrāqī's erudition regardless of accuracy or inaccuracy of the reported age. The same source gives a detailed account of the poet's love for a young minstrel boy whom he pursues from Isfahān to India and ultimately to the presence of the grand Sufi master Baha' al-Dīn of Multan.[49] As a poet, ʿIrāqī is equally daring. While experimenting in a wide array of traditional genres, he makes a substantial contribution to the lyric genre of ghazel, leaving his personal mark on the genre. *Ruba'i* is short and memorable. It can shock and delight like a flash of lightning. It is, among other things, used to deliver short effective messages designed to stay in the reader's memory. But it does not provide the space required for a more substantial portrayal of experiences in any developed form. The genre of *masnavi,* rhyming couplets, is used for that purpose. However, masnavis are dedicated characteristically to narration or didactic discussion. Unless narrating a romance, they are devoid of lyricism.[50] The ghazel provides the ideal space for the intermingling of the sacred and the poetic. It is shorter than masnavi, longer than ruba'i, and has had a tested history of lyric expression by 'Irāqī's time. By the thirteenth century, however, the ghazel developed a tendency to avoid thematic coherence for lyrical purposes and became an unlikely candidate for any extended discussions of developed themes. With admirable autonomy, as well as control over the artistic medium, 'Irāqī produced ghazels that expand the generic norms and transform the genre into the witty, thematic, and *shath*like (ecstatic) vehicle needed for effective lyric expression. At the same time, the standard ghazel length, varying from six or seven to thirteen or fourteen verses, provided him with space in which to develop his flashes of romantic encounter with the sacred. Some of these innovative moves are extensions of earlier innovations in ghazels of Rūmī and others.[51]

'Irāqī's poetic structures are well developed in configuration. They are refined, carefully crafted, and polished in texture. To better utilize the space of a ghazel, he often maintains thematic coherence relying on broad Qur'anic themes, resonant mystical/literary tropes, or popular folk themes. Condensing longer narrative structures into their essential components, he interprets and reformulates them into fresh and witty ghazels. The example I start with is an account of the creation of Adam, rendered romantic, and embellished with interpreted details. Still giddy with the primordial love that immersed everything at the time of creation, human beings are here to continue the clamor and stay giddy. They have to remain connected with the sacred through this intoxication until the day that the memory of the moments of union, dusted over with the multiplicity of the world, is recovered. Forgetful and distracted, humanity nevertheless is a mirror that reflects the divine beauty, the same beauty that roses have written on their every petal. Human beings, however, need to develop the ability to see themselves in this splendid role. The long road is carefully sign-posted for those willing to read. The world's distractive multiplicity is as chaotic as the beloved's disheveled curls, but the straight path is mapped clearly on the beauty of her upright figure:

> What a hubbub in the wine house!
> The clamor has spread everywhere.
> What mutiny did her eyes plot, this time?
> The uproar comes from all directions.
> What wine did her lips serve?
> A sip intoxicated every soul there is.

***

Oh cup-bearer! One more cup, I am giddy with love
The wine that got to my head is still there.
Love's outcry is ringing all around me
The charm is as strong as ever.
My life, is chaos like your long untied hair
Without your upright figure, there are no straight paths for me.
You are the destination for the journey that is my being
Cups have no purpose but to hold pure wine.
My soul is a mirror for your countenance,
Your face reflected in it clear as daylight.
Flowers all have the color of your face,
Why else would they look so handsome?[52]

In a similar ghazel that develops some of the same themes in varying shades and colors, the main frame is restructured. The wine house is moved to the space of the lover's inner world. In this version, *we* are the sites for the mutiny. In the wine house that is our being, the primordial wine is mixed with the clay that fashions our human form. The wine is the sacred essence described in verse 29 of the sura *Al-Hajar,* the breath of God generating life in the human prototype.[53] The parallel drawn between wine and the Qur'anic description of God's life-giving breath is daring. But most fascinating in this ghazel is the simple, down-to-earth, and intimate portrayal of the omnipotent creator as he adds to his creation step-by-step with the kind of love and interdependency that a human artist feels toward his/her work of art. Paradoxical and hazy precincts of our view are kept in the foreground through a deliberately ambiguous shifting of the agency of creation from God to love and vice versa. Halfway through the poem, this God/love creator transforms into a calligrapher himself made up of letters he uses as model to inscribe the human existence. The merging is gradual and subtle. The beloved arranges a grand show of revealing his beauty only to himself as the blind, inactive, and groggy lover inches his/her way with difficulty toward this center of activity. At this point, in the ninth verse in the ghazel, the lover's union with the beloved occurs. In an intimate moment of "self-display" (*kirishmah*), the beloved empowers the lover with every gift that defines and distinguishes the divine aptitude. From this point on, the movement is reversed. The lover now returns to the world not less clamorous or mutinous—because mutiny is in love's constitution —but revived with the sacred energy. However, the lover's clamor is this time a different kind matching his/her newly endowed divine abilities. S/he now has the beloved's eyes to see with and a spark of his gnosis with which to unravel the divine mystery spread far and wide. In a delightful ending strategy, 'Irāqī summons the beloved to the scene of transformation riveting and warlike! The beloved is ready to plunder the lover's heart all over, a reminder that the cycle of love and growth has no end:

Love left a mutinous core in our being,
Putting our lives to a permanent test.
Words, it put in our mouth,
And a quest, deep in our hearts.
A drop, it took from the wine barrel
    and mixed with the clay,
The life in Adam and Eve came from that drop.

***

Every moment love appeared in a fresh garb,
Every instant it arrived in a new place.
Because He did not have a designated house,
Wherever there was room, He made his residence.
He copied the letter that Himself was made of,
That inscribed letter he named Adam and Eve.
To Himself, He was revealing his own beauty,
Though the pretext was the lover.
His own eyes enjoyed His own glory,
The poor-sighted lover caught in the display.
He revealed Himself to Himself with such intensity
That a flash of love reached every being young and old.

***

Farhad's desire, and the inner longing of all of us,
He manifested in the sweet lips of the beauteous Shirin.
For the union to be enjoyed by everyone,
He bestowed sight on every blind eye.
For the perfection of His knowledge to become manifest,
He spread divine mysteries across vast open fields.
A riotous uproar took the world over,
As the divine beauty came out of ambush to plunder.
In the eye of the storm, He looked and saw ʿIrāqī,
"That prelude to all mutiny!" He exclaimed.[54]

Knowing God through knowing oneself is a theme familiar to many mystical tra-
ditions. ʿIrāqī expands on that theme with conviction. There are no ways to reach
the sacred Other than through our seemingly imperfect human form. No matter
where the divine resides, the road to that residence is imprinted on us:

There is a big city, I reside therein.
Life is water, I am the jar that holds it.
I have sensed a [divine] scent at some point,
My life is sustained with that scent and the breeze that carries it.

> Don't toy with me O master! Don't take me lightly,
> I am a description of His unparalleled glory.
> Hit with life's polo stick
> I am running like a ball on a playground.
> I have acquired the nature of His attributes,
> No one knows, truly, my nature.[55]

The human nature of the divine, or the divine temperament manifested through humanity, is "truly" unknowable. This is in part due to its hybrid nature. Neither is the relation between the two parts—human and divine—free of quarrel. In one of his most celebrated ghazels, 'Irāqī starts in the traditional poetic style of juxtaposing parallels:

> Blessed is the pain to which you are the cure,
> Blessed is the road to which you are the destination.
> Blessed is the eye that beholds your countenance,
> Blessed is the land in which you are the king.[56]

The repetitive patterns establish a stable and familiar background. The pairs such as pain/cure or road/destination presented in a rapid succession are easy to visualize and musically flowing. The refrain "you are" (*tu bashi*) is expressed in conditional subjunctive introducing a humorous *if* into the statement. The pleasant swinging between parallels, however, is interrupted with cries of pain and confusion when the abandoned lover points a finger at the divine:

> Do not question concerning faith and infidelity the one who has
>   given his heart!
> He, whose faith and infidelity is none other than you.
> Do not hide from the lover, whose day and night
> Whose hidden and revealed worlds are none other than you.[57]

"He Gave the Air to the Birds, the Sea to the Fish": Exactitude and Sobriety

Side by side with the intoxication and daring unconventionality of 'Irāqī and his peers, a current of sober, conventional, and well-contained behavior in relation to the sacred develops in premodern Persian literature. This current is no less mystical or love-conscious in its orientation toward the sacred. Yet it views the world in a less mutinous and more orderly fashion. In this worldview, things are more possible to be predicted and controlled. The values such as the purity of intentions, breaking the idol of the self, and detachment from the world are still central. So is the absolute power of God as the ruler of the universe and the designer par excellence of all things. Still, this master of creation is not undecided or temperamental as is Khayyám's creator. Nor is he a playmate or a dance partner to humans, as is God/beloved in Rūmī's scheme of things. He is not ʿIrāqī's passionate and ravishing beloved comforting a mutinous creation with the rupture of momentary union. Carrying a touch of each of these sacreds in itself, the sober astute divine is distinguished from them by attention to every detail in his creation. These intricacies he loves and plans generously and vigilantly. His expectations of humans are challenging and hard to meet but are not mysterious, conflicting, or confusing. As a result, despite the divine's absolute power, and less intimate relationship with the world, human beings stand a better chance of predicting the divine will and satisfying it through pious and disciplined behavior. Abū al-Majd Majdud ibn Adam, Sanāʾī (d. 1130), is one of the forefathers of this balanced and well-rounded vision of the sacred.

> O King, I praise thee, for thou art pure, thou art God
> I won't traverse except on the road that thou point me to.
> Thou art generous, thou art kind, thou art great and bountiful
> Thou showeth your exultation, thou art worthy of praise.[58]

Approximately a century after Sanāʾī, Saʿdī (d. 1292) refined and perfected this sober poetic expression of the divine in the generically diverse corpus of his poetry. In the works of Saʿdī, this cool, orderly, compassionate, but predictable God comes to life (one might even say comes of age). On the one hand, Saʿdī affirms the sobriety, exactitude, and systemic nature of the divine will through portrayal of the creation as complicated yet fully balanced. On the other, Saʿdī's own poetic language mirrors, in precision and orderliness, this perception of the divine. Just as Rūmī's dancing divine is reflected in the dynamic poetic dance that comprises his lyrics, Saʿdī's polished and carefully crafted syntax reflects his vision of the universe. Earlier, Khayyám's creator made an exquisite jar one instant and broke it the next. Even Abu Saʾid's God dealt with the affairs of his creation in less than a perfect manner. Saʿdī's creator is a keen mastermind with plenty of attention and patience to lavish on details. He does not break at whim what he has made. Neither does he permit creatures to overstep their boundaries and deprive each other of that which has been allotted to each species:

> Through generosity and bounty to His slaves
> He gave the air to the birds, the sea to the fish.
> Each has his share, the rich and the poor,
> Daily sustenance is allotted to every mosquito, every bird.
> He would know through his knowledge of the unseen,
> The needs of an ant at the bottom of a well, beneath a rock.
> He creates life out of semen, sugar from sugar cane,
> Fresh leaves from dry wood, water from stony earth.[59]

The subtleties of this divinely tamed cosmos are not apparent to the imperfect human mind. The intoxicated gnostic *'arif-i madhush,* however, is given the inner faculty to discern the divine will behind every baffling complexity. In truth, not just the tongue of the mystic but every limb in the human body sings the praise of the divine artistry.[60] Witnesses to these marvels are many, the physical beauty of the fair-faced ones being one of the most special sites of presence:

> In your face the mysteries of the craftsmanship of the Lord
> Is visible as is water in a fine crystal jar.[61]

Variations on the theme abound and lead to subthemes, for example the intoxication of the world with itself because of it being the site of the presence of the sacred. The world is, therefore, by nature a happy place, just as those are happy who can see the divine agency of love in its constitution:

> I am happy in the world, for the world is gladdened by Him.
> I am in love with the world, for the world is all from Him.
> Treasure the morning breeze! And you will bring life into dead hearts
> It is the breath of Jesus my friend! It is all from Him.
> The celestial spheres are impoverished, the angles empty-handed
> Compared to that which we all carry in our innermost being, all
>   from Him.[62]

While the intoxicated Sufis downplay the significance of formal worship, the sober school makes more frequent allegorical reference to performance of daily rituals such as prayer, fasting, or pilgrimage. Performance has to be augmented with right intentions. Nevertheless, emphasizing the significance of the rituals to all indicates the logical and predictable nature of the God/human relation regulated by standard worship. Sometimes allusions to rituals are for allegorical purposes. Sa'dī is fond of such metaphors and often adds to their effectiveness with a touch of humor. *Sama',* the mystical dance during which the exuberant dancer might tear his clothes, is one such example in the following verses:

> No journey feels long to a true seeker's feet,
> The one who died for Him is eternally alive.
> When the spiritually intoxicated rise to dance,
> Not just clothes but their skin fails to contain their joy.[63]

The stages on the Sufi path form equally subtle allegorical spaces in which the poetic message weaves the lyrical and the spiritual into a colorful tapestry. *Taslim* (complete surrender) to the divine will is unconditional, *sabr* (patience) is the desert to be traversed in the journey to the *Ka'bah* of visual contact with God, and the station of *rida* (contentment) must be perfected to the point of drinking poison and surrendering oneself to the divine sword if so desired by the beloved. The end is the complete annihilation of the lover, complete union.[64]

In this world, carefully sign-posted by prophets and saints, human beings make few choices. The sacred is present everywhere and the journey toward him is ultimately unavoidable. With or without the ritualistic tools preparing the wayfarer for the path, everyone will in the end make the journey that has started with their birth. Still, even this methodical world is not without its paradoxes. Despite God's distinct presence, and the inevitability of ultimate contact, the formless nature of the sacred plays tricks on the seeker. Neither does almighty have any likeness in the world detectable to human senses:

> I cannot describe you the way you truly are,
> For this is a fabric too wide to fit in the textile bazaar.
> I will no longer surrender my heart to any created form,
> Being with you is not the encounter that fits into the form of *didar*.[65]

The good news is that this fabric "too wide to fit in the textile bazaar" is on sale everywhere. The apparent absence of the sacred is due to easy accessibility of his hidden form. Humanity is aided with the gift of God's names in its attempt to renew the primordial covenant and to renew the lost memory of the presence of the sacred. The music of love is not a well-guarded secret; it is the rhythm of daily life:

> The heart comes to life with the hope of loyalty to the friend,
> The soul rises to dance hearing the voice of the beloved.[66]

The forgotten truth is formless and recovering the memory difficult. However, surrendering to God's power, listening to the music of love, and opening up to the novelty of the love's games make it worthwhile. The God/human relation in this context is that of a master and slave. Somewhere in the exchange, however, there is a message of hope for an intimate love leading into eventual union.

FAMILIAR THREADS, NEW TAPESTRY

In less than a century, Sa'dī is followed by Hāfez of Shīrāz (d. 1388?) another master of ghazel writing. Despite his reputation as the *lisan al-ghayb* (the tongue of the unseen), and although viewed as the writer of "ghazal at its summit," Hāfez has received little critical attention. The fifteenth-century literary historian Dawlat Shah of Samarqand in the *Tadhkirat al-shu'ara'* (Biography of poets) considers Hāfez's lyrics to be "beyond human creative capacity." In these ghazels, Hāfez combines order and mutiny, intoxication and sobriety, as well as discord and surrender. The edifice that Hāfez has erected deserves extensive analysis in an independent monograph.[67] Here, I limit the discussion to a general outline of the portrayal of the sacred in the world. In a playful and changing tone, which affirms the human weakness and strength in comprehending the sacred, Hāfez moves between conflicting positions with ease. One instant he reminds the reader that no one will ever know the divine secrets, only to declare in the next:

> The face of the beloved is completely unveiled
> Wash the sand off your eyes so you may be able to see.[68]

Sharp Khayyám-like encounters with the divine are not uncommon:

> A flash of lightning from Layli's quarters brightened the dawn
> Ah, what did it do to the harvest of Majnun's existence?
> Give me wine, O cup-bearer! For it is not apparent
> What the painter of the unseen did behind the curtain of mysteries.

More specifically, in the controversial verse known for its candid cynicism:

> Our master said there have been no errors in creation!
> Blessed is his pure vision, his kind indulging judgment![69]

Yet, for Hāfez, this faulty and bewildered creation is the site of presence of the sacred in a Rūmī-like all-embracing manner that transcends the limits of specific religious conviction:

> The grand Magus is my master, what difference is there?
> No heart is devoid of divine mysteries.
> In the monastery of ascetic and the seclusion of the Sufi
> There are no prayer niches other than your arched eyebrows.[70]

In this diverse land fertile for the cultivation of the sacred, the poet's own words are often presented as the mirror depicting the purest of divine manifestations. Hāfez's talent in the poetic art of sacred making is displayed best when his divine-revealing "mirror of words" transforms into simple songs that praise the beauty of the worldly beloved:

> O hidden from sight! O companion of the heart!
> I send you words of prayer and songs of praise.
> In [the beauty of] your own face, see the divine craftsmanship,
> For I send you a mirror that reveals God's face.
> So the musicians tell you of the eagerness in my heart,
> I send you ghazels grafted on melodious songs.[71]

Beyond sporadic allusions to the sacred, Hāfez produces entire ghazels that carefully craft a poetic scheme to solve the ontological dilemma of human imperfection. In these ghazels, which maintain thematic wholeness in tightly constructed verses, readers participate in dramatized primordial scenes of the ensoulment of the human prototype. The success of these ghazels, which are among the best known in the *Divan* of Hāfez, is in the ease with which they blend the earthly human and the divine sacred together. Hāfez does not seek to revolutionize the traditional poetic language itself. Rather, he makes the transformation through skillful use of existing poetic devices. His tone is candid and sharp, and his images complex. The resonance of the anecdotes is enhanced through a rich combination of allusions to Qur'anic and other intertextually familiar sources:

> Last night, I saw the angels knocking at the door of the wine house,
> Where they measured the clay of Adam and mixed it [with wine].
> Those beings from high heavens protected by God against sin,
> Shared drinks with a homeless poor wayfarer such as me!

Far from insignificant, the "homeless poor wayfarer" is celebrated for his human poverty, capacity to love, and willingness to take risks. The adjective *divanah* (crazy), used in the following verse to describe the human prototype, serves the multiple purpose of denoting all the above while resting the responsibility of human imperfection on God. Equally significant is the allusion in the adjective to the seminal role of love in human disposition:

> The sky could not carry the load of His trust
> Who should be selected to carry the load but a crazy one like me?
> O forgive the endless disagreements of the seventy-two sects,
> The truth was kept from them, they opted for tales.
> Still, praise be to the Lord for the peace between me and my beloved!
> Fellow Sufis have since been celebrating with cup after cup!
> I wouldn't call fire the flame reflected in the candle's laughter,
> Fire is that which burns the moth's existence into ashes.[72]

Notorious for exposing the hypocrisy in the institutionalized religion, Hāfez produces a wide critical repertoire to reveal the corruption of the clergy engaged in display of pious behavior guarding their respectable public image:

> The preachers appearing piously on the pulpit and facing Mecca to pray,
> Do that which is not preaching and praying where no soul can see.
> Pray ask the respectable expert in the assembly to answer my question:
> How is it that those recommending repentance rarely repent themselves?
> It is almost as if they have no faith in arrival of the hour of judgment!
> Why else would they consider their false coins acceptable to a discerning
>   judge?

The sarcastic and overly grim outlook of the poem is gradually brightened with the talk of love. The cure for the hypocritical small-minded human being who hopes to trick God into accepting his faulty coin is a cup from the wine house where the hearts are "empowered" with one sip. Here the Sufi concept of *husn* (beauty) utilized by Abu Sa'id comes to play again; the wine is none other than the essence of divine beauty:

> As the divine beauty slays lovers in vast numbers,
> Another group come to life with love and emerge from the unseen.

> Come angels, praise the Lord at the threshold of love's wine house!
> For that is where Adam's clay is in perpetual making.

Again, all this is connected intrinsically with human ability for verbal self-expression and with the poet's own words in particular:

> There was a hubbub in high heavens early this morning,
> It seems like the angels are memorizing the words of Hāfez![73]

The public fight with hypocrisy, and the effort to nurture the true self, has a personal side that develops into an equally prominent theme. Being true to the self is the absolute precondition for being true to the sacred. Sincerity should be manifested on the more limited personal scale before it can become a social virtue. Hāfez is particularly interested in the interplay between the two. Still, the wide range of variations on the theme would not allow a full treatment here. More relevant for us are discussions of the nature of the sacred built around the need to fight hypocrisy and false pride:

> In the Magus's tavern, I see divine light,
> What light! What unlikely place! How is this possible?
> O, guide to the caravan of pilgrims to Mecca! Don't boast of your
>   privilege
> You [arrive there and] see the building, I the owner of the sacred house.

***

> A heart burning with desire, tears at dawn, calling on God in the night,
> These are gifts you have bestowed on me with your grace.
> Every instant, your beauty enchants my imagination again!
> Who will understand if I describe what I see on this canvas?[74]

The poets who, following Hāfez, continue the poetic art of sacred making, expand the repertoire of God/human encounters. By the eighteenth and nineteenth centuries, elaborate long *qit'ahs, tarji'bands,* and other generic forms are devoted completely to the theme and its variations. Rarely did such examples present completely original ideas, novel approaches to the sacred, or fresh strategies for encoding poetic massages. When they did display signs of originality, they met with great public success. The tarji'band with the refrain "wahdahu la ilaha illa hu" (he is one, there is none other than him) by Hatif, the eighteenth-century poet of Isfahān, is one such example. The poem is among the best-known examples from the last phases of premodern Persian poetry. It combines a tolerant Sufi vision of the unity of all persuasions with colorful imagery and brief dramatic descriptions of Sufi gatherings. These elements are brought together in the frame of a natural syntax comfortably fitting in the poem's light melodic rhythm. While the simplicity and memorability of the rhythm explain much of the success, the poet's revolutionary openness to certain supposedly foreign doctrines such as the trinity add an air of novelty that catches the readers' imagination. In the second section of the poem, the doctrine of trinity is justified with the argument that silk will remain silk even if it is referred to with three different names *parnian, harir,* or *parand.*[75] More significant than justifying the Christian doctrine is the fact that the argument is not presented to us by the poet but rather in the voice of a Christian, and a woman at that. As she couches her argument in the metaphorical silk called three different things, the church bell rings echoing the poems familiar refrain: *"wahdahu la ilaha illa hu."*

Another significant later development in the poetic expression of the sacred is the panegyric or the elegiac verse written in honor of the holy Shiite figures, the Imams. This pattern gains prominence from the early sixteenth century in the Ṣafavid Iran due to the overt support of the ruling dynasty for Shiite sentiments. The thematic genre survives and reaches the twentieth century side by side with the "modernized" poetry that expresses its religious/spiritual sentiments in entirely different ways.[76]

In general, it would be safe to argue that while the sacred remains central to poetic expression, at least in exploring the broader patterns, patterns of sacred making do not go through structural change in seventeenth and eighteenth centuries. In the late nineteenth and early twentieth centuries, however, the sobering encounter with modernity disrupts the flow of traditional cultural expression and makes an impact in this area too. Since emerging paradigms in poetic expressions of spirituality in the twentieth century are the main focus of the rest of this monograph, I deal with them in detail in chapters to come. In the meantime, the premodern landscape that we explored in this chapter should provide us with a clear idea of the plurality of the traditional background in poetic expressions of the sacred. It is against this background and in contradistinction to it that the modern poet makes his/her poetic contribution.

"I Was Heading for God's Quarters"

Resignifying the Poetic Idiom for Modern Spiritual Expression

The two revolutions that shook twentieth-century Iran reflected the urgency felt in the entire region for change in the social and political system.[1] The events themselves are the concrete manifestations of long processes of social and intellectual reform rooted in the nineteenth century and earlier. As with the European enlightenment, here too, the proponents of social change viewed it as intrinsically connected to linguistic—particularly literary—reform. Similarly, the literary reformists understood the process to be connected with broader changes. Ahmad Karimi-Hakkak has demonstrated that influential nineteenth-century figures such as Akhundzadeh, Kermani, and Malkom situated their program for revitalizing the Iranian poetic system of signification and communication at the heart of the debate on social and cultural reform. As a part of larger agenda to modernize Iran, they sought to "free" poetry from a "pathological obsession with an idealized sense of beauty" and stylized expression.[2]

The twentieth-century modernist poets agreed with their predecessors on the need for revitalizing the poetic system. When targeting specific problems, they highlighted religious belief as the major obstacle on the way to progress. Deliberate dissociation from institutionalized Islam permeated the poems and critical remarks of such figures as Suhrab Sepehri (1928–81), Ahmad Shamlu (1925–2000), Forugh Farrokhzad (1935–67), and others. In the process, these prominent figures of twentieth-century poetry seemed to distance themselves equally from their classical literary forefathers such as Rūmī, Hāfez, and Saʿdī. To contemporary historians such as Nikki Keddie, they appeared to disregard the passionate Shiʿi sentiments of a largely devout Muslim population.[3] Keddie described the scene in twentieth-century Iran as "the two-cultures phenomenon," arguing for a schizophrenic cultural self-perception in which the "secular" elite lived completely cut off from the rural and popular classes. According to her, by the middle of the century, the breakdown between the elite and the populace was complete.[4] Keddie's categorization may be challenged on many grounds. First, as the present work demonstrates, the rubric "secular" will prove seriously insufficient to describe the variety of intellectual and spiritual tendencies demonstrated even by the handful of major figures named above. Furthermore, her categorization excludes many young inquisitive minds firmly rooted in the Islamic tradition such as those described in Roy Mottahedeh's colorful account of the 1979 revolution, *The Mantle of the Prophet.*[5] Included among these, and disregarded in Keddie's paradigm, are prominent figures, such as 'Ali Shari'ati, who exerted formative influence in the 1979 revolution and were rooted in the elitist intellectual as well as the religious tradition.[6]

More important, the distance assumed between the Iranian elite, the so-called secular poets of this century, and their literary/spiritual forefathers (i.e., Rūmī), as well as the religious populace, is exaggerated. For the most part, this is a critical misreading of the seditious posture of modern poetry beneath which a deep desire for a spiritual identity fuels the creative impulse. As the society moved toward modernization and exponents of the literary tradition renewed and redefined it, new avenues of religious and spiritual expression were explored. In the process, modern Persian poetry became the vehicle for a gradual process of resignification of premodern mystical/religious concepts that led to the formation of new literary/spiritual paradigms. It is important to realize that the entire resignification process may remain unnoticed if critical inquiry continues to recognize as religious/spiritual only the familiar poetic structures such as Qur'anic allusions and ignores the paradigm shift. If, on the other hand, the old paradigms are abandoned and new poetic patterns are sought, a rich unexplored domain of spiritual expression opens before us. We can observe, in this domain, the cultural and linguistic embeddedness of the notion of spirituality in twentieth-century Iran and its success in coexisting with the inherited notion of the supremacy of reason. In this chapter, and those that follow, I explore the formation of new spiritual paradigms and the formulation of new literary strategies leading to the creation of a new space for the sacred that appears to have been displaced by the onset of modernity. A fascinating feature of this cultural/literary phenomenon is that, far from cutting itself from the past, in the process of creating "new" paradigms, it relies consistently on interaction with and renewal of the past. While some such efforts meet with limited success, others lead to formation of effective new patterns.

Before examining the renewal process more closely, a clarification is in order. The present work does not include the "revolutionary" poetry produced in the last two decades of twentieth-century Iran. The argument for the exclusion is manifold. It is chiefly based on the understanding that the post 1979 revolutionary literature needs to be acknowledged as an independent genre with its own variety of subgenres, all forging their specific norms and conventions. Furthermore, a good deal of the poetry produced in the post-1979 Iran demonstrates a fascinating backward-looking posture. This is a feature most probably motivated, among other things, by the desire to revive traditional indigenous patterns that are capable of replacing those inspired by European poetry. While this backward glance is by no means devoid of the impulse to renew and expand, it leads, at least from a formal point of view, to the revival of traditional qasidah and ghazel writing. A detailed independent study will be required to explore the formation and development of this "revolutionary" formalistic revival still in its formative stages.

Let me now step back and outline the literary reform movement that started long before the 1979 revolution and led to the emergence of concepts refashioned to suit the "modern" world. My focus remains narrow deliberately to keep in view the poetic expressions of the sacred in its journey of evolution.

The Call to Modernity

In their first encounters with modernity, eighteenth- and nineteenth-century Persian historians (Rustam al-Hukama', author of *Rustam al-Tavarikh*, and I'timad al-Saltanah, author of *Mir'at al-Buldan,* for example) attempted to rechart the past in order to designate for Iran a more central place in history. Language, and specifically poetry with its highly personalized discourse, played a crucial role in providing the semantic tools for the process of dissociating Iranian national identity form its Muslim counterpart.[7] Not only was language the tool for articulating the new vision and therefore necessarily subjected to crucial changes, but, as Mohammad Tavakoli-Targhi has observed, in the nineteenth and twentieth centuries Persian debate on modernity language was often foregrounded as a formative element. Mirza Aqa Khan Kirmani, for example, argued that the Persian word *nivishtan* (writing) was derived from the root *naw* (new) and therefore denoted the original act of creating something new.[8]

To fill the vacuum caused by cutting ties with the Islamic culture, attempts were made to revive, or rather construct, an inspiring past. Early classical poetry, which had flourished in the tenth to twelfth centuries in northeast Iran, provided a suitable source. This poetry embodied a worldview with fewer apparent religious tendencies, more passion for life, and an equal desire for contemplating the beauty of the carnal world. In this milieu, the canonical status of such verses as the following by 'Ali ibn Julagh Farrukhi (d. 1037) were reinstated:

> So lush is the earth, as if it were the open sky,
> The open sky is a garden in bloom.
> In the fields, the tulip is a pair of ruby lips,
> The nightingale is the voice of the green tree.
> The flowers are night-lights for the gardener,
> The eglantine tree is the slender figure of the beloved.[9]

These and similar poems, picturing a carefree past undisturbed by sociopolitical upheavals, were recirculated as genuinely Persian artifacts through a revivalist movement, which became known as the movement of *bazgasht* (return).[10] Poets as renowned as Mohammad Taqī Bahār (d. 1951) contributed to the movement by producing qasidahs that succeeded in capturing the imagination of popular readership. Despite its initial aesthetic appeal, the "return" movement failed to provide a viable literary option because it failed to participate in the domestic intellectual debate. Rapid social change led to a general ambivalence demanding flexible and dynamic poetic modes to respond to its changing and self-scrutinizing impulse. How should the Iranians envision themselves in the world? How would national identity form? Would the Iranian nation include non-Muslim members? Who would define the role of such minorities? To what extent should religion interfere in the daily realities of living in a rapidly changing world? The return movement was simply inadequate in responding to such crucial questions.

THE SPIRITUAL IN RE-ENVISIONING POETRY

New literary paradigms had to develop to reshape the ideal role that poetry was to play in these changing circumstances. These paradigmatic notions were inspired predominantly by what was understood to be the cultured, strong, and free Europe pioneering a progressive approach to literature. In demonstrating selectively ideal features, this Europe came close to the idealized Iran of centuries past. It demonstrated only positive cultural tendencies and a curious affinity with the "authentic" cultural features of classical Iran. In the heat of the desire to find such similarities, some intellectuals went so far as finding Persian etymologies for certain key concepts in European languages. Thus the French term *histoire*, according to Mirza Aqa Khan Kirmani, was derived from the Persian term *ustuvar*, meaning "firm and sturdy." Similarly, Iranians were claimed to be the initiators of the custom of eating at the table, which was later adopted by Europe, for how could otherwise the Persian term *mizban* (host), literally "the one responsible for the table," be explained?[11]

The poetry inspired by this glorious past and suitable for "modern" Iran was to be multifaceted. Not only was it expected to rid itself of the norms and conventions that had over the centuries given it a distant and depersonalized demeanor in order to connect to its immediate surroundings. The modern poet had to be ultrasensitive to his/her social responsibility because with the artistic talent came grave social and moral obligations. If learning about the past became relevant, then it was the poet's duty to learn history. Nima Yushij (1895–1959), who came to be known as the father of modern Persian poetry, demanded that a poet be able "to sit in the place a stone is sitting and feel the storms of centuries past with his own body."[12] The modern poet had to have all the virtues of an intelligent, knowledgeable, sensitive leader for taking the society through hard times as well as putting the concern of others before his/her own.[13] Whereas the classical poet received gold as appreciation for his words of praise, the modern poet was to expect no rewards for the heroic contribution. Rather, the reward came with being crowned as a modern poet, a considerable honor in itself. To continue to remold Persian poetry was at the heart of such poetic responsibilities and not just from a formalistic point of view. In Nima's words:

> Our classical poetry has an artificial air about it which is caused by its connections with, and subordination to, music. When we take a poem out of its formal metrical pattern, we see that it produces a different effect. I have done this to Persian poetry, I have freed it from this horrendous captivity, redirected it to its natural course, and have endowed it with a descriptive tendency. . . . I realized, not just through looking at Persian poetic meter but through examining its function, that this poetry has to be essentially remolded, I repeat not just from the point of view of form but function as well.[14]

Interestingly enough, in this re-envisioning of the poetic process involving form and function proposed by Nima, there was no visible concern for spirituality. It was almost as if the need for the spiritual was a thing of the past that would be remedied with the onset of modernity. Classical Persian poetry had been deeply devoted to spirituality. The poets in this tradition had forged for themselves identities solid enough not to fade with time and malleable enough to provide variations on recognizable themes. As we can judge even from the brief overview in the previous chapter, love, wit and humor, ethical leadership, and spiritual conviction all had a place in that complex identity, which received selective emphasis to meet the contextual and generic demand. Modernists had to forge an independent identity. They had to cut the umbilical cord, as it were, and become their own source of strength. To enforce the process of separation, they did what all teenagers do on the way to adulthood: they exaggerated beyond proportion the "undesired" dimensions of the classical identity. By mid–twentieth century, claiming an idealistic Layla and Majnun brand of love raised questions about the mental health of the poet and assuming ethical leadership or expressing spiritual conviction ran the risk of being counterproductive. In the poem *Ma'shuq-i man* (The One I Love), Farrokhzad, one of the most prominent poetic voices of this century, rewrote the sickly and passive Majnun into an assertive lover. This was a "savagely free" lover, a frank expression of natural instincts in the flash of whose teeth a thirsty Berber dreamed of a prey's warm blood. The contrast between him and Majnun went from subtle comparisons and sporadic allusions to a clear claim to superiority:

> The one I love
> means something clear, inevitable
> as nature herself.
> He proves
> true the law of force
> in my defeat.

He's savage and free
as a healthy instinct
in the heart of a desert island
He wipes the dust of the street
from his shoes with rags
torn from Majnun's tent.[15]

Expressions of hopeless love and contentment with suffering were not romantic
anymore, or worthy of poetry. The same was true of assuming ethical leadership.
Claims had to be verified in some variation of a "people's court." Poetic invention
was to result from uninterrupted dialogic contact between fictive creation and the
reality of the poet's daily life. Farrokhzad dismissed "distance from real life" not
just in Majnun's exaggerated love, but in every aspect of the poet's existence. She
said in a radio interview:

> Poetry is essentially a part of life. It cannot exist independent of life and
> outside circle of impacts that the real life events create on the individual.
> . . . If poetry remains oblivious of the conditions in which it comes to
> existence and evolves, it can never be called poetry. Unfortunately, in our
> present-day poetry, the one to which we refer as modern, even though
> there is a pretence of loyalty to reality, there is a considerable distance from
> real life.[16]

In her more pessimistic moments, Farrokhzad saw no constructive roles for reli-
gion in this reality she tried to remain loyal to. She objected particularly to the
institutionalized version of religion, followed *blindly* by the generations past. In
this scheme of things, God was little more than a delusion conjured by the
believer's fear of punishment:

All of Mother's life
Has been a prayer rug
Spread at the gate of hell's terrors.
Mother hunts for sin's footprints
Under everything
And believes the garden's been fouled
By some sin's blaspheming.
Mother prays all day long
Mother sins naturally
And blows on all the flowers
And blows on all the fish
And blows on herself
Mother awaits the coming of heaven
And the descent of forgiveness.[17]

Pointing a finger at religion for all shortcomings was in fashion. There was a pride in the newfound courage to question God's role, even existence. Poets such as Nadir Nadirpur (1929–2000) who belonged to less subversive reformist traditions, joined forces with the skeptics in putting God on trial. In the poem *Shi'ir-i khuda* (God's Poem), he endowed the devil with God's creative status. In this poem, locked in a literary binary opposition, Satan and God are appraised for their poetic achievements. All pleasurable experiences, such as love, singing, and wine drinking, are associated with sin and constitute the devil's poetic corpus. God, on the other hand, has but one poem: *gham,* the meditative sorrow, which is his masterpiece. Although in the closing stanza Nadirpur added to God's literary accomplishments the possible existence of unknown poems, and although he privileged God's single poem gham over the devil's entire pleasure-inducing collection, the fact that Satan was permitted to challenge God remained.[18] Even the relatively subdued Nadirpur exhibited stronger iconoclastic tendencies when dealing with the liturgical aspects of institutionalized religion. In a poem that gained instant fame, and was named after the cradle of Shiite conformity, the city of Qom, he portrayed what he viewed as total decay in an institution that had had a strong hold on the masses.[19] To portray the town, Nadirpur structured the poem in short disjointed phrases selecting only rigidity and lifelessness for description. In the poem *Qom,* there are no signs of the lucid blue sky, the fragrant nature, and the vivid colors that are well known to Nadirpur's readers. There are, instead, "old crows resting on piles of stone," "ponds half-filled with stale water," and "a garden devoid of green." The only colorful image that may bring a positive feeling into the poem is that of a "golden dome," which quickly loses its visual attraction as the following line converts it into a resting place for "old storks." The characters that people the poem are equally hard to relate to. They are either a part of the faceless mass of *chandin hazar zan* (a few thousands of women) and *chandin hazar mard* (a few thousands of men) or more specifically they are *anbuh-i sa'ilan* (the crowd of beggars). Of human activities, we only hear about two absences: the absence of speech and the absence of laughter. In the poem's powerful ending, Nadirpur's quiet elegy of decay and sorrow is disrupted with a final loud cry. This is a description of the inherent evil of religion in the black faces of the clerical figures in the crowd and in its sharp contrast with what symbolizes the clergy's neat and conforming appearance: their white turban.

REINVENTED POETIC PATTERNS OF SPIRITUAL EXPRESSION

Nadirpur's attack on religion was one among many. The tapestry of inner spiritual desires seemed to have been left with a large hole in the center caused by the intellectual fear and dismissal of the "irrational faith." Whether the hole was real or illusory, the artifact itself was not discarded regardless of the defect. Despite the great insistence on critical reflection on the value and nature of faith, it was impossible to step outside the culture to get a completely distant objective view of the situation. Georgia Warnke has prudently observed that critical reflection often does not undermine loyalty to the authority of the tradition because the critic cannot get "outside" of the tradition to subject it to independent criticism.[20] This would describe the attempts to scrutinize religion in the early and middle part of twentieth-century Iran accurately. However, in attempts to free oneself of old traditions, according to Richard Rorty, poetry is a great ally to hermeneutics. Poetry has a strong tendency to "create and appreciate new ways of acting and speaking." It is willing to explore unfamiliar territory by reinterpreting our "familiar surroundings" in exciting "unfamiliar terms" of new inventions.[21] We feel secure and comfortable in familiar environments that protect us against the anxiety of facing the new by blending them into the obscurity of the familiar. Poetry dares to challenge that. It foregrounds these elements and makes them visible despite the murkiness of the familiar environment. Twentieth-century Persian poetry fulfilled exactly that role. Side by side with the above polemical gestures, it took the tradition through a colorful process of inventing and rearticulating the desire for the sacred in freshly encoded poetic messages. These messages were too complex and varied to fit under a single rubric. By and large, though, they exhibited one general characteristic: extensive positive use of religious themes and concepts. In what follows, I sift through these themes and concepts in search of patterns that go beyond isolated individualistic use, demonstrate repetitive but evolving presence, and possess broad intertextual visibility and endurance.

EARTHLY PSALMS: ADOPTING SCRIPTURAL STRUCTURES

Poetry has to rely on resonance. If its subject matter, imagery, rhythm, structural composition, or some constituent elements do not strike familiar cords, it will not evoke any response that would live beyond the page. As the relatively small number of examples I quoted in the previous chapter show, classical Persian poetry relied heavily, for resonance, on religious spiritual elements. These could range from direct extensive quotes from the Qur'an and the hadith, Sufi aphorisms and tales, to ethical teachings of religious figures or well-known writers. The persona of various prophets vibrated with strong individualized—yet resonant—qualities suitable for breathing life into poetic messages aimed at reaching broad audiences. Even poets with overt antireligious sentiments such as Ahmad Shamlu made regular use of this strategy. In the poem *Lawh* (The Tablet), for example, the poetic persona is that of a prophet, albeit a prophet whose mission is to avert a thoughtless crowd from their long and desperate search for another divine revelation. To warn the crowd against "mourning some crucified Christ," the poet disguises himself as Moses holding up a clay tablet and preaching his three commandments of mercy, friendship, and honesty:

Then I held up the clay tablet crying unto them:
"This is all there is; and sealed
It's an old inscription, aged and worn, lo! Behold!
However tainted with the blood of many a wound
Mercy it preaches, friendship and honesty."[22]

Such use of religious personae, often in redefined contexts, became so prevalent that I devote a section to it later in this chapter. By mid–twentieth century, however, most varieties of religious themes and contents were seriously out of fashion. A Qur'anic quotation, for example, would raise questions about the political affinity or the rational/progressive nature of the poet's contribution. Allusions to the hadith or resorting to ethical guidance would amount to a literary suicide. As we shall see with Muhammad Riza Shafi'i-Kadkani's experiment later in this section, certain Sufi figures such as Hallāj were in the "acceptable" zone due to the possibility of interpreting their actions as a variety of political activism. Still, care had to be taken for them not to be associated too closely with institutionalized religion. Even a poet as established as Sa'dī was criticized for propagating "rigid" ethical values.[23] In general, new ways had to be invented to encode poetic messages celebrating the presence, and the significance, of the sacred without the negative implications evoked in the process.

One such successful invention soon polished, developed into subgenres, and adopted by a number of poets was the poetic adoption of various formal scriptural patterns. While religious personalities had clearly defined messages and temperaments, scriptural structures were broad, ambiguous, and compositionally complex. They could be adopted in varying degrees of closeness to the original thereby incorporating a carefully measured dose of textual impact. As a result, they could resonate with authority with the readers without evoking specific religious context if not so desired. Farrokhzad's *Ayah'ha-yi zamini* (The Earthly Scriptures) is a perfect example. Not only does the title draw attention to this formal adoption, the poem itself opens in the same fashion as the book of Genesis. Here, the choice of a Jewish/Christian scripture is significant in itself. One might assume that in this work Farrokhzad was addressing the Iranian Christian minority. While she did not wish to exclude such readers, the audience she specifically tried to reach is beyond doubt the mainstream—predominantly Muslim—reader. Perhaps her choice was, in part, motivated by the fact that this largely Muslim readership, particularly the educated segment, would recognize the pattern without getting unavoidable religious connotations that would have resulted from evoking the Qur'an, for example. In Iran, Christianity had not been explored in depth, except by those motivated with missionary or polemical purposes. The so-called intellectual elite was not familiar with the doctrines to any significant degree. Association with the prestigious Christian West, however, by the middle of the twentieth century, had endowed Christian images and themes with a prestigious status in high artistic circles. Though a poet of Farrokhzad's caliber would not fall for shallow fashionable patterns, she would be aware of the powerful resonance that Genesis could generate.[24] At the same time, through adopting the biblical structure, she paid her personal poetic respect to the Christian minority, who despite association with the prestigious West were not acknowledged or appreciated in a meaningful way.

Although *Ayah'ha-yi zamini* opens in the same way as Genesis does, Farrokhzad skillfully turns the pattern against itself by, ironically, reversing the narrative line. In Genesis first there is darkness and God commands the light to be, but her twentieth-century earthly scripture opens as the sun dies and all life perishes:

> Then,
> The sun went cold,
>   and prosperity left all lands.
> And grass withered in the fields,
> And fish perished in the sea.
> And from then on
>   the dead were not taken in by the earth.[25]

Farrokhzad gives us a chance to recognize the biblical rhythm and consequently associate the poetic message with prophetic clairvoyance. She, then, jolts us into the present time by evoking the most prevalent metaphor of her poetic tradition for social and political stagnation: the image of a lingering night. The night is taking hold not just on the horizon but inside individual windows like a dubious vision (*yak tasavvur-i mashkuk*). The roads, symbols of contact and communication, abandon their destinations. No one dreams of love or victory anymore, indeed no one dreams of anything anymore. As we feel the loneliness that abounds and the absurdity that reigns and witness the people's blood, which smells of bhang and opium, we receive our first hint concerning the group that is the prime target for Farrokhzad's anger: the supposed intellectual elite. Shallow, inert, and pretentious, this is the class that is supposed to be the culture's navigator in the journey to modernity. But instead, in Farrokhzad's view, it does little more than talk, self-destruct, and self-deceive. Her reference to opium, a fashionable drug for intellectual escapism, mocks the elite in their current state of paralysis. The chilling description that follows rules out the promise of any hopeful change in the near future:

> Pregnant women
> Gave birth to headless babies.
> And cradles hid themselves with shame
> In graves.[26]

In this stanza, a harsh trope reversal turns the proverbial statement (perhaps even a hadith) "seek knowledge from cradle to grave" into a parody of itself. She would not stop at that: not only are the intellectuals disappointing but the very nature of things is undergoing a fundamental decay and metamorphosis. Even mirrors misrepresent colors and shapes just as sacred halos form around the heads of clowns and whores instead of saints. We are still not finished with the intellectuals, who are now keeping company with clowns and whores, together sinking into swamps of alcohol covered with "vile poisonous vapors." The gravity of the plague of inaction is further emphasized with the appearance of mice nibbling at gold illumined pages of books in old bookcases. This is all because:

> The sun had died
> And tomorrow had a vague confusing sense
> in the mind of children.
> They showed the strangeness of the concept
> in their homework,
> With a large black blotch.[27]

As we get immersed in contemporary issues, the biblical effect begins to wear off. Farrokhzad revives the rhythm by distancing herself from the problems of the intellectuals and turning to the larger disasters befalling the society as a whole. Warning of calamity and description of mass punishments restore the scriptural rhythm. But most of all she affirms her deliberate use of the structure by depicting the "hungry prophets" (of her age) abandoning their sacred commitment, a negligence that leads to calamity. Aimless morbid masses, then, "wander from exile to exile" as if "carrying the weight of their own corpses on their shoulders." Alienation kills their human spirits and the desire to kill swells in their hands. Still, they are completely passive. Paralysis has reached a point that all they can do to gratify the desire to kill is to watch public executions and participate in imaginary crimes. In a way, we behave like the sleepwalkers in the poem. Haunted by the morbidity of the descriptions, and the darkness of the world she has created, we do not notice the seed of action, which she has planted in the above stanza. Nevertheless, the seed begins to grow and return as a question demanding an answer. What is the sun that has died? What is the cure for these sick and sorrowful people drowning in their own fear and sin? She now gives the *janian-i kuchik* (petty criminals) of her earthly scripture a flicker of life. It is *yik chiz-i nim zindih-yi na maghshush* (a half-alive confused thing), but it is a flicker nonetheless, a possibility of redemption. As they gather in the public squares to watch the executions, they stare at the water fountains in the middle of the pond, a sign that they wish to believe in the "purity of the song of the water." Even that faint desire to believe in the sanctity of something is a window opening on a better world. With that flicker of hope, she closes the poem on a clear biblical note stretching the horizons somewhat by combining faith and reverence to nature, which is the hallmark of her sacred making. The attempt of the petrified masses to "have faith in the purity of the song of the water" is connection to life but a conditional one. The connection will take hold only if they realize that the calamity befalling them is caused by one absence alone: the absence of the "sorrowful dove of faith."

As I argue in the following chapter, Farrokhzad was the architect of a complex poetic/spiritual edifice, which went beyond the concerns of the *Ayah'ha-yi zamini*. Combining the sanctity of her feminine force, and the mystery of nature, she turned the edifice into a sanctuary for all life. The above poem, however, was the closest she came to acknowledging the need of humanity to guard the sacred dove that nested within and flew on wings of faith.

Swearing by Sight: A Qur'anic Search for the Jewel in the Palm of the Earth

Sepehri, the poet of *The Expanse of Green,* experimented with scriptural structures in an equally effective, and certainly not as morbid a poem. As is the case with the *Ayah'ha-yi zamini,* the title of Sepehri's poem *Surah-yi tamasha* (The Chapter of Sight) reveals the scriptural connection. In this poem, Sepehri opted for the Qur'anic rhythm, particularly that of the early revelations, which emphasized God's existence and manifestation in the beauty and strength of nature. Important as it was for him to portray the sanctity of nature, he paid equal attention to the miracle of human creativity with words—his own poetry. Thus we see the two mingled from the beginning: God's natural verse and the flowering of human thoughts in words:

> I swear by sight!
> And by beginning of speech
> And by the banishing of the pigeons from memory
>   What is in the cage is merely a word![28]

Here, Sepehri made a deliberate decision to stay close to the Qur'anic rhythm. Whereas Farrokhzad moved quickly after the opening stanza to contemporary issues, he opted for evoking the oppositional relation between the prophets and the stubborn members of the congregation paying little attention to heavenly warnings. From the opening lines of the poem, Sepehri's prophetic status is reflected in his allusions to the sermons he has delivered to the crowd. Later lines contain glimpses of selective, poetically embellished, excerpts from these sermons:

> My words were as clear as a patch of grass.
> I told them:
> There is a sun at the threshold,
> It will shine on everything you do
>   if only you open the door.

> And I told them,
> Stones are not to decorate the mountains
> Just as the metal piece on an ax is not an ornament.
> Hidden in the closed palm of the earth is a jewel
>   —a jewel the eyes of all prophets dimmed with its glow!
> Seek the jewel!
> Take your moments to the pasture of prophethood!

With a clear mission outlined here, and the news of a jewel—not known to the populace—handed out, the poet's prophetic role is reinforced. What takes place in the poem at this point is a deliberate stretching of the scriptural rhythm, a step beyond what Farrokhzad attempted. With a subtle twist, Sepehri expands his own role, as well as the Qur'anic pattern, introducing a biblical touch into the tale. He has now transformed into John the Baptist paving the way for the arrival of Jesus:

> And I gave them glad tidings of the arrival of the messenger
> Of the nearness of the day, the increase of color
> And of the echo of the red rose behind the hedge of lofty words.[29]

Sepehri's poetic success, beginning here and continuing till the end, consists in wrapping in a fine garment of mystery the simplest and most obvious of daily events that take place around us. His prophetic strength, his miracle underlines the poetic mission all the way through: curing the prevalent colorblindness to the spectacular miracles of nature. If only we could look at a piece of wood and see the garden that it once was a part of! We have put our faces in the wind of "unending ecstasy!" If only we could make friends with the birds of the air, our sleep would be the most peaceful in the world! The poetic miracle is now in full motion; he is clearly excited with possibilities of the Qur'anic rhythm that he has adopted. In case Sepehri's prophetic status is not fully established, we get a detailed account of a miraculous instance that silences the skeptic crowd around him:

> We stood under a willow tree
> I picked a leaf from the branch above my head:
> "Open your eyes!" I said, "Do you want an evidence clearer than this?"
> And I heard them whisper to each other:
> "Sorcery! He knows sorcery!"[30]

The embodiment of divine performance in a single leaf has been acknowledged before Sepehri—in an oft-quoted verse—by his classical forefather, Sa'dī.[31] Sa'dī declared each leaf a book of Gnostic wisdom to those possessing intelligence. Sepehri's contribution is reviving Sa'dī's humble wisdom-bearing leaf and entering it into the scriptural edifice he has erected to serve his poetic purpose. Like everything else in the poem, the green leaf expands to include additional connotations needed to support Sepehri's poetic/prophetic voice. For example,

the mingling of the sacred and the jewels hidden in the palm of the earth intro-
duces a naturalist tendency into the picture, which diverts attention from the reli-
gious dimension and defuses possible opposition to promotion of Qur'anic views.
As a result, Sepehri is able to play with resonant Qur'anic themes, which could—
in the case of less religious readers—meet with resistance. He has borrowed the
authority of the Qur'an and the poetic subtleties of the verses without the asso-
ciations they might evoke with literalist or superstitious practice. He is now free
to play the game he has prepared the readers for.

As the Qur'an deplores the human forgetfulness of the primordial covenant
with God, *Surah-yi tamasha* mourns the loss of the mythical memory that con-
nected humans to nature. As the Qur'an suggests constant remembrance of God
to remedy the forgetfulness, the poem encourages the unremitting quest for the
jewel in the palm of the earth. And finally, just as the Qur'an promises its follow-
ers a happy life and afterlife, the poem promises the restful sleep referred to ear-
lier. Even the confrontation with the crowd and daring them to stay unconvinced
in the face of a miraculous leaf from a willow tree is an echo of the Qur'anic chal-
lenge put before the unbeliever, to produce an evidence sounder than that pre-
sented by the Qur'an or be convinced. Qur'anic reverberations are not only in
the mode of argumentation but also in the use of natural elements as evidence
for the sacred. There are, of course, similarities between what is here defined as
Qur'anic and the communicative rhythm in other holy scriptures. However, the
fine details I have just touched on as well as intentional use of Qur'anic terminol-
ogy such as *sūra* (chapter) and *rasul* (messenger) suggest the Qur'an as the proto-
type for the poem's structural development and organizing impulse.[32]

I cannot close the discussion without reference to another masterful use of
scriptural rhythm for poetic purposes. This is the opening poem named *Dibachah*
(The Opening Chapter) in Shafiʿi-Kadkani's celebrated collection *Dar khucha
bagh'ha-yi Nishabur* (In the Garden Alley Ways of Neyshābūr).[33]

Shafiʿi-Kadkani is different from Farrokhzad and Sepehri in that he speaks
from within the Islamic tradition. Not only does he have an established reputa-
tion as a Muslim poet, he shows no reservations in adopting the Qur'anic rhythm
with full respect to its institutional authority. Before the readers reach the poem
Dibachah, the collection opens with a brief quote titled "for blessing purposes"
from the twelfth-century martyred mystic and judge ʿAyn al-Qudat of Hamadān.
Executed for blasphemous views on *nubuvvat* (prophethood), ʿAyn al-Qudat is
one of the youngest, brightest, and best known casualties of free thinking in the
Islamic tradition. The quote, which is from a letter the Sufi master wrote to a
friend, reads:

> Don't you see that the hand and the pen write without being aware of what
> they do? And that the paper, which is written upon, is the same? Alas, any
> scribe that is not the heart will write without awareness [of what s/he

writes] and everything that is written upon, if not the heart, will be the
same [in lacking self-awareness].[34]

The choice of the quote makes it clear that from the outset the author stipulates
a special demand in his contractual relationship with the reader: an attentive
reading of the central message of the volume, social awareness and action. The
choice of a mystic/poet/martyr adds a footnote to the message: in the poetic en-
counters awaiting us in this book of poems, the borders between faith, poetry,
and activism will be blurred. As a whole, the poems in the collection verify this
initial impression. Compared to the two previous poets, Kadkani has a more
pointed political agenda. He anticipates, and cherishes, the arrival of an Islamic
revolution. For this reason, political figures from the Sufi tradition, particularly
those who lose their life in defense of their opinion such as ʿAyn al-Qudat and
Hallāj, have a particular poetic/political appeal to him.[35] Kadkani demands our
acceptance of these figures, rooted firmly in the tradition yet subversive enough
to be prosecuted by some of the upholders of the same tradition. The spiritual/
political conviction that the he asks of his readers is far from simple or predictable.

The poem cast in Qurʾanic rhythm is the first in the collection, a deliberate
choice of place. It opens with "Recite in the name of the red rose in the deserts
of the night," echoing the Qurʾanic verse "Recite in the name of thy Lord who
created." Anyone with the least knowledge of the Islamic scripture knows that the
above verse is accepted as the first verse in the long series of Qurʾanic revelations.
In this way, the poem establishes close rhythmic, thematic, as well as temporal
affinity with its scriptural model. The association, in the first line, of prophetic
recitation and the deserts of the night, establishes a quick connection between the
sacred mission of the scripture and the "revolutionary" dynamism of Islam, which
was sent to abolish the darkness of ignorance and injustice. That Shafiʿi-Kad-
kani's agenda is more immediate, radical, and action oriented (than that of Far-
rokhzad and Sepehri, for example) is apparent in part in going beyond prophetic
authority and becoming God's own mouthpiece. The populace, who receive this
"divine" message, are then expected to take prophetic action by reciting just as
prophet Muhammad did with his response to the angel Gabriel, which led to the
spread of Islam to half of the civilized world in a quarter of a century. From a lit-
erary point of view, this is an innovative use of the poetic voice that expands the
pattern and empowers the poet through an original utilization of the scriptural
rhythm. In what follows, the poem itself spells out the desired outcome of the
prophetic mission put before the readership:

> Recite in the name of the red rose in the deserts of the night!
> So the gardens awaken, [so the trees] bear fruit.

And here the poem presents us with a brave restructuring of the first Qurʾanic
revelation. The Qurʾanic verse reverts its attention from the imperative "recite!"

after it gets to "in the name of thy Lord who created." From the point of the appearance of the divine in the verse, the Qur'anic focus shifts from humans to the deity and his accomplishments. Admittedly God's accomplishment in this particular case centers on educating the humanity by means of a pen. Nevertheless, the humanity represented in this Qur'anic verse is addressed only once. Shafi'i-Kadkani's poem, however, diverges from the model by returning to the imperative repeatedly, thereby shifting the emphasis from God's creative act to the prophetic mission, which is now to be taken over by the reader:

> Recite! Recite again! So the white doves
> Make their journey back to their violated nests.
> Recite in the name of the red rose! In the colonnade of silence,
> So the waves and the height of their musical flow take the plains over.
> So the brilliant message of the rain
>   —pouring from the indigo rooftops of the night—
> Be taken to all corners on the shoulders of the breeze.[36]

As these opening verses demonstrate, Shafi'i-Kadkani's revelation borrows nature's colorful garb for effective poetic expression. Instead of God, we recite in the name of the red rose displaying its natural beauty in the color that symbolizes the martyrs' blood. But the red rose is not an exception; everything that has a message of freedom and life acts from within the natural world. So does the fear-mongering enemy, who has spread the false rumor of a drought. We are, however, to have faith and face that prospect with courage:

> Are you afraid of drought? What on earth for?
> Many are dams they erected
> Not just on the way of [flowing] waters,
> But on the way of light
> To kill songs
> To kill even the desire to sing.[37]

And so in these times of suppression when the poets are given license "to praise only false love in sleep-inducing songs," the mission is clear: sing to remove the barrier of silence, to disperse the darkness of self-imposed fear, and to hasten the arrival of the spring.

Shafi'i-Kadkani's impressive poetic achievement in this poem is in the ability to develop the poetic message into a number of diverging directions concurrently. On the one hand, he succeeds in sending a clear action alert without reducing the poem into a slogan, a cheap invitation to join a specific political party. On the other, he makes effective use of nature to achieve his political end without abusing or trivializing his natural tools. Amid the Qur'anic echo and revolutionary cries, we celebrate the arrival of spring crossing the fence and the purple flame of the violet enlivening the drought-stricken desert. Most significantly, the poet remains close to his scriptural model while refusing to be straitjacketed into a one-track-minded focus on the faith. The horizons are wide open. We know this from the mirrors that have come to life to flow in all directions in the manner that the rivers do:

> A thousand mirrors flow
> A thousand mirrors
>   this instant
> Pulsate whole-heartedly
> To echo your heartbeat.[38]

Shafi'i-Kadkani ends the poem evoking a poetic/spiritual forefather, Hāfez of Shīrāz. This is an excellent choice, not just because the free-spirited *rind* in Hāfez's poetry is probably the closest that any classical personality can come to a contemporary revolutionary but also because Hāfez is by far the most suitable candidate to embody sociopolitical opposition to corruption. Shafi'i-Kadkani's poem is expressed with a combination of literary excellence and wholehearted devotion to the Qur'anic ideal. When the poem ends with a single verse quotation from the master, "Tell the story of love in the language that you know best," Kadkani has hit two birds with one stone. On the one hand, he has warned us not to remain limited to the subject matter of his poem. On the other, of all the classical masters, he has united us with the one known for expertise on the Qur'an, the text that has generated the creative rhythm of the very poem we have read.

Re-employing Prominent Religious Personae: Meaning in Every Inch of the Canvas

Besides borrowing the structural rhythm of holy texts, the reformist poetry of twentieth-century Iran made use of another old poetic paradigm with powerful literary resonance and capacity for sacred making. This was evoking prominent religious personae and placing them in reconstructed settings that allowed their personalities to evolve and display new traits. Figures such as Jesus, Moses, and Hallāj were familiar enough to fit in the Iranian historical, literary, and religious memory. Yet they were redefined in fundamental ways to act in harmony with the contemporary agenda. It is time to evoke James Elkins's superb study *What Painting Is,* one more time. Commenting on the sensations we experience by looking at oil paintings, Elkins observes that the feeling generated in the viewer comes from attention to seemingly minor components of each composition. In other words, it is the very small movements of the brush, the finest of details, in paintings that create the complex nuances of meaning. Elkins's insight suggests that general subjects, though important, are not what paintings are about. Rather the meaning is in every inch of the canvas.[39] I would suggest the observation to be applicable to art forms other than painting. In our current discussion, it applies to the impact of the reconstructed portraits of the religious figures used in reformist Persian poetry. While it is significant that such classical personae were re-employed, the intricacies of the part they played become apparent when we focus on every inch of the canvas. The exact way in which they were each re-envisioned sheds light on the evolution of the concept of the sacred. Prophets and saints were prominent among these re-employed religious personae.

"Restlessness" in Moments of "Prophetic Perception": New Faces for Prophets

Prophets were suitable for this purpose. They could come from a different religious tradition and yet resonate with Muslim readership. Enough of an outsider to introduce fresh concepts and expand the borders of the discourse, they remained within the borderlines of the acknowledged Qur'anic universe not to present the tradition with too much challenge. Particularly the prophets of the *Ahl al-kitab* (*The People of the Book*) possessed fairly well-defined yet vibrant personalities. Jesus was one such figure. In classical Persian poetry, Jesus was the soul, the exalted being riding the donkey that represented the flesh with its earthly attributes.[40] In addition, Jesus was the life giver, the miracle worker whose breath brought the dead back to life. As Sorour Soroudi has observed, however, Jesus as the sacrificing sufferer and the symbol of the struggle of the selfless individual to save humanity is notably absent from the literature of that period:

> Jesus image as a persecuted man who bore his burden with love and who did not give up his belief even at the cost of his life which he sacrificed to save others does not receive attention in classical Persian poetry nor, indeed, in Muslim writing in general. There are examples in classical poetry in which slanderous talk against Jesus, his intended crucifixion, and his ascent to heaven, are mentioned. But classical poets, even the persecuted ones, rarely heeded the social aspects so essential to Jesus's personality as depicted in the New Testament.[41]

The explanation for what surprised Soroudi, of course, lies in the fact that Iranian classical poets did not know Jesus through the New Testament but rather through the Qur'anic narrative. In the Muslim scripture, the life-giving triumphant dimension of the prophet's personality looms so large that it overshadows the sufferer. The twentieth-century Iranian poets, however, used a different vantage point. Eager to look beyond the Arab-Muslim worldview, and able to interact freely with the Iranian non-Muslim population, they discovered the Jesus of the New Testament. Ahmad Shamlu devoted an entire poem to the crucifixion of Jesus entitled *Marg-i Nasiri* (The Death of the Nazarene), which was part of the newly born tradition of celebrating things Christian observed earlier in

Farrokhzad's *Ayah'ha-yi zamini.*[42] Themes and concepts associated with Jesus, Mary, carrying the cross, sacrifice, and the like were familiar for Persian readers by mid–twentieth century. In a superb visual aggrandizement, Shamlu's poem carved out and highlighted only the last moments in the life of Jesus. Then, to underline the vital dynamism of the sacrificial moment, it opted not to linger on details but take the reader on a fast-paced walk through the scene: the wreath of thorns, the cross on his back, the suffering, and the death. There is no mention, here, of the triumphant life-giving Jesus. Instead, Shamlu used the prophet to expose the ignorant and heartless society that inflicted suffering on him. The short and effective narrative crystallized into a clear allegory aiming criticism at the society in which the poet himself was subjected to censorship and prosecution. This explains why the poem ended not with elegy for Jesus but for the *avaz-i ruy dar khamushi-i rahm* (dying voice of mercy). As Elkins observed with paintings, it is not the broader story line—in this case the crucifixion—that tells us our Jesus is not the old one. It is rather the fine details. One such remarkable detail revealing the resignified personality of Jesus is the name used in the poem to refer to him. He would normally be called 'Isa (Jesus). However, Shamlu was aware of the resonating array of themes and concepts associated with the name. Realizing that it would be almost impossible to dissociate 'Isa from his triumphant self and transform the miracle worker into a dying sufferer, Shamlu refrained from using that name altogether. By calling Jesus "Nasiri" (the Nazarene), rather than the standard "'Isa," Shamlu succeeded in identifying the prophet to his readers without evoking his common attributes.[43]

BEYOND THE MONOTHEISTIC HORIZONS

In 1965 Mehdi Akhavan Salis (1928–1990), one of the major poets of twentieth-century Iran, whom I have not referred to yet, published a fascinating collection of poems composed from 1960 to 1965. Akhavan titled the collection *Az in Avesta* (From This Avesta), a direct reference to the Zoroastrian scripture Avesta.[44] In this collection, which contains an unusual combination of poetry and literary critical writing, the poet combined the two strategies of encoding poetic messages that have been discussed in this chapter so far. He adopted scriptural rhythms, and within these scriptural frames employed specific prophetic figures. Akhavan was an established poet with a reputation for firm control over his artistic medium and mastery of techniques in classical Persian poetry. He had already made his mark on the reformist poetic movement in more than one way. On the social front, he was a time-honored activist with prison records resulting from political allegories such as *Zamistan* (The Winter), which had taken the ruling regime to task for the chilly policing climate and gained instant success.

More significantly for the present discussion, he was the architect of a poetic vision that defined poetic creativity as "the result of human *bitabi* (restlessness) in moments of *shu'ur-i nubuvat* (prophetic perception)."[45] In its Persian version the alchemical interaction of restlessness and perception, in Akhavan's view, led to successful poetic permutation if the poet had full awareness of the unique pre-Islamic culture that Iranians had created. A thousand years of exposure to Arab/Islamic sensibility had in his estimation led to an amnesia that had literally buried the resulting cultural riches.[46] It is not surprising that the poet named his collection after the Zoroastrian scripture Avesta.[47] It is, rather, fascinating that disappointment with over a thousand years of "Arabic Islam" did not put him off the need for the sacred, or the notion of a prophetic perception at the core of poetic creation. He opened his epilogue with the familiar generic pattern of praising the divine (though emptied of Islamic content and filled with parallel Zoroastrian nuances):

> In the name of Ahura Mazda, the great just creator, creator of goodness and worth, decent acts and beauty, the nurturer of betterment, that which is better, and He who is the best . . . worship and praise be to the best offspring of the glorious heaven and the earth Zoroaster.[48]

The entire epilogue has a humorously exaggerated tone. Akhavan's goal was clearly not to propagate the Zoroastrian religion but rather to underline the need for reviving ties with the past and tapping into the cultural riches that can nourish and revive nobility through art. In his own "restless" moments of exposure to "prophetic perception," Akhavan was aware of the resilience and resonance in the personality of the prophets. He knew each prophet would set off splintering allusions to unforeseeable corners of folk tales and sacred literature alike. Akhavan did not wish any of the allusions to lead to the Arab-Islamic vision, which had "masked" the "true" Iranian heritage. Instead of leaving the prophets out of the picture, the poet opted for those not usually included in the standard list of the "People of the Book." In a short, lucid, and tightly structured piece titled *Va nadanistan* (And Not Knowing), Akhavan summoned the Buddha, Mazdak, and Zoroaster at the same time to answer the questions of a seeker of the truth:[49]

> The spring rain had washed everything, everywhere
> A pure divine night it was
> And that was clear.[50]

In this poem, against the backdrop of a cleanly washed lucid night, friends are on a hill "together" yet each "alone" in their space. The brilliance of the moon, the openness of the horizons, the vastness and serenity of the universe at the beginning of the poem tell of the riches that are coming their way, and indeed ours as well if we stay with the poem. Soon, the silence of the night is interrupted with the seeker's question:

> I have heard
> From now till the end of the world

There will always be a line between knowing and not knowing.
Tell me Mazdak! What do you know
Of the other side of this invisible line?
What is there?
Who would know the ins and outs of the other side?[51]

The question sums up the main concern of the poem: mysteries are behind a cur-
tain and even the prophets who can cross to the other side cannot do more than
stir up the seeker's desire to know. Akhavan has less groundwork in the form of
redefinition of the personality of the prophets he features in this poem as none of
them clashes with progressive/intellectual sensibilities of the time. He, therefore,
has them all perform within the borderlines of what is expected of them. Mazdak
sees only the concrete world around him; the Buddha emphasizes the significance
of not knowing; and Zoroaster wishes he could show the materialist Mazdak the
mysteries of the unseen. The seeker's presence is intentionally well defined and
foregrounded. S/he asks the question without hesitation in a number of long and
carefully worded sentences, an indication that s/he is overpowered in the illustri-
ous company of the prophets. Furthermore, the closing stanza confirms his/her
knowledge of the line between knowing and not knowing presented initially as a
question to the prophets. Although we are no wiser concerning that which is
beyond the line, we walk away—mostly thanks to the seeker—empowered with
our "not knowing." This poem and the collection *Az in Avesta* in general are fas-
cinating examples of the empowerment brought to the emerging poetic voice in
need of the depth and resonance emanating from the rootedness of these prophetic
figures. Even a poet such as Akhavan who felt disenchanted with the prophets of
the Abrahamic tradition, and viewed their contribution as stifling to artistic cre-
ativity, felt the need for the prophetic depth and resonance. He reached out for the
sacred, albeit in its nonmonotheistic manifestations, to sanction the poetic search
when it came to a concept as paradoxical as the knowledge of not knowing.

The Red Song of "I Am the Truth":
Reinventing the Saints

Sufi sheikhs were another category of poetic personae associated closely with the
spiritual/literary past and available for poetic redefinition. They were not as pub-
licly known as the prophets, a characteristic that made them less resonant with
general readership. The same quality, however, allowed them more mystery and
complexity, two fountainheads of poetic energy. They had other advantages. To
begin with they were much larger in number, providing a wide array of tem-
peraments, personalities, and cultural/geographical backgrounds to select from.
Furthermore, most of them had produced a colorful corpus of prose or poetry
often flexible and universal in outlook to be incorporated into evolving modern

worldviews without much difficulty. I have already discussed Kadkani's use of a quotation from 'Ayn al-Qudat of Hamadān, the young and learned Sufi judge and martyr, to preface his collection *Dar khucha bagh'ha-yi Nishabur* celebrating a politicized Islam. The iconoclastic trait in the personality of most Sufi sheikhs was an attractive quality to the modern poet, and one that reduced the need for redefinition of the character. Martyred or otherwise, most Sufi figures had challenged seriously the traditions they were rooted in, if not aggressively defying these traditions. This made them desirable for an emerging poetic tradition that could not deny its connections to the past yet wished to subject the past to scrutiny in order to assert its nascent identity.

The mysterious and malleable mission of the Sufi masters enabled them to move discretely between the ranks of the prophets, saints, and pious members of the community capable of vision and leadership. I have already, in the previous chapter, pointed to Abu Sa'id Abu al-Khayr walking the fine line between skepticism, sobriety, and intoxication. While cherishing the love that imbues the universe like rays of the sun, Abu Sa'id questions the fragility of the human ability to benefit from it as dark clouds threaten to cover that sun at any given moment. Eccentric and colorful personages abound: take the daring Abu Yazid of Bistam—known as Bayazid among modern Persian speakers, for example. Bayazid's words offer endless poetic possibilities, beginning with a daring redefinition of the Qur'anic praise of God into the human-centered exclamation "Glory be to me! How exalted is my place."[52]

Besides glorifying humanity, Bayazid spoke of a personal experience that by virtue of being told publicly exalted humanity beyond anyone's wildest dreams and caught the imagination of a twentieth-century Persian poet I have introduced already, Shafi'i-Kadkani. This is an appropriate moment to look at Bayazid's description of this experience as we are turning from prophets to Sufi figures. Bayazid spoke of a nocturnal journey, which enabled him to "gaze upon God with the eye of certainty" putting himself afoot with the "Seal of the Prophets." In this echo of Prophet Muhammad's celebrated *mi'raj* (nocturnal journey), Bayazid supposedly explored the heavens and gazed on the entire creation through the divine light. In the *Tadhkirat al-awliya'*, 'Attār presents Bayazid's daring and detailed account of his encounter with God as follows:

> I gazed upon God with the eye of certainty after He had advanced me to the degree of independence from all creatures, and illuminated me with His light, revealing to me the grandeur of His He-ness. Then from God I gazed upon myself, and considered well the secrets and attributes of my self. My light was darkness beside the light of God. . . . When I looked again, I saw my being by God's light. I realized that my glory was of His grandeur and glory. Whatsoever I did, I was able to do through His omnipotence.[53]

Bayazid was respected enough for the above episode not to be viewed as bold rivalry with the Prophet and instead to be taken in a very positive light. The piece is included in ʿAttār's collection of anecdotes from Bayazid's sayings and writings under the title *Mi'rajnamah*, normally given to writings that explicate the Prophet's nocturnal journey. Indeed, in ʿAttār's retelling, the episode has found such poetic depth and intricacy that it will remain a source of inspiration to Persian readers for centuries to come.

In his 1978 collection titled *Az budan u surudan* (Of Being and Making Songs), which sold out in three months and reappeared in a twenty thousand copy edition, Kadkani presented his readers with a long poem inspired by Bayazid's *Mi'rajnamah*. To give his poem the resonance of Bayazid's ascension as well as that of the original prophetic mi'raj, he gave the poem the same title.[54] In Bayazid's style, Kadkani's poem opens with the striking moment of ascent to heaven in the belly of a red bird soaring and creating a sudden dramatic impact:

> Then I soared above the stars
> More liberated than the breeze, the light
> And opened my eyes like Viraf.
> That red bird
> Swallowed me like a seed
> Opening its wings to carry me high.
> In dazzling heights of freedom
> On waves of light, and of conquest
> Flew the bird.
> And opened before me in every moment
>   in its green belly
> An endless galaxy of colors.[55]

The poem is a watercolor, a dazzling blend of heavenly blue and natural green against the exotic Qur'anic fruits and flowing rivers of milk. Amid this heavenly display of color, the process of poetic resignification begins with the powerful black light of *Iblis* (Satan) overshadowing the angelic glow, evoking a daring Sufi reading of the devil, and directing our gaze back toward the earth. This is an earth on which—in the East—the bloodied dawn pulsates with "the bright echo of the lovers' song" signaling struggle and sacrifice. From this point on, we know that the poetic ascent is for no reason other than exposing the injustice that pervades the eastern horizon and the silence that allows the injustice to continue. Far from longing to be annihilated in the divine, our Bayazid is concerned with what goes on below. His mission is to inform the inhabitants of the earth of the broken rod of Solomon and of his throne consumed by termites, ready to collapse with the first wind. With this symbolic collapse of the ancient prophet we are signaled to look for sources of strength closer to home. The visions of our ascending poet/prophet tells us of heads—presumably of activists—severed from their bodies and grown on celestial trees like fruits, where they continue to expose injustice. From this point on, what is exposed fits smoothly with the sociopolitical condition of the country. It is indicative of the poet's courage in the face of the shah's secret police but hardly in need of being revealed in a nocturnal journey. The statue of the old wolf carries a fake light, the inhabitants of cities metamorphose into pigs and crabs, and the supposed intellectuals walk around with headless bodies. A remarkable resignification in the poem is the expansion of the inner power of the journeyer himself to include the sacred. At various points in the poem, when he needs to understand the morbid scenes he witnesses on earth, instead of appealing to the unseen God, he speaks to *surush-i dil-i khvish* (the angel of his own heart). The inner angel is candid in expressing regret at headless poet/intellectuals succeeding to an office once occupied by such worthy figures as Omar Khayyám, the embodiment of eastern wisdom. Later, the angel bursts into a song trying to excite the will to act in those living behind closed windows and indifferent to the darkness of injustice that invades their worlds. As the angelic recitation, or the poet's inner voice, ceases, the poem concludes with a vision as sudden and as striking as the one that opened the piece. In his usual love for memorable endings, Kadkani presents us with a rare mixture of poetry, spirituality, and politics, an execution blending into a red sunrise:

> Then in the moment
> That the clocks stopped
> And the sparrows sang on aspens:
> "History stops here,"
> And I saw in the piercing sound of the bullet,
> A man carrying the dawn on his shoulders.
> His forehead broken,
> And his blood sprinkled across the horizon.[56]

Colorful and explosive as the above account of Shafi'i-Kadkani/Bayazid nocturnal journey is, it is not as popularly known as his poetic retelling of the martyrdom of Hallāj, the iconoclastic Sufi figure of the ninth century.[57] The long political turmoil that led to the demise of Hallāj is not known to the public. His martyrdom is attributed solely to his outspoken expression of oneness with deity. In *Dar khucha bagh'ha-yi Nishabur*, the collection prefaced with 'Ayn al-Qudat's words to which I referred earlier, Kadkani presents his readers with a poem created around the figure of Hallāj and named after the mystic.[58] Dissociated from acts of renunciation or surrender to destiny, in Kadkani's poem Hallāj is transformed into a political activist protesting the social injustice with the *surud-i surkh-i ana al-Haqq* (red song of I am the truth) on his lips:

> In the mirror
> He has appeared again
> His hair like white clouds in the wind
> The red song of "I am the truth" on his lips.

Though primarily a social commentary on the oppressive regime of the time, the poem is imbued with vibrant spiritual pathos. Hallāj is presented as a higher being, his image reflected in a "mirror," a common metaphor for the pure heart. His hair is flying in the wind, as if he were suspended in the air or standing on a high pedestal, as he whispers persistently his "ana al-Haqq" in the manner that the Sufis repeat their formulaic meditative prayer, the *dhikr*. Later in the poem, the mystic's candid self-expression, which led to his persecution, is referred to as reciting *namaz-i 'ishq* (the prayer of love), evoking the rite of Muslim daily prayer. We respond to the worship-related imagery because in their metaphorical role they evoke larger social concerns. At the same time, signals such as the redness of the song of "I am the truth" prepare us for a change of course in the direction of more politically charged themes. Once again, Hāfez and his rebellious rinds serve as the bridge connecting the two thematic clusters:

> Your name is the code
> Whispered by the *rinds* of Neyshābūr
> In moments of intoxication,
> daring moments of revealing the truth.

Lahzah'ha-yi masti (the moments of intoxication) embody the rapturous poetic force that propels us out of the limiting details of daily religious practice into the hazardous but exciting sphere of political action. With the intercession of Hāfez and his *rinds* begins the rapid takeover of current political themes. Thus we see the gallows erected bearing the body of the martyred mystic and catch in the process an unflattering view of ourselves, a flock of "overlooking vultures" (*anbuh-i karkasan-i tamasha*) overpowered with submissive silence. In case shame has not shaken us into action yet, we are portrayed as co-opted by "the appointed police" (*shihnah'ha-yi ma'mur*) watching everything dutifully and blindly. If the blood of Hallāj the mystic, as it trickled on the ground, formed the word *Allah* according to the legends, from the ashes of Shafi'i-Kadkani's Hallāj, "wherever the wind scatters them," grow men worthy of the battle to save humanity from enslavement. The fact that, by the end of the poem, the spiritual impulse is converted entirely into the urge for political action does not undermine the religious significance of the allegory. Much sacred has infused previously mundane spheres of our daily action.

The fact remains that out of numerous historical personalities and occasions, in the poems quoted in the last segment of this chapter and in many we shall see in chapters to come, the martyrdom of figures such as Jesus and Hallāj are selected to convey the dynamic sociopolitical action bordering on self-sacrifice. The sacred energy emanating from these figures is central to the overall success of the poetic composition. So is the access to the classical literary tradition that contributes to the solidity and resonance of the poetic structure. Kadkani closes the song of Hallāj with another successful grafting of the contemporary political outcry on the longer lasting Hāfezian echo of ecstatic singing. He blends the "red song" of his Hallāj with the happy nocturnal melodies of the intoxicated ringing in the night to evoke discretely but surely the fourteenth-century master of ghazels with strong social overtones.

4

>⊶⊷⊙⊶⊷<

In "the Fragrant Core of a Fertilized Egg"
Merging the Feminine, the Natural, and the Spiritual

Forugh Farrokhzad, whose earthly scriptures mourning the loss of the "sorrowful dove of faith" are explored in chapter 3, was the architect of an impressive poetic edifice in which her special brand of spirituality played a key role. In this finely designed multilevel structure, the human body and its intricate relation to a mysterious life-giving nature provided the vocabulary for poetic expression. Though original, Farrokhzad's edifice was more than a personal invention. It was an articulation of her generation's collective desire to empower poetry beyond stylistic excellence to echo the paradoxes of modern life. It was an attempt to activate the lifeline that poetry provided in increasingly mechanistic environments that despite their superficial dynamism encouraged stagnation and decay. Above all, it was the culmination, in Persian poetry, of the desire for a personalized individualistic discourse celebrating the human potential to remain sexual and spiritual at the same time. Nineteenth- and twentieth-century intellectuals had situated modernization of Persian literature at the heart of their agenda for social and cultural reform. For Farrokhzad, too, the poetic word itself was more than a means to verbalize the above needs and aspirations. It provided the vital bridge that kept humanity connected to its very soul, its past, present, and future.

THE WINDOW OPENING ON EXISTENCE

In her extended radio interview published as a separate booklet in 1977, Farrokhzad described her interaction with her poetry by underlining the significance that her generation attached to the art from. Particularly essential was the ways in which the poet's own personal growth was considered to be correlated with poetic creativity:

> Poetry is like a window for me that opens by itself every time I approach it. I sit at this window, I look, sing, shout, cry, mingle with the images of the trees and know that at the other side of the window there is a space. [In that space] someone hears, someone who might live two hundred years from now or three hundred years ago. That does not make a difference. Poetry is a means for remaining connected with being, with existence in its

broad sense. The good thing about writing poetry is that one can say "I, too, exist" or "I, too, existed." Otherwise, how can one claim to exist? I do not search for anything in my poetry, I find myself in it.[1]

Farrokhzad invited her readers beyond the window to do the same, to open it when they wished to see, scream, and remain connected to life. It opened to her world of poetic creation in which much was happening. It was vibrant with sexuality, fascination with nature, and self-explorations of all kind. Significant for the present discussion is a conscious process of sacred making, which took place on a continuous basis. The process, which can be traced back to her early writings, picked momentum in the last years of Farrokhzad's career and generated, during its evolution, a distinct vocabulary, a rhythm, a set of spiritual principles, and a teleological orientation. The journey had started in raw fascination with sexuality in her early collections *Asir* (The Captive, 1952) and *Divar* (The Wall, 1957). In its later phases, it developed into a deeper exploration of life always struggling with terror of decay and uselessness. First in *'Isyan* (Rebellion, 1959) and later in *Tavalludi digar* (Another Birth, 1964), the fear of decay was alleviated by tapping into the evergreen fountain of life in nature. As her closeness to nature began to border on a love affair that led to merging with one another, a search for the sacred—an integrating force of life and goodness—started to direct her creative energies. In her last poetic explorations, Farrokhzad succeeded in integrating nature, the sacred, and the human body in a poetic continuum that formed a sanctuary for life. In this sanctuary all life-forms had a right to freedom, growth, and self-expression. This arrival at a moment of safety calmed the restlessness that had been the hallmark of her earlier years. In these latter years, although songs continued to "well up" in her and "the eager hare in the pupil of her eyes" still "went venturing to unknown meadows," she overcame the restlessness.

At ease with her sexuality, fortified through connection with nature and empowered with poetic word, she became the archetypal fertile woman protecting and nurturing this sanctuary of life. Her lively and carefully crafted poetic messages were rooted in the cultural grammar of the human body while at the same time transcending it to explore life in its fuller dimensions. The idea of the sacred envisioned and articulated within bodily boundaries was, of course, not new.[2] To revive the metaphor of painting I have borrowed from Elkins's study, Farrokhzad's special contribution did not lie in the re-envisioning of the broad strokes that defined that paradigm. Rather, her personal contributions manifested themselves in minute details in every inch of the canvas. Her work was an uninterrupted exploration of fresh poetic possibilities, each piece pointing in a new direction that will continue to intrigue modern Iranian poets for decades and be identified as the hallmark of her work. As Karimi-Hakkak has demonstrated with the poetry of Nima Yushij, what appears in the works of a single poet as a purely

personal breakthrough is often the culmination of long and gradual processes that
have begun with previous writers discretely.[3] Farrokhzad's contribution is no
exception. Her work provided the appropriate moments for already existing
undercurrents to come to the surface. These are currents that will continue to
evolve in contemporary Persian poetry. And so her poetry provides the opportu-
nity to explore a trend rather than the output of a single author. In what follows,
I explore this trend, the landscape she spread before the reader. While the primary
focus is on every inch of the canvas, I ask you to step back periodically to iden-
tify broader compositional structures.

The One I Love

One unexplored avenue opened by Farrokhzad for twentieth-century Persian
poetry was the legitimization (if not canonization) of the female erotic voice pre-
viously deemed improper for poetic expression. Her frank sense of entitlement to
the unacknowledged female right of self-expression in moments of intimacy and
in description of male physical beauty, as Farzaneh Milani has skillfully demon-
strated, was spirited and unapologetic.[4] Timing had much to do with the way this
fresh vision was received. Farrokhzad was opening a new chapter in the corpus of
Persian love poetry in the decades prior to the 1979 revolution when political
commitment took center stage and emotional self-expression of any sort was
branded as a betrayal of the social cause. In *Shi'ri ki zindagist* (Poetry That Is Life),
a poem that became the manifesto of modern Persian poetry, Ahmad Shamlu had
mocked the traditional poet as captive in "the ridiculous snares of the beloved's
hair." The poet of "today" according to Shamlu was a branch from the forest of
the masses and his/her poetry primarily a weapon.[5] Although Farrokhzad's beloved
made his way into the poetic arena under judgments harsh as the above, he made
his presence felt, despite not serving a revolutionary cause, by being a total shock
to the old system. Far from succumbing to the underhanded occupation of set-
ting "ridiculous snares" for the lover's heart, he stood up tall and expressed the
"naked" beauty of his "rebellious limbs" with the frankness of a "healthy instinct."
In the poem *Ma'shuq-i man* (The One I Love), to which I referred earlier, Far-
rokhzad was particularly cautious for erotic imagery not to be interpreted as
metaphors for something else. She adopted a clear and completely unambiguous
language that celebrated its own strong sensuous tone:

> The one I love
> Stands on strong legs
> Like death's shameless, naked body
> Nervous, swollen lines
> Following
> The firm outline
> Of his rebellious limbs.[6]

In the poem, almost anything else was subordinated to the concreteness and physicality of the beloved's body on which the poetry was grafted. Aware of the traditional objection to the level of frankness in expression, Farrokhzad insisted that the physical presence be kept in the foreground—through repeated reference— as the main poetic force that animated the poem. As readers, we are left with no choice but to feel and to acknowledge the inevitability of this natural force:

> The one I love
> Means something clear, inevitable
> As nature herself
> He proves
> true the law of force
> in my defeat
> He is savage and free
> as a healthy instinct
> in the heart of a desert island.[7]

Later in the poem, this departure from tradition crystallizes, as I pointed out in the previous chapter, into a direct challenge. To "prove true the law of force," Farrokhzad's lover does not just "stand on strong legs" or "defeat her." He pushes the age-old, pale-faced, love-stricken Majnun off the poetic scene completely by wiping "the dust of the street" from his shoes with "rags torn from the poor lover's tent." This was yet another reaction to an exaggerated fear of decay on Far- rokhzad's part. Majnun, as far as she was concerned, was dead and so were poets who would hold uncreatively onto his inherited lifeless ghost for lack of energy to rejuvenate artistic expression.

The Tartar's Ongoing Ambush

Farrokhzad, however, did not just push the old overboard. Her remarkable con- tribution lay in the ability to redefine and rearrange the building blocks for fresh poetic construction, which she achieved without breaking ties with the past. She re-envisioned the body, nature, and the sacred to fit into the modern poetic dis- course, taking full advantage of their complicated poetic resonance within the old tradition. Her strong objection to stock characters notwithstanding, she de- monstrated impressive awareness of the significance of the literary memory that supplemented a considerable portion of the reader's subtext. Even in her most rebellious moments, when she lent her beloved rags torn from Majnun's tent to wipe his shoes, Farrokhzad remained aware of the power of conventional imagery and the poetic potential they had to offer. Thus, in the same poem, we run into the familiar Tartar beloved in the acts of ambush, capture, and kill, which Persian poetry had used metaphorically to portray the forceful challenges of love for centuries:

> The one I love
> Seems to have come from generations out of mind
> As though a Tartar
> were lying in ambush for some rider
> in the bottom of his eyes
> As though a savage
> in the glinting brightness of his teeth
> were enthralled by the prey's hot blood.[8]

Significant for the present discussion is the particular way in which all this "savage" freedom to acknowledge male beauty and aggression served the overarching purpose of refashioning literary conventions. Furthermore, the encounters with the naked beloved, departing Majnun, or the savage Tartar were placed within a larger control structure, which had a persisting spiritual connotation. In the most adventurous moments of exploring the forbidden in Farrokhzad's work, the reader knows that things are going to be fine because some overarching sacred/natural law underlay all that is important in life. If we recognize this force in nature and in ourselves, it does in turn connect us to the sanctified core that is in the center of our human existence even in the "shamelessly" naked body of the beloved. Thus, before the poem "The One I Love" concludes, we are reintroduced to the beloved, who "from his first hour" has been:

> Like the god of a Nepalese shrine
> He is a man
> Out of centuries long gone
> A token of beauty's truth
> He always arouses
> Innocent memories around him
> Like a baby's smell
> He is a happy popular song
> Rough, and full of feeling.[9]

And we should not be surprised at the end of the poem, when the beloved is converted into a "simple human being" hidden in the "thicket" of the poet's "breast" fully sacralized and placed in a high orbit of his own:

> Like the last relic of a marvelous religion
> In this hideous country of uncouth things.[10]

His Dark Pupils in Sama':
Further Rearranging the Old Building Blocks

Farrokhzad's utilization of images and concepts from the past often goes further than a momentary borrowing of the Tartar in ambush. The poem *Vasl* (Union) is an example of mobilizing the complete symbolic universe of mysticism to give expression to the simple human exchange in lovemaking. In this poem, her daring utilization of a sacred structure complements the challenge she brought to the tradition by verbalizing the experience in the first place. She displays remarkable control over the technical mystical details as well as the natural/sensual exchange from the opening stanza, in which a mystic lost in the rapture of the spiritual dance *sama'* becomes a metaphor for eye contact in moments of intimacy:

> Those dark pupils, ah
> Those simple hermit Sufis of mine
> fainting, rapt
> in the music of his eyes.[11]

The exchange had to be sanctified and raised above the restraining and trivializing forces of everyday life. She needed her sanctuary, the safe haven in which she frequently cleansed all human action of selfishness, smallness, and decay by grafting them onto nature in order to access its green vibrating life. So, in the poem "Union," natural forces are summoned to the love scene. Not only do they purify/sanctify the intimate exchange at the heart of the poem, they bridge the moment with eternity where time is no longer a constraint:

> I saw him breaking over me in waves
> Like the red glow of fire
> Like a watery reflection
> Like a cloud tremulant with rains
> Like a sky breathing summery warmth
> toward infinity
> spreading
> beyond the life here.[12]

This is not a simple borrowing of natural imagery for descriptive purposes. In the poem, major alchemical transformations are underway through which the "marrow" of the poet's being melts just as the beloved is purified in "the aura of the flames." During "that long reach of desire," much more than sexual gratification is taking place when the shadowing weight of his eyelashes "stream from the depths of darkness" down to her "lost roots." Purified by the alchemical transformation of love, empowered by the life-giving forces of nature, and connected with her lost roots—the sacred core within her—she now expands beyond her physical being:

> I saw myself released
> I saw myself released
> I saw the skin encasing me split by my swelling love

At this point, Farrokhzad displays a remarkable sense of poetic precision. She makes the exchange between her and nature as mutual as the one between her and her lover. Connected to her sacred inner core, and free from bodily limits, she is now able to access nature and return the sanctifying favor. Her poetic persona enriches the heavens by allowing her "molten mass"—purified in love—"smelt slowly and pour out":

> On the moon,
> The moon sunk in the deep,
> the dark, stormy moon.[13]

We will never know whether the dark stormy moon mirrored the poet's dark and stormy emotions or whether its vulnerability is revealed to us so the human love exchange could find a moment to display its transforming nature. With the kind of poetic harmony she is able to orchestrate, however, the union with the moon—the process of give and take with nature generated in the poem—closes at the same instant in which the exchange takes the lovers through the instant of their union, where they had "madly lived in one another." The Sufi experience of *fana'* (annihilation) leading to the station of *baqa'* (subsistence) is borrowed and completely refashioned to endow the human love for one another and for nature with the transformative quality attributed traditionally to the alchemical grace of the divine.

The poem "Union" is not an exception. Throughout her last collection, *Tavalludi digar* (Another Birth), which is the focus of this chapter, Farrokhzad demonstrated remarkable poetic resilience in moving between universes that centered on human (particularly female) sexuality, the forces of nature, as well as personal acts of sacred making. While utilizing the poetic potential in each domain according to generic and contextual demands, she demonstrated an impressive ability to transcend traditional boundaries and not to remain captive to the limits of the respective discourses. The same may be observed of her sociopolitical concerns. At a time when Iranian intellectuals polarized into leftist, national-front sympathizers, religious activists, or others with similarly confining affiliations, Farrokhzad escaped factionalist/sectarian tendencies. Respect for human independence and individual space remained a chief concern of hers just as she did not ever compromise her distinct style of political commitment. Her poetry remained open to universal concerns rather than particular brands of politics. I now sift through a few facts about her life before returning to her work in search of broader patterns that outline her major poetic moves.

Farrokhzad was born in 1934 in Tehran in a conventional family and grew up with artistically talented siblings each acknowledged in their own right. Her sister, Puran, herself a writer, described their colonel father as bitter, cold, and frightening, "a real soldier." When the military mask of the soldier was temporarily removed, however, he demonstrated strong emotions for people, for poets he loved, and the books that filled the house.[14] Farrokhzad published her first collection of poems, *Asir* (The Captive), at the age of seventeen and the second, *Divar* (The Wall) five years later. These two collections, which I use infrequently in this chapter, display the joys and anxieties of a fresh and restless mind searching for moments of self-expression under the watchful eye of an established and domineering tradition. *'Isyan* (Rebellion), published two years after *Divar*, showed signs of intensification in the struggle for freeing her creative energies, which were now in serious need of release. In a later interview Farrokhzad described her struggle in the latter two collections as "being out of breath in the last moments of kicking and screaming before freedom." She allegorized her evolving relationship with her poetry as cohabitation turned into full union:

> In *Asir, Divar*, and *'Isyan*, I was a simple narrator of the events in the external world. At that time, poetry had not yet infiltrated me, rather it cohabited with me like a husband, a lover, like all the people who are with you for a while. But later, poetry grew roots in me and for this reason its subject matter changed as far as I was concerned. I no longer considered poetry to be a means of expressing an isolated feeling about myself. As poetry permeated me deeper, and I expanded further, I discovered new worlds.[15]

The above description downplays the poet's agency, assigning the more active role to the infiltrating poetic energy. While potency of poetry was of special interest to Farrokhzad, she did acknowledge elsewhere her own conscious efforts in the process of evolving into a full-fledged modern poet. In these comments, she elaborated with pride on her courageous encounters with painful evolutionary stages in her poetic career, referring to the breakthrough as "arriving at a moment of thinking":

> One arrives at a moment of thinking. During youth, emotions have weak roots but their pull is stronger. If they are not guided with thoughts, they will wither and die. I looked at the world around me, the objects that surrounded me, the people that surrounded me and discovered the chief outer lines of this world. I discovered this world, but when I wished to speak it, I realized that I needed words, fresh words that belonged to this fresh world. Had I feared, I would have died. But I did not fear, I imported the words [thinking to myself] what do I care if they don't yet have poetic license, they have life, I shall make them poetic![16]

In *Tavalludi digar*, published in 1964, Farrokhzad had arrived at that moment of thinking. She no longer struggled with the right to express her sexuality, or to acknowledge the gripping beauty of nature that gave her the freedom she had been denied socially. She had mustered the courage to look for the fresh words that belonged to her newly discovered world. Especially relevant to our discussion is the centrality of the art of sacred making in this world. This is a sacred rooted in nature, concrete, and intimate with the mysteries of the body. The poetic processes that lead to the emergence of the sacred in its various configurations are multifaceted and interconnected. In *Tavalludi digar* Farrokhzad feels aware of the intricacies of her poetry and entitled to devoting her life to it. Above all, she feels her creative goals to be within her artistic reach.

Even in similar social and personal life conditions, poetic expression—the details in every inch of the canvas—differs in inexplicable ways from one artist to another. Part of the charm in artistic expression comes from the idiosyncrasy of these unpredictable details. Farrokhzad's contemporaries dealt with issues similar to hers in different manners. Sepehri, for example, in his resignification of poetic/spiritual expression, which I bring to the center of discussion in the next chapter, relied equally heavily on nature. In the poetic edifice that he built, however, the building blocks can primarily be traced back to the familiar poetic space of premodern Sufi writers. His nature is neat, peaceful, and remote, away from the messy earth and the complications of acknowledging "savagely" free instincts. Farrokhzad celebrated noisily her nature, and within it her colorful vision of the sacred, carved on tree trunks and on her own body with striking vividness. Not only did her version not avoid the untidiness of the instincts, but it crossed the border between the plant and the animal kingdoms when the need arose for the horizons to expand. To her, untidiness is a sign of reality, of life. On her fingers, she preserved the stains of ink—the proud indications of writing poetry. And when the time came, she planted the same fingers in the garden for them to grow and to become nests for swallows, which would lay their eggs in "the hollow of her ink-stained fingers."[17]

I start with a few general observations. It is important to note that sacred making was not a luxury, an ornamental detail in Farrokhzad's poetic edifice; it formed a main supporting pillar. The question might arise as to why this was the case. Her possible personal quest aside, as a master poet, she was aware of the resonance, ethical value, and depth that the sacred brings to the process of generating meaning. There is no need to justify the attraction or to look for associations between her and religious authorities or believing literalists.[18] Furthermore, everyone engages in the process to some degree. The sacred, as Veikok Anttonen observes, is a special quality in individual and collective systems of meaning. Although in religious thinking the concept is always associated with situations and circumstances that refer to the "culture-specific conception of the category of God," in "non-theological contexts," the category can be replaced with some supreme principle of life such as love, freedom, equality, justice, and so on.[19] Thus, contrary to the standard view that the sacred must be constructed in some remote unknown condition, people at large participate in the process of sacred making actively. It involves a process of signification according to paradigms provided by the belief systems to which the participants adhere be they religious, national, or ideological. The making of the sacred is not always smooth and problem free. Paradigms of sacralization may originate unequivocally in mythic histories of organized religions, national traditions, or political ideologies. They could, however, be rooted ambiguously in conflicting and multivalent symbolic constructions of syncretic worldviews and life strategies.[20] While such ambiguous processes may cause problems for anthropologists, or social scientists, aiming to unravel the process, they are treasures to a poet seeking to utilize the productive ambiguity in the structure. Farrokhzad made use of such ambiguities for poetic purposes.

In various belief systems, existing religious structures are desacralized on a periodic basis to make room for new, nonreligious forms of sacralization to be invented. Farrokhzad was aware of the over-reliance in modern discourse on rationality and on logical unraveling of the ambiguous that had, for centuries, enriched the mythical as well as the religious expanses of the culture. At the same time, as we saw in *Dilam bara-yi baghchah misuzad* (I Pity the Garden), she detested superstition and blind religious obedience as major pitfalls on the way of learning and evolution. In this poem, "mother's prayer rug" spread at the gates of the fear of hell and living in a time "that has lost its heart" are two extremes that trouble her.[21] She worked toward building a sacred that could point in the direction of finding the heart, and nurturing it, without encouraging small-minded devotion that imprisoned the heart and the mind. When frustrated with this narrowness, Farrokhzad turned to the mythical world for a similar otherworldly impact. Myths and epic narratives have often been identified as the supernatural worlds in which such gods and spirits can be located "beyond" and "beneath" the spaces and territories of human habitations. These otherworldly places are often situated in deserts, forests, lakes, and islands. Human dwellers in inhabited areas discover evidence of this "other world" beyond in anomalous objects, times, places, and phenomena that contradict and "threaten" the normal categories in terms of which the world is perceived in the flow of everyday life.[22] Although not in a threatening manner, "wandering islands," "oceans," and "sad little nymphs" often brought the mythical space into Farrokhzad's work. The poem "Another Birth," and with it the collection named after the poem, ended in the music of such a "sad little nymph" who carried in her daily mythical rebirth the promise of perpetual regeneration in Farrokhzad's poetic discourse:

> I know
> A sad little nymph
> Who lives in the ocean
> Playing the wooden flute of her heart
> Gently, gently

> A sad little nymph
> Who dies of a kiss every night
> And comes back to life of another every dawn.[23]

I now turn to the poems in *Tavalludi digar* (*Another Birth*), the collection that echoes many of the concerns of twentieth-century Persian poetry and consequently makes Farrokhzad a major figure in the era. In addition to poems from *Tavalludi digar,* I look at some posthumously published poems of equally wide recognition. The search, however, focuses primarily on the process of sacred making in these poems. Generally speaking, I examine compositional structures that stand out as paradigmatic in her broader poetic landscape. These may be found in varying shapes and in different places. Concrete formal structures—such as the scriptural structure she adopted in *Ayah'ha-yi zamini*—are among the more easily detectable.[24] While I attend to these broader patterns, I stay mindful of less visible, yet equally significant, elements such as inner rhythm or the finer details of her poetic morphology and syntax.

Fascination with Sexuality

By the time *Tavalludi digar* was published Farrokhzad already had a reputation for frank expression of her sexuality and intimate experiences. In particular, the poem *Gunah* (Sin) in the collection *Divar* had caused controversy. Not only are the expressions unabashed, the references to sinning are clear about the extramarital nature of the relationship. A woman in her early twenties has transgressed the boundaries of propriety:

> In arms burning and hot I sinned
> A sin that utterly pleased me
> I sinned in his arms, and burning
> Iron strong and avenging was he
>
> In that dark and silent meeting
> The eyes I saw were full of mysteries
> My heart in my breast shook, anxious
> To answer his hungry eyes' pleas
>
> In that dark and silent meeting
> I rested in his arms, undone
> From his lips desire poured out on mine
> And my wild heart's gloom was gone.[25]

The poem sought no ethical or philosophical resolutions. Neither was it meant to allegorize an exchange of a nonphysical nature. It simply celebrated the intimacy between two lovers. Much has been said about Farrokhzad's venturing into this forbidden arena.[26] What has not been acknowledged is that she did not wish to celebrate human sexuality at the cost of the sacred dimension. Rather, these were not conflicting opposites as she understood the complexity of her own being. From a traditionalist perspective, the subject matter was not suitable for public debate to begin with, certainly not by a young woman. She was branded "notorious" and "sinful." Farrokhzad rose to the challenge. She treated the attacks, on this and other frank poems, in the time-honored poetic tradition of the classical era by composing poems in response. In the poem *Pasukh* (Response), she used a long-established poetic style, standard imagery, and a tightly structured meter that followed premodern stylistic conventions. Composed in the formal genre of *qat'ih*, the poem is an impressive display of control over the classical idiom. It was an attempt to outmaneuver the traditionalist opponents with their own weapon, so to speak. Thus, she lashed back:

> God showers me with glances full of laughter
> Though I have not landed on the shore of His grace
> For like wrong-doers hiding in robes of renunciation
> I have not covered my sins from Him in a far-off place.[27]

In case it was not evident that the guardians of the institutionalized religion were the prime target, she provided clear indications in the following stanza:

> A face darkened with the stamp of a deadly sin
> Better than marks of hypocritical prostration on the forehead
> Never saying God's name is a hundred times better
> Than whispering it loud in the hope to be overheard.

To take on the religious authorities in a deeply traditional society that struggled with change was daring, but the poem achieved more than that. On one level, it voiced her desire for a glance from God, albeit a smiling God that preferred sincere shortcoming and transgression to following the rules hypocritically. This much was not new. Indeed, it echoed the Sufi outcry for sincerity from the depths of the classical era. She acknowledged the Sufi source of inspiration by quoting Hāfez, himself a target of clerical dismay in a different time, in the last stanza of the poem.[28] On another level, however, the poem demanded much more. It expressed the desire to maintain the godly glance, without losing the perfectly human privilege of exchange with a lover. God, as far as she was concerned, had no problem understanding her humanity:

> Not to worry if the Shaykh in the circle of his followers
> Happily closed the doors of paradise on me
> He will hear my pleas and open that door
> He who created me of love's sweet melancholy.

Last but not least, the poem demanded the right to an unsuppressed feminine voice for celebrating that humanity, and the emotion of love, in her poetry.

By the time *Tavalludi digar* was published, another development had taken place. Farrokhzad had formed a deeper and more sophisticated understanding of the problem of self-expression. She was no longer troubled with particular individuals or social classes. "Arriving at the moment of thinking" had diverted her attention from small personal "enemies" to broader patterns of human perception. She now realized that the compartmentalization of her being into mundane and spiritual had to be corrected at a deeper level within. This perceptual correction was as, if not more, important than reforming the social norms imposed by the institutionalized religion.

In the poem *Aftab mishavad* (The Sun Coming Up), the above maturation is visible. Here she was not dealing with enemies but with events and processes. Furthermore, she did not allow the magnetic force of the erotic to absorb all her poetic energy. Feelings were now as multivalent and nuanced as was the language she had developed to express them. In "The Sun Coming Up," the beloved comes from the distanced *sarzami-i 'atr'ha u nur'ha* (land of perfume and light), which are basic components of a holy shrine. He sets her on a skiff made of ivory, crystal, and cloud and carries her to the *shahr-i shi'r'ha u shur'ha* (city of passion and poems).[29] In this journey that connects her to mythical space, "star-scorched," "fevered," and filled with wonder, she is a simple goldfish in the pools of night. This is a full-fledged nocturnal journey, if not prophetic then fairly close to it. In her nocturnal ascent, however, unlike Bayazid and Kadkani, Farrokhzad does not leave her beloved—her human passions—behind. If there is one goal attached to this ascent, it is to connect the heaven and earth. It is to realize that the remoteness of the sky has been a function of nearsightedness on the part of the inhabitants of the earth and caused by a inability to expand beyond one realm to reach the other:

> How remote from the blue porches of the skies
>   our world once lay
> Your voice
> Comes to me again now
> White wings of angels sounding
> Do you see how far I have come?
> As far as the Milky Way
>   beyond space, beyond time.[30]

She had ascended to bless her humanity in heavens, or the heavens with her humanity. They both were parts of the same continuum. The point was precisely to see the faulty nature of the distinction. Now that she had achieved the "height" affording her the privilege of a new vantage point, what she wished to do among the stars, the waves, and the clouds was to celebrate her womanhood:

> Now that we have reached the heights
> Wash me in the wine of waves

> Wrap me in your silky kisses
> Want me through unending nights
> Never let go of me
> Never take these stars from me

"The Sun Coming Up" ends with the beloved rising as the sun, the morning that follows this star-studded night. That he is the ending point in the poem underlines the conviction that, in Farrokhzad's view, the human presence was not to be overshadowed by the heavenly and the mythical. Equally remarkable is her revival, at this point, of the emphasis on the role of the poetic word. The ascent that had begun with the beloved to "the city of passion and poems," has led to the opening up of a poetic horizon above the cradle of her words, a half-mythical half-real space to be illumined with the dawn of love:

> And above the cradle of my poem
> see yourself
>   rising
>   the sun coming up.[31]

"The Sun Coming Up" is one of Farrokhzad's more subdued variations on a theme one might call conciliation between sexuality and spirituality. A more dramatic attempt at the fusion of the two appears in the form of an extended allegory on sexual union in the poem *Vasl* (Union), which I discussed earlier in this chapter.

Farrokhzad's search for an inner life force, a soul if you will, extended beyond her own body to the world around and particularly to nature, which was to become a major tool in her later poetic ventures. The interaction with nature that in later poems transformed into complete union—and at times organic grafting on one another—in its early stages had demonstrated a strong narrowly defined sexual overtone. In the poem *Abtani* (Bathing), as she undresses and bathes in the spring, nature comes alive with desire that seeks instant gratification. She wants to share her sorrow with the spring, whose "cool brilliant" waves pull her in with soft crystalline hands. The natural elements become increasingly more human as the poem progresses. The strong scent of wild mint carried by the wind mingles with her breath as she gives herself to the spring wholly, "like a woman embraced by her lover." By the last stanza, *cheshmah'sar-i gunah'kar* (the sinful spring) has demonstrated full agency in the union that has unfolded before our eyes.[32] The poem is rare, not just in modern Persian poetry or as an example of women's writings, but in eroticizing nature to the degree that justifies attaching sins to its potent character. Artistically speaking, although one of her less developed earlier pieces, this is a delightful poem. It captures a carefree moment and brings it to sharp focus by celebrating every exquisite detail. Her physical presence, her feelings, and the natural beauty of the spring are held together with a bouncy rhythm that stays fresh and playful till the end. While the sexual content may feel fore-grounded to some readers, to others the joy and the play of the encounter, which is full of surprises, takes precedence.

In the evolutionary journey that took Farrokhzad through stages of writing, *Abtani* occupied a place close to *Pasukh*. Both poems belonged to a period in which strong, and relatively simple, emotions were expressed with vividness and zeal. They focused on elevated or angry moments delivering strong blows and heading for clear destinations. Unambiguous and powerful as these poems were, they lacked the sophistication displayed in her later writings, where the complexity of minute details allowed a more nuanced expression.

In *Dar khiyaban'ha-yi sard-i shab* (In Night's Cold Streets), Farrokhzad had achieved that level of sophistication and nuanced articulation.[33] The poem opens with a shocking, yet effectively ambiguous, declaration of self-sacrifice, a voluntary surrender to an execution. The self-destruction begins to make sense when placed, in the next stanza, against the backdrop of "night's cold streets," wrapped in silent dark and empty of all sounds but good-byes. By the third stanza, the surrender has expanded its semantic umbrella and been infused with new meaning. It is now clear that the surrender is not meant to evoke self-destruction as much as it is intended to allude to breaking out of an old pattern of existence and moving toward new horizons. We know this because the poet's heart now "flows on the other side of time," looking beyond horizons of ordinary possibilities. She is released from temporal captivity:

> I have no regrets
> As though my heart flowed on the other side of time
> Life will utter my heart again
> And the dandelion's wisp sailing over the wind's lake
> Will utter me again.[34]

On the surface, this is another fusion with nature and the empowerment that came with "being uttered by life" again and again in endless natural cycles of rebirth. A closer examination reveals Farrokhzad's newfound ability to bring much more to the work through the sheer force and inevitability of her own sexuality. This is a sexuality no longer satisfied with playful erotic encounters with the spring. It is as mysterious and powerful as it is deep and sacred. It seeks fuller encounters with life, opportunities that can afford her explorations of unlimited dimension. Furthermore, she now carries within herself the fountain of life she once sought elsewhere. She possesses the sexual potency, the life-giving womanhood, and the nurturing love needed for generating perpetual growth:

> Ah, do you see
> How my skin is splitting
> How milk's forming in the blue veins of my breasts

How the blood
begins
growing its cartilage in my patient loins

I am you   you
And the one who loves
And the one who suddenly finds
In herself a dumb grafting
To thousands of unknown, lost things
And I am all of earth's ferocious lust
Sucking all the waters into herself
Making all the fields conceive.[35]

All she has to do now is to encode into poetry the mystery in this organic grow-
ing life and, at the same time, the vulnerability. Depending on our level of aware-
ness and care, this mystery can wither away or expand itself to horizons of
mythical dimension. She has mocked on numerous occasions the devotion to
sacred when it is trivialized and reduced to mechanical blind worship. Now she
can demonstrate that in its healthy state, making the sacred and venerating it has
genuine roots in the pulsating core of life. Were the mysterious incantations of
the mornings, the silence of the mirrors, the depth of dreams, and the tireless
heartbeat of life to be understood properly, the concept of regret would disappear
from our treasury of words and ideas. Regrets are meaningless where no one
remains captive to the physical boundaries of the body or limitations of time:

Listen to my voice far off
In the dense mist of morning's incantations
And see me in the silent mirrors
Touching once again the deep dark of all dreams
With what is left of my hands
And tattooing my heart like a bloodstain
On life's innocent luck
I have no regrets
Speak to me
O my beloved, to another me
You will find once more in the night's cold street.[36]

Once again, the poem ends addressing the beloved placing human presence and
contact at the heart of growth and renewal.

When the Lagoon's Water Has Lost Its Flow

Farrokhzad's insistence on freeing the human, particularly female, sexual potential
from cultural taboos and elevating it to a sacred force went beyond the need to

remedy social injustice. It was closely connected with her fear of artistic stagnation and her almost obsessive need for growth and renewal. As far as she was concerned, growth and renewal were the only shields that protected humanity against the perpetual danger of death and decay. To understand this fear, and her ways of dealing with it, is key to understanding her poetic sacred making, which was always expressed through frankly erotic processes of sensual give and take.

Remember that by the time *Tavalludi digar* was published, Farrokhzad could see that there were threats bigger than clerical dismay. She now talked about the human tendency to surrender to inertia, being numbed into passivity by blind faith, intimidation by technology, paralysis caused by comforts of "modern" life. Since the struggle to defeat the tendency for decay and paralysis had to be continuous, it informed her every creative move. She wrote for theater, appeared in minor parts in cinema, and made documentaries. What mattered was to stay alive, and to grow, which were both correlated closely with the ability to express oneself. In one interview she said:

> That I wrote poetry my whole life does not mean that poetry is the only means of self-expression. I like cinema. I will work with any other medium that I can, too. If I do not write, I'll act on stage. If not active in theatre, I'll make films. How long will that continue? I don't know, as long as I have something to say.[37]

Of all artistic media she tried, however, poetry provided the scene for the liveliest struggles against decay. The struggle acquired such broad dimensions and varied strategies that it may be defined as the central paradigmatic feature of her work. Her confessions in various interviews that she wrote in order to avoid death found fascinating proportions in her poetry. This poetic thirst for vitality and allegorical search for the fountain of creativity/life is worth a brief investigation.[38]

LOOKING THE MONSTER IN THE FACE

When the fear was tangible and close to the surface, the struggle took place in the open. On such occasions, Farrokhzad looked the monster in the face and described it directly by thematizing the fear. The poem *Murdab* (The Lagoon) is a case in point.[39] From the opening stanza, the simple descriptive phrases signal the presence of death and decay. The night is "black and diseased," insomnia prevails and life is an "old long held breath." In this "wasteland" with its "cardboard sun" and "cardboard moon" everything happens in insurmountable isolation. Even birth does not bring any glad tidings, as the fetuses already aging in the womb claw its walls to work their way out. We are not spared any details of this devastating decay and morbidity. Indeed, we share the vantage point of the poet who has isolated herself like an "earthworm burrowing in musty ground," watching her own execution from the rooftops of her lonely existence. "Addicted to the scent of her mate," she looks for him from street to street, and at times even finds him, but to no avail:

> Sometimes finding him, but doubting it's he
> Her mate, someone lonelier yet than she
> Both trembling and fearful of each other
> Ungrateful, bitter-tongued to each other
> Their love a madness that must be condemned
> Their Union a suspect dream that must end.[40]

"The lagoon's water has lost its flow." If we wish to be honest with ourselves, we need to take a look at the lagoon in which we live and admit that it has gone "stale, stagnating and sinking low." Fear does not solve the problem just as denial does not provide a way out. But if we stay with the poem, we are about to learn a poetic lesson: life is infectious; grafting someone else's vital dreams on one's fading memory of being alive can bring us back to life.

It is not consistent with Farrokhzad's way of handling problems to allow death to take over. As we feel the chilling fear of decay in our bones, she musters her creative strength and turns the tide. This is a delicate operation. On the one hand, she does not wish to alleviate with an easy resolution the pain she has induced carefully. On the other, change is desperately needed. She chooses the transforming potential of her poetic language as the vehicle for enacting the change. In one of the most spectacular examples of poetic contrast, she appeals to life-giving nature once more, and turns the last seven verses of the poem into a nostalgic yet exuberant dream of finding a path to the sea. She is now herself the lagoon pleading with the deer to salvage her from the depths of her decay by remembering, in their free ventures in the fields, her longings for the sea. In the process, she uses the deer's memory as the canvas on which to display nature's watercolor of revival and buoyancy, the antidote to wasting away in stale waters:

> Deer, O deer browsing free in the field
> If, near crossroads that wildflowers conceal
> You sometimes find a singing rivulet
> That meanders towards the sea's violet
> She's riding the chariot of her flood
> She's flowing like silk on the moving flood
> Fingers laced in the mane of the wind's horse
> The red soul of the moon trailing her course
> Parting grassy green thighs in acquiescence
> Stealing from bushes their virgin fragrance
> Overhead, as in each bubble's reflection
> The unexhausted image of the sun

> Remember that sleep of the sleepless one
> Remember that dying in the lagoon.[41]

Even though the last verse of the poem evokes death in the lagoon, by this time the fear of decay has almost vanished. Life has been remembered with such vividness and color that defeating the paralysis is now a true possibility. She has voiced the captivity of the lagoon, borrowed the memory of the browsing deer, and empowered us to taste the liberating fantasy of reaching the sea.

Still, Farrokhzad understood that the power of dreaming could be turned against itself, that like any other powerful weapon it was a double-edged sword. Dreaming was stepping into a world of mythical proportions, a world in which our rational estimations of danger, reward, and punishment no longer held true. Every time we stepped into it, we were facing another unknown. The unknown could be a sea overflowing with life or a deadly trap ready to swallow everything we had. Nonetheless, decay was the true demise and all life a struggle with death. Under these circumstances, we had little choice but inventing new strategies of living in our dreams. When running out of such strategies, we would graft our dreams on those of the deer, the fish, and others who knew how to stay alive.

There were instances of failure as in the case of *'Ali Kuchikeh* (Little Ali). Little Ali is the protagonist in one of the best-known poems in the *Tavalludi digar* written in a conversational style. Ali has dreamed of a fish:

> A silver fish like coins in a pile
> Like a bolt of beautiful silk
> Bordered in the beaded style
> And sewn all about with silk
> Like the petals of the tulips of the field
> With diamonds smooth and round and cut for rings
> Playing hide-and-seek in her eyes.[42]

Although enthralled with the fish, Ali has resisted jumping into the pond where the fish lives for the fear of the unknown lying in the bottom. All attempts to catch the fish have failed. Every time "he reaches for that floating color" there is lightning and rain, the water turns black, and the golden lights disappear. Then, Little Ali is left with the same old night spreading itself overhead: "no dreams, no fish, no signs of spring." Every night, Ali runs literally a hundred times between the desire for the silvery fish and the fear of falling into the pond.

Little Ali's lagoon, with its stale water and perishing life, is outside the pond that holds the fish of his dream. It is his everyday life, yet it is less visible than the one portrayed in the previous poem because it is covered up with lies, threats, and promises of peace and comfort. When Ali clears his head of all the noises that disrupt thinking and listens to the fish, he knows that in the pond life is real and vibrant. In contrast, the world outside the pond—an allegory for Iran in the 1960s with its stagnating social conditions and policing state—is the lagoon. Even the god of the lagoon follows "hoods with knives," yet few see the absence of life in this world because a "blaring noise" masks its emptiness:

> This world where dowager bitches meet
> Falling in behind its god
> Whenever He shows on the street
> Preceded by some hoods with knives
> A world jammed wherever you go
> With the blaring noise of the radio
> She takes him away
> takes him away from this sack of trash, worms and disease.[43]

So Little Ali dives into the pond one night and meets his death, which is sitting in ambush in the bottom of the pond, probably an allegory for the destiny awaiting those who opted for armed struggle against the forces running the lagoon. Whatever our reading of the allegory may be, Ali's tragic death is by no means a defeat. There is a difference between a death in pursuit of the silvery fish of one's dreams and one caused by sinking into the lagoon of unawareness and inertia.

The sources of the stagnation and decay that fueled Farrokhzad's persistent fears were varied and numerous. Inaction, self-delusion, and self-importance were among them. The "inert intellectuals" drowning in the poem *Ayah'ha-yi zamini* (The Earthly Scriptures) in "the swamp of alcohol" and "vile poisonous vapors" were not victims in a distant world. She felt herself in danger of falling prey to the same kind of self-delusion and inertia. The poem *Dar ghurubi abadi* (In an Eternity of Setting Sun) contains a series of dialogues in search of ways to infuse life with meaning. A voice responds to another that suggests "working" as a solution:

> Yes, but in that big desk
> There lives a secret enemy
>   who softly, softly chews you
> The way it chews up wood and notebooks
>   and a thousand more useless things
> Till you sink at last in a cup of tea
>   like a boat in a whirlpool
> And see nothing in the heart of the horizon
> But thick clouds of cigarette smoke, and meaningless lines.[44]

GOD IN A NAMELESS GRAVE

By far the most deadly source of stagnation for Farrokhzad was blind faith and ritual practice emptied of spiritual vitality and vigor. There was the god who "showered" his creation "with glances full of laughter" and the god "preceded by some hoods with knives" and followed by "dowager bitches" whenever he showed on the street. They were worlds apart; one could be a fountain of inner life and the other a source of decay. Farrokhzad provided a vivid visual description of gradual death in the grips of lifeless empty faith in the poem *'Arusak-i kuki* (Mechanical Doll):

> Head bowed you can kneel your whole life long
>   On the cold floor of a holy tomb
> You can see God in some nameless grave
>   Recover faith with a mere penny
> You can rot away like an old chanter
>   Of prayers in the chapel of some mosque
> You can remain the one constant, cipher
>   Through manifold calculation
> Your eyes seeming bleached buttons
>   On old shoes in the bag of their anger
> You can dry up like water in your own ditch.[45]

Beneath the fear of decay and the desire to defeat death, there was a deep yearning to find the heart and the soul that propelled the universe pulsating with life. Parallel with the hope was the anxiety that entrapment in a degenerating world, and neglect of this heart and soul, have driven a wedge between us and our sacred inner core. In *Didar dar shab* (Encounter at Night) Farrokhzad echoed centuries of Sufi warnings that the spiritual faculties will be numbed if life is shaped merely by habitual patterns:

> Perhaps addiction to being
> And living on tranquilizers
> Have led our simple human desires
> To complete degeneration
> Perhaps the soul has been exiled
> To a remote deserted island
> Perhaps I have heard the cricket's voice
>   Only in a dream.[46]

The following stanza in the poem, which I quote below, testifies to Farrokhzad's insight into the culture's memory, her awareness of ties with the past. While the poem is not restrained by the premodern tradition, it is grounded in it. No search for life's sacred core can afford to overlook connections with the past preserved in the culture's collective memory. The quote is also a statement of Farrokhzad's disappointment with the "intellectual milieu" that underestimated this continuity. It expresses shock at the lack of resemblance between the inspiring figures of the

past and the contemporaries sinking deeper and deeper into their thinly disguised
lagoons:

> Then these infantry
> Leaning patiently on their wooden spears
> Are those swift riders?
> And these figures
>   bent, emaciated, and given to addiction
> Those pure free thinking Sufis?[47]

This is one of Farrokhzad's harshest statements of disappointment with the intel-
lectual community. Closeness to nature has taught her that survival requires
growing roots and reaching deep into a tradition. Even Majnun, whose tent she
used to wipe the dust off her lover's shoes, has something to offer his contempo-
rary counterparts. The treasures passed over the hedges of history—the legacy of
the culture that once possessed a soul—ought to be preserved. Otherwise, there
is no hope for an arrival, a prophecy, a door opening into a world with meaning-
ful inner life.

Tavalludi digar testifies to many moments of despair in Farrokhzad's life.
These were times when she doubted her own survival let alone that of the tradi-
tion she infused with life in its harsh encounters with modernity. In *Didar dar
shab,* the unknown face beyond the window does not spare her feelings when she
needs to hear the truth. The air is cold, and the night silent: "not even a leaf stirs."
There is no hope for an arrival:

> Then it is true that humanity
> No longer awaits an arrival
> And girls in love
> Have pierced their naively believing eyes
> With their knitting needles.[48]

As time passed, however, things changed. Just as Farrokhzad's early flashes of
anger at individual enemies had subsided into a more perceptive assessment of
the larger processes behind feelings and events, so did her need for an arrival. The
more she explored the strength and beauty of nature and the mysteries of her own
feminine evolution, the more she understood the gradual and intangible nature
of the arrival. These sparks of perception first occurred in passing poetic moments.
In the poem *Daryaft* (Insight), as she sinks slowly to the bottom of the hole like
"stagnant water," all she can hear is "a loathsome mouse in its burrow, coarsely
singing."[49] However, amid morbid observations of decay, she is able to recall the
day of "her first menses" and her body

> Marveling innocently, opening itself
> To merge with darkness, silence, mystery.

After this recollection, the first "trembling line of light" yawns itself "up in a little bubble."[50] There are many such glimmers of light brightening corners of her darker poems for brief instants. During a relatively rapid process of poetic maturation, these fleeting moments expanded into longer more lasting instances of personal awareness. The result was a level of integration of experience that can be viewed as the hallmark of her latest work.

"HAS THE TIME NOT COME FOR THIS WINDOW TO OPEN WIDE, WIDE, WIDE . . . FOR RAINS TO FALL?"

It did not take long for Farrokhzad to perceive and acknowledge the interrelated nature of her encounters with the world around her. Her marveling at her own emerging feminine voice, her craving for the "sorrowful dove of faith," and her need for grafting dreams of the deer on hers were all happening along one exploratory continuum. They all faded into one another and resurfaced again with a tendency to form one integrated poetic whole. The presence "beyond the window" expressed the same tendency: it was time "to open the window wide enough for rains to fall" on everything.[51] The riches that "the eager" restless hare "living in the pupils of her eyes" found in its daily ventures in "unknown meadows" had to be integrated in the crucible of her poetry.[52] Her greatest success in sacred making occurred after this integration.

There was much that needed integration. The beloved, for example, went through the full process of integration into the cycle of human/nature interaction. In the poem *Bad ma ra khvahad burd* (The Wind Will Blow Us Away), the beloved is "green from head to toe" and when he holds her hands the wind blows the two of them away.[53] This full-fledged migration into nature was the culmination of many isolated images and sporadic allusions that had prepared the way for crossing the borders between nature and human body. The poem *Tavalludi digar*, in which she plants her ink-stained fingers in the garden, follows the same goal of rescuing the beloved from decay by grafting him on nature:

> My entire being is a dark verse
> That repeats you like a refrain
> Taking you thereby
> To the dawn of eternal growing and blossoming
> I sighed you in this verse, I sighed you
> I grafted you in this verse
>   on trees, on water, and on fire.[54]

Not all the mingling with nature was as straightforward. In *Dar ab'ha-yi sabz-i tabistan* (In Summer's Green Waters), *to be* is a floating and fluctuating experience for her and her lover, who move between plant and human existence. In this poem she portrays his green, fragrant, and diffuse presence, which thrives in her emotional space. She relates to this presence in much the same way that she

would to a mysterious garden on a bright summer day. These are new chapters in
a literature that had rarely recorded female expressions of feelings let alone those
with such strong erotic overtones:

> Here you are
> Like the odor of acacias
> Diffusing through the lanes at dawn
> On my breast, heavy
> In my hands, hot
> In my fainting hair, burnt, abandoned
> Here you are now.[55]

She has appropriated the calm and composure of his "natural" presence in these
peaceful moments of love and togetherness. She has made him hers, as one might
in inhaling the scent of acacias. Separation is meaningless. She can now rest, she
can forget the prospect of decay once and for all, even escape temporal limitations
by allowing herself to close "on the arriving moments like a door." Anxiety fades
away like the "vague . . . distant hubbub of a noisy day" in the moment of falling
asleep. And there is such affinity with nature that falling asleep feels like being
"plucked from the surface of a pool" or "being picked from a branch":

> Something vast, dark, and dense
> Something vague like the distant hubbub of a noisy day
> Hovers around and spreads itself
> On my closing eyelids
> Am I being plucked from the surface of a pool?
> Am I being picked from a branch?
> Am I being closed on the arriving moments
> 　　like a door?
> Am I . . .
> I do not see anymore.[56]

In "the Fragrant Core of a Fertilized Egg": Building a Sanctuary for Life

I conclude with a reading of the poem *Divar'ha-yi marz* (The Frontier Walls)
from the collection *Tavalludi digar*.[57] "The Frontier Walls" is one of the most
remarkable instances in Farrokhzad's poetry in which the paradigmatic patterns
identified in the present chapter display full integration. Furthermore, the piece
has an organized and directed structural order that leads to a sense of complete-
ness and closure. It is as if Farrokhzad has composed the piece to leave her read-
ers with a poetic manifesto, her philosophy of life, and her perception of the role
she played in it. In this poem, Farrokhzad builds frontier walls around a poeti-
cally cultivated space vibrating with life and turns it into the sanctuary she desires

for all life-forms. Within the sanctuary, she takes her readers on a fascinating tour of frozen seasons that come to life with the warmth of love and back to the "fragrant core of a fertilized egg."[58]

The poem opens with the building of the basic structures of the sanctuary, the "forbidding walls" that might at first seem to put her in captivity:

> Now forbidding walls
> Frontier walls rise again
> In the quiet night like plants
>   Sentries posted on my love's state.[59]

Her agency in building the walls, however, shows itself in the approving tone that she uses in describing the protected space. Not only does the city's "dirty clamor" move from her shores, but we can foretell her feelings by looking at the trees now able to "shed barks," and the "earth's pores" sucking "the atoms of the moon":

> Now the City's dirty clamor
> moves from my dark shore again
> like a school of fish disturbed
> Now windows see themselves opened
> to pleasant scattered perfumes again
> Trees in the sleeping garden all shed their bark again
> and the earth's myriad of pores suck down the atoms of the moon.[60]

The fresh air has filtered in through the open windows, the moonlight has cleansed everything, and the trees have felt safe to disrobe in this nightly perfumed garden. The sanctuary is now hers, and that of all humanity. "The love's longing beat" that now spread through her "tribal limbs" is not just an expression of womanhood, but an occasion for the regeneration of all life, for reinvention of the desire to be. This is an intensely sacred moment in which life's perpetual evolution has eradicated all possibility of decay. Farrokhzad expresses the potentials of the moment in which "all stars" are "making love" with the simple confession that she knows it when it is "time to pray." In this sanctuary, the regular artificial distinctions between physical and spiritual evolutions are not going to prevail. The rewards for being a part of this sanctuary are numerous. Not only can she gift her "young green hot climate's tropic flowers" to the beloved with no anxiety of punitive social measures, she can be "blown on the last breath of air, through the sanctuary of the night" and rain on all as "madly" as she wishes. This is not a place to stop, not a place to end explorations. Indeed, it is just the beginning:

> Come with me
> to that star come with me
> to that star a thousand thousand years away
> from the frozen seasons of the earth and its senseless balancing

And where no one
fears the light.[61]

But the main journey is to the core of life itself, where artificial compartmentalization has not yet prevailed. This is the place in which the sacred has a vast meaning not yet fragmented with smallness and greed:

Come back with me
Come back with me
to the start of creation
to the fragrant core of a fertilized egg
to the moment I was born from you
Come back with me
You've left me incomplete.[62]

With a refreshingly unabashed tone, she alternates her allusions to light, to prayer, and to the sacredness at the heart of life with descriptions of her physical longing for love. These exquisite descriptions of "doves taking wings" on the tip of her breasts and kisses cocooned in her lips fill the sanctuary with lively and concrete expressions of union. Yet they all end in highly sacralized moments of prayer in phrases such as

Now
my body's an altar
ready for the rites of love

and with confessions to the inexpressibility of the moment.[63] The closing stanza to the poem is a model of a successful poetic closure. It is perhaps the most suitable poem with which to end the present chapter. In brief articulate phrases, she first merges the feminine, the natural, and the sacred in the crucible of her poetry then celebrates the alchemical miracle that results. In that sanctuary filled with the moon, where her feminine voice is unsuppressed, her poetry has built walls of protection, and decay is unimaginable, another Jesus could come to life:

Let me conceive by the moon in the sanctuary of the night
Let me be filled
By small raindrops
By infant hearts
By the weight of children not yet born
Perhaps my love could be
the womb of another Jesus.

This is the ultimate immaculate conception, where the physical and the sacred merge and alter each other beyond recognition.

"Infinite" Fruits in the Basket of Poetry

Resignifying the Mystical Idiom for Spiritual Expression

In twentieth-century Iran, within the spectrum of religious visions, mysticism seemed particularly attractive for remaking the sacred and expressing the spiritual self in a changing world. The reformist tendencies of the modern Persian poet did not clash with the conventional mystical-lyrical sentiments. The Sufi conceptualization of the world as capable of direct contact, even union, with God as well as the abundance of colorful and mulitlayered Sufi motifs in the poetic discourse of a millennium were inviting.[1] The poetry of Suhrab Sepehri, on which I focus in this chapter, was the culmination, within the reformist movement, of a prevalent desire to engage the poetic discourse at the heart of the age-old Sufi tradition. The engagement, I argue, had numerous dimensions, including admiration, rivalry, struggle, cohabitation, mingling, as well as renewal. Before we get to the intricacies of this evolving poetic encounter, however, I would like to make a few clarifications. In the course of our discussion, the term "mysticism" will evoke the Sufi spiritual outlook permeating premodern, as well as contemporary, Persian culture. Though at times problematic, the category *mysticism* is the most suitable rubric widely recognized by the English-speaking reader available for use here. However, I first highlight some of the defining features of the category itself before I begin to apply it to our modern Muslim Persian context.

Like all categories we use to capture the essence of complex social phenomena that surround us, mysticism refers to a cultural construct. The term was initially coined by western intellectuals "to refer to that phenomenon or aspect of the Christian tradition that was understood to emphasize religious knowledge gained by means of an extraordinary experience or revelation of the divine. This has remained a constant theme in the academic study of the subject." In his *Orientalism and Religion,* Richard King follows the above characterization with a variety of specific attributes of mysticism put forth by various historians of religion such as Margaret Smith and Evelyn Underhill. These include such main features as "the revolt against cold formality and religious torpor," establishing "a conscious relation with the absolute" in order to find "the personal object of love," "union between God and the soul," or "a process of sublimation." These predominantly Western Christian features, King reminds us, are applied to all forms of mysticism throughout the different world-religious traditions, even when in conflict with the mystic's philosophy as in Hinduism and Neoplatonism.[2] Interestingly, none of what King summarizes here as hastily universalized Christian features of mysticism present problems, at least in their broad outlines, when applied to the specific context of the material I discuss in this chapter.

King's broader point is, however, well taken concerning the problems with such postenlightenment definitions as mysticism. His dissatisfaction echoes similar complaints on the part of contemporary historians wishing to break free from the essentializing discourses of the Enlightenment era. As I have shown with Timothy Fitzgerald's discussion of the category religion, there is a clear need for revising discourses that straitjacket culturally boisterous phenomena denying them their diverse nature, their subtle differences arising from their historicity.[3] Invented universalizing rubrics such as mysticism can hardly do justice to strategies of sacred making and interaction with deities, which have been a consistent feature of human life throughout history. Each culture, each era, has witnessed different ways of imagining the sacred and equally different ways of interacting with it. Indeed, this is one of the reasons for the close examination of the poetic strategies of sacred making by Sepehri and his contemporaries in this chapter. It is a rare glance at what they and their generation wove into this already colorful tapestry of spiritual visions.[4]

Sometimes appropriate for our context and sometimes not, the universalizing definition of mysticism carved out of Christianity emphasizes a few structural points. It presupposes the Christian notions of God, communion, and the soul. As an extension of the above, it assumes implicitly a monotheistic belief at the heart of all mystical traditions even when it does not make explicit references to it. At the same time, it presumes a predominantly experiential nature to any mystical perception of the world. Examples of poetry produced in the twentieth-century Persian cultural setting, used in this chapter, show varieties of mystical understanding of the sacred with features different from the above.[5] Yet geographical and temporal distance does not automatically lead to difference. Indeed the map of cultural exchange in the modern world is far from simple or predictable.

Twentieth-century poets from various parts of the world might share more than we see at first glance. For example, they frequently come from literate environments. With the Eurocentric orientation of the world's educational institutions, it is not surprising for these poets to be familiar with, even influenced by, literary works colored with postenlightenment features of modernized thought. This may alter, even Europeanize, their representation of certain features of their own local cultures. Sepehri's poetry, for example, seems to present the sacred within his mystical tradition as more of a private personal discovery rather than as a communal phenomenon. There is little doubt that the Persian traditional mystical experience is still rooted predominantly in communal experience.[6] One might argue, then, that Sepehri looked from a personal vantage point colored by the Eurocentric perspective rather than by that of his indigenous culture. Indeed, King categorizes the "privatization" of the mystical experience as a particularly post-enlightenment European perception of the sacred.[7] While this may be the case, on another level, Sepehri's work and lifestyle maintained its particularities and demonstrated awareness of the limits of the Eurocentric perspective on the varieties of human interaction with the sacred. He traveled to south and southeast Asia, for example, and showed fascination with the mystical traditions within these cultures. He, then, gave poetic sanction to the value of such traditions in *Sida-yi pa-yi ab* (The Footsteps of Water) and in later poems. The celebrated reference to the city of Varanasi being illuminated with eternal light is one such passing reference.[8] His awareness that patterns of universal exchange were rooted in culturally specific experiences of daily life went beyond making sporadic allusions. At times, he expressed this awareness as a theme in more developed passages:

> I am from Kāshān
> My roots may be traced
> To a plant in India, a piece of pottery in Sialkot
> I may be traced back to a whore in the city of Bukhara.[9]

While Sepehri's Eurocentric education had prepared him for a personal and private notion of the mystical, attention to detail in his poetry reveals a keen understanding of his communal rootedness. From these details, which one might call regional patterns, as well as the poet's personal style of codifying them into poetry, rich and fresh portraits of the sacred emerge. This is the only hope for transcending standard studies devoted to textualized world religions as sole representatives of "religious experience of humankind" and enriching these studies, at the same time. No Qur'anic commentary or compendium of speculative mysticism will provide the details, or the perspective, offered in the poetic portrayal.

King notes that virtually all contemporary studies of mysticism fail to appreciate the sense in which notions of the mystical are cultural and linguistic constructions dependent on a web of interlocking definitions, attitudes, and discursive processes.[10] These culturally complex sets of exchanges can hardly be captured through studies conducted within any single discipline, particularly disciplines not attentive to the linguistic embeddedness of cultural perception. In this regard, the present literary study has a timely role to fulfill. On the one hand, it highlights the linguistically embedded cultural specifics that cannot be deduced from historical narration or quantitative social/economic analysis. On the other, it remains aware that, as a category, the mystical is socially constructed and questions of power, authority, and gender find different degrees of relevance to it. This investigation, therefore, does not attempt to replace various disciplines in social sciences but rather works with them as an ally. Its main purpose is to unravel the definitions, attitudes, and discursive processes mentioned above by seeing them in a new light and by getting deeper into the forms of life and historically specific practices that they are tied to. These are complicated processes that cannot be understood properly unless their generic conventions—the linguistic behavior of systems of signification within which they have been codified to convey meaning—are decodified. Here again, the sensitivity of literary inquiries to generic conventions serves as a useful methodological tool for decoding the varieties of mystical expression.

There is no need for probing deeper to show the difficulties involved in a proper study of mysticism. The sheer awareness of its shifting cultural, political, and semantic patterns throughout history makes one thing clear: any abstract search, in any cultural context, for an essence of mysticism is fundamentally misconceived. In this chapter, I pursue two broad, interrelated, and equally important objectives. The first is an exploration of Sepehri's poetry to grasp the particular poetic articulation of the mystical tradition in the specific historical moments in which he and his contemporaries tried to make sense of modernity and change. The second objective is to use this opportunity to understand the ways in which the strategies of sacred making in the mystical tradition contributed to the evolution of a fresh system of encoding poetic messages. If there is a conclusion to the chapter, it is that interaction in the modern context led to the alteration of both, mysticism and poetic possibilities of self-expression. This mutually formative interplay stays at the heart of the present inquiry.

Difficulties of defining mysticism, and complexities of the above interplay notwithstanding, our exploratory journey begins by recalling a simple historical fact. Mystical themes had persistently been a favorite subject matter in Persian poetry since the classical period. Certain defining and relatively constant features of the mystical tradition must have been responsible for this long-lasting historical interaction. I call such features "structural features." Even in specific historical periods and places, structural features of mysticism had not remained fixed, limited, or constant. Besides, specific social and political conditions would bring certain features to prominence at any given time. At the time of Sepehri and his contemporaries, for example, mysticism's general tolerance for "otherness" constituted a structural feature and a main attraction. That the traditional mystical outlook had, in many cases, reached beyond the Arab-Muslim communal aspirations to accommodate a wider notion both of deity and humanity served a number of purposes. On the one hand, it made the tradition conducive to challenging a narrowly defined past from a philosophical or literary perspective. On the other, the same tolerance made mysticism a brand of spirituality inclusive of varieties of religious practice. Finally, and perhaps most significantly, the openness of the Sufi discourse had endowed it with a concurrent complexity and flexibility capable of tolerating the infiltration of new elements. This past feature is of particular relevance to our discussion. Karimi-Hakkak has provided an interesting reading of literary change and renewal in contemporary Iran. Bearing Bakhtin and Lotman's theoretical insight on the process of change in Persian poetry, he has noted that in encoding new poetic messages the old and the new can cohabit the cultural space until the new gains more currency and relevance. In this light, the smooth cohabitation of the reformist and conventional mystical-lyrical tendencies mentioned here are remarkable examples. The existing mystical tradition was strong and confident enough to absorb new shapes and patterns without fear of losing its identity or falling apart. The mystical tradition had a strong "sense of itself," to use Karimi-Hakkak's term, which was not easily violated by infiltration of new elements. As a result, the existing system could tolerate change without being subjected to structural crisis.[11]

I have noted in previous chapters that the struggle with modernity did not eliminate the Persian poet's need to seek a spiritual identity. If anything, the socioeconomic and cultural/educational reforms further strengthened the need. Farrokhzad's journey to the "fragrant core of a fertilized egg," Sepehri's search for proof under the willow tree, even Shamlu's antiprophetic prophet insisting on the futility of expecting a Messiah, all demonstrated that the question of spiritual identity remained at the center of the self-image that these poets attempted to reconstruct. The broad mystical outlook of the world as the manifestation of the divine provided at least two characteristics desperately needed under the circumstances. Vertically, it elevated the world, and with it humanity, to being worthy and capable of reuniting with the divine. Horizontally, it showed the tolerance for others, the elixir that seemed to be absent even from the seemingly progressive agenda of modernity. All in all, the mystical outlook offered a suitable infrastructure for reconstructing the indefinable sacred and the much desired spiritual self.

This freshly articulated spiritual tradition was by no means monolithic just as its classical forefather had not been. As a strong and prevailing worldview, the poetic/mystical outlook had made a diverse, direct, as well as intertextually implicit impact on centuries of Persian literature. At any point, it had retained certain constant features just as it had revised and altered others. "Modern" minds were no exception in their exposure to this evolving tradition. Although in their attempts to rearticulate they altered and enhanced its complexity, the new production did demonstrate certain recognizable trends. One such trend was the loyalty to the legacy of influential mystic poets such as 'Attār (d. 1220) and Rūmī (d. 1273).[12] This was not influence or imitation in an outward stylistic sense, but a loyalty that should be appreciated for its self-awareness and complexity. For example, the modernist discourse showed signs of continuity and sympathy with the classical tradition by endorsing much of the former's conceptual core. As a competing tradition, however, it tried to replace the old. A tendency that, as

Alasdair MacIntyre has observed of rival traditions, presupposes a "significant" but different understanding of the rival. In this case, the understanding entailed a sharper focus on renewal and "enrichment," which led to conceptual and linguistic innovation.[13] The works of Suhrab Sepehri provide examples of this concurrent understanding and rivalry, sameness and difference.

Sepehri, the main focus of this chapter, was one of the chief architects of the freshly articulated spiritual tradition born from a mystical encounter with modernity. Yet it would be wrong to assume that the tradition was extant only in his work just as it would be wrong to view it as monolithic. I have already referred to at least two successful examples of such mystical expressions in Shafi'i-Kadkani's "Hallaj" and Farrokhzad's "Union."[14] Still, Sepehri stood out in comparison to either poets because of his deliberate and full-scale assimilation of the mystical tradition into a consciously reformist discourse. His was a sustained and successful effort to merge the two into a natural and seamlessly integrated poetic idiom. He further distinguished himself through the richness and scope of his experimentations. Applying MacIntyre's concept of concurrent understanding and rivalry, for example, Sepehri's works yield fascinating examples. These examples combine wholesale adoption of particular Sufi concepts with fundamental resignification of others. His concept of deity, for instance, sheds its specific Muslim/Sufi garb in favor of a generalized force of goodness and beauty, whereas the *Parsa*'s renunciation of the world remains loyal to conventional Sufi piety. I will now turn to his poetry, to details in every inch of the canvas as it were, for specific examples of this refashioning.

There Is Kindness, There Are Apples, and There Is Faith

I noted earlier that in "The Chapter of Sight" Sepehri prepared the poetic space for the presence of the sacred through adopting Qur'anic patterns of expression. Furthermore, he often associated nature with acts of piety such as likening the plains to prayer mats and the wind to a muezzin reciting the call to prayer from cypress trees. I demonstrate in this chapter that these were the more evident aspects of a complex process of sacred making, tips of an iceberg submerged in deep waters of his poetic discourse. By the end of the chapter, it is clear that Sepehri pursued remarkably consistent strategies of sacred making while navigating these waters. In particular, I note a poignant subversive tendency, contradicting Sepehri's reputation as a quiet and conforming poet. Beneath the quiet surface is the active and persistent poet fashioning a new outlook for the sacred in Persian poetry. In this outlook traditional hierarchies collapse, and "kindness," "apples," and "faith" fit into the same basket.[15]

Born in the small city of Kāshān in a family given to poetry, music, calligraphy, and painting, Sepehri enjoyed the company of loving and literary-minded women. His grandmother Hamideh is mentioned among women poets of her generation. The restless search in the treasure house of nature that is the hallmark of Sepehri's poetic contribution was matched by a desire to travel and see the world. The longing took the poet as far to the east as Japan and to the west as the United States. Though we shall not explore his life here, it is important to remember that Sepehri's contribution as a painter is to be acknowledged and studied. He experimented with shapes and patterns on the canvas even before discovering the medium of poetry and pursued painting on technical as well as philosophical levels till the end of his life. In his paintings, too, Sepehri remained an avid observer and admirer of nature's lucid poetry. Although the flourishing of his poetic career overshadowed his contribution as a painter, more recent studies of his life in Persian language have acknowledged that dimension of his work.[16]

Just as Farrokhzad's edifice was not a purely personal invention, the new outlook Sepehri was forging had a multitude of constituent elements that reflected broader generational desires for rebuilding a viable modern poetic voice. From a religious point of view, this new outlook did not exactly challenge the legitimacy of the Muslim perspective. Yet it questioned and reconceptualized some of the most basic precepts of the old perspective to construct its own. This paradigmatic cohabitation of understanding and rivalry brought a productive instability to Sepehri's poetry that displayed open conflicts and daring contradictions in the emergent spiritual tradition it nurtured and expressed. For this reason, his poetry is an ideal site for the study of the formative behavioral patterns in the new tradition. I base my analysis on one of Sepehri's collections of poems and two of his long poems. The first long poem, *Sida-yi pa-yi ab* (The Footsteps of Water), composed in 1964 and considered widely as his most original contribution, has already been cited in this chapter. The second long poem, written two years after the first, is called *Musafir* (The Traveler). Though not as famed as "The Footsteps of Water," the traveler did make considerable impact. My primary focus, however, is on Sepehri's last major collection of poems, called *Hajm-i sabz* (*The Expanse of Green*). The collection, published in 1967, brought the poetic seeds first planted in the two long poems to major fruition. Sepehri's poetic output is considerably more extensive, but it was with these poems that he rose to widespread fame, demonstrated maturation of personal style, and best articulated themes and ideas central to our discussion.[17]

"Infinite" Fruits in the Basket of Poetry

Following his unproductive trip to the fruit market in the poem *Sida-yi didar* (The Sound of Encounter), Sepehri answered Mother's query concerning purchase of fruits with "How could infinite fruits fit in this basket?" Mother's desire for including the nutritious fruits in *khurak-i zuhr* (the mid-day meal) mirrored the poet's desire for articulating their infinite presence as they sang and emanated color in the morning market. His feeling was more of triumph than failure. In his mind, Mother's disappointment had transformed into awe and wonder as pomegranates had expanded to overflow his basket of perception and expression. What was needed was a language capable of encoding this boundless existence into poetry. By lunchtime that day, the mirrors had expanded the image of the quinces to the far-off edges of life. Sepehri's poetry was about to do the same.[18]

I suggest that this happy overflowing basket of colors was not isolated or accidental. Presenting a view of life as extended beyond physical tangible surfaces was at the heart of Sepehri's poetic art of sacred making. He did so with utmost simplicity and a flat refusal to explain the collapse of conventional borderlines. The impact was tremendous. Making use of his contractual right as a poet, he maneuvered around in the world of make-believe avoiding the slightest entanglement in any logical/ conceptual justification for this alternative worldview. His strategy is a reminder of Saint-Exupéry's Little Prince, who asked many questions but never answered any.[19] Like the Little Prince, too, he allowed the reader a glance at his rare planet from his unique vantage point. From that vantage point, the readers saw a boundless world with a logic of its own, shrouded in mystery yet presented in simplest of terms. They fell in love with it.

Not only were the fruits *bi-nihayat* (infinite) in this world, and "the shadow of an elm tree" extended to "eternity," but in the "nameless expanse" and the "distant" unknown there was always a voice, which called unto him.[20] In the poem *Dar Gulistanih* (In Gulistan), evoking nostalgic images from his early years, Sepehri did not look for a concrete object lodged in his childhood memory. He searched, instead, for a hazy "dream," an indistinct "pebble," or an elusive "light."[21] Even the "innocent heedlessness," the component of childhood that was inviting, called him from behind the poplars after having turned into an invisible presence. Nothing was merely what it seemed. The wind blowing through the reed bed whispered something; even the lizard that crossed his path signaled a moment of wakefulness and the beginning of a journey. In this world that had broken out of its conventional frame of activity, every atom was attentive and eager to communicate. When life reached a level of intensity difficult to follow, the earth with its dependable sturdy nature, and its capacity to witness and forget, offered a refuge. Sepehri stayed close to the earth for its quiet and constant presence, its stability. Even this stability was one that masked movement and change leading to transformative moments of greenness. These moments that connected humanity with trees and animals created yet further opportunities for poetry to capture and crystallize the joy of expanding, of defying limits:

> How green I am today!
> How sober are my limbs!
> What if an unexpected sorrow arrives?
> Who is behind the trees?
> Ah, no one . . . just a cow grazing in the pastures.[22]

Neither the infinitude of the fruits nor the life-giving green of nature remained content with a neutral self-celebrating existence. For the poet who observed, the joy of internalizing the green did not stop at the edge of a simple love affair with nature either. In this boundless world of energy and color, there was a vivid and constant struggle to reach beyond and to unravel. Nature—as well as the unknown—always looked in the direction of another destination beyond the tangible green where they had started:

> Life is not empty
> There is kindness, there are apples,
>   And there is faith.

Connecting with the presence that filled the vacuum, tasting the apples, and living the kindness were only the beginning. Even reaching out for the faith was a mere initial response to the distant call that had revived within:

> There is an indescribable in my heart
> A thicket of light perhaps,
>   an early morning siesta.
> And I am so excited
> I want to run the plain to the edge, the mountain to the top.
> There is a voice in the distance, a voice that calls on me.[23]

One may ask why this revered presence is considered to be more than a vague sacred existence occasionally approaching the borders of some sort of a faith or devotion. What are the conditions that transform these poems into poetic expressions of sacred making in a serious and sustained manner? Indeed, critics have been inclined to take the association of the apple with faith and the nature of the "voice in the distance" as vague and inconclusive infatuations with "nature mysticism."[24] Such readings are more than standard instances of hasty judgment. They are, often, genuine attempts to salvage the "rational" identity of a "modern" poet who got dangerously close to religion.

   Sepehri, however, used clear markers to give the natural/spiritual concoctions prepared in the crucible of his poetry an explicitly religious flavor. The markers he used ranged from broad structural moves such as fashioning the cosmos around God's presence to adopting terminology that carried unambiguous allusions to Islamic notions of piety. The fineness of details in the allusive nature of his descriptive strategies is fascinating. Whether it is in the *tapish-i bagh* (heartbeat of the garden), the mystery of the shadows, or the purity of *marduman-i dih-i bala'dast* (the villagers next door), God is always present in some form or fashion. We shall return to his poetic articulations of God due to the centrality of the notion. As for the piety-related terminology, it comes in both metaphorical as well as plainly referential modes. Allegorically speaking, the world and its constituent parts are often portrayed as worshiping Muslims whose actions mirror acts of reverence ranging from momentous to insignificant. The poppies on the hill perform the prophetic mi'raj "the nucturnal journey" of Prophet Muhammad while the simple fish reflect on the image of the red carnation quivering in their pond as a window to paradise.[25] While the religious significance of some such metaphorical terminology may be considered secondary, there are numerous instances in which these and other terms, such as *paki* (purity), *jazbeh* (rapture), and *rastgari* (salvation), were used with unambiguously religious overtones.[26] It is a good time to move from these details to broader structural patterns that highlight the strong sacred-making impulse within these poems even more. I do so by identifying a number of general patterns emerging from the poems beginning with the sense of mission that connects the poetic to the prophetic.

"I See the Way in the Dark, I Am Full of Lanterns!"

The basket of fruits was revived in the poem *Va payami dar rah* (And a Message on the Way) to be emptied of sleep and filled with the red apple of the sun. Here, however, it is not the trope but the prophetic mode in which it is presented that gives the apples a distinctly sacred flavor. In a triumphant revelatory fashion, the poet declared his glad tidings:

> I shall come one day
> And I shall bring a message.
> I shall fill the veins with light
> And I shall declare:
> "Oh, your baskets filled with sleep!
> I have apples for you
> The red apples of the sun."[27]

The rest of the poem is a reiteration of the poet's impending arrival summarized in the above stanza as bringing morning to those overwhelmed by sleep. The poetic tension generates from subverting habitually accepted patterns, a pitfall familiar to all instigators of social and psychological reform. The parallel drawn between the poetic utterance and a prophetic mission is further affirmed through recurrent use of the images of light and water, universal metaphors for knowledge and life bestowed on humanity through divine scriptures:

> I shall describe to the blind the beauty of the garden.
> I shall be a peddler walking the alleyways announcing
>   dewdrops for sale!
> A passer-by shall say: it is a truly dark night!
> I shall give him a galaxy.
> On the bridge sits a girl who has lost her legs,
> I shall hang a string of stars around her neck.[28]

"And a Message on the Way" demonstrates that the revelatory nuance in "The Chapter of Sight," discussed earlier, is not momentary or whimsical. It fulfills a structural role in the larger poetic schema that emerges if Sepehri's poetry is sifted through in search of representative general features. The two poems, however, vary in what they foreground. In "The Chapter of Sight," the poet's prophetic mission has been subordinated in favor of special attention to the scriptural rhythm of the composition, but in "And a Message on the Way," the agency of the poet/prophet plays the central role. In another poem from the collection *The Expanse of Green* called *Raushani, man, gul, ab* (Light, Me, Flower, Water), Sepehri affirms the poet's prophetic virtues in unequivocal terms. The setting is a day filled with light. The scent of bread, cheese, and fresh basil is in the air and *rastgari* (salvation) is a few steps away, among the flowers in the yard. Before the poem ends, all seemingly insignificant objects have either performed a sacred role or a mission of cosmic proportion. Even the old ladder leaning against the wall helps the morning to descend on earth. In the lucidity of this ordinary yet rare day, and through a crack in the wall of time, the poet glances at himself. This self-vision is inclusive of the universe with all its ordinary and extraordinary things. Central to the vision is the poet's prophetic ability to ascend and see the way in the dark:

> I ascend high, to the zenith,
>   I am full of wings!
> I see the way in the dark, I am full of lanterns!
> I am full of light and pebbles,
> And full of trees,
> Full of the way, the bridge, the river, the wave
> I am full of the shade of a single leaf on water:
> And inside, I am all solitude![29]

Besides poems that have entire sections devoted to the prophetic trope with varying focus on the messenger or the message, allusions to the theme permeates various other compositions. Among these is the poet's mandate to take the complaint of the waterless fish to God in *Paygham-i mahi'ha* (Message from the Fish) cited earlier in this chapter for its reference to paradise. The most notable among such examples, and the most relevant to our current discussion, however, is the celebrated poem *Niday-i aghaz* (The Call to Start).[30] It is built around the nostalgic theme of migration, which it keeps in the foreground through refrains such as "Where are my shoes?" "Who was it that called 'Suhrab'?" and "I must leave tonight." The poem creates a masterful dialectic between the disillusionment with the status quo—fueling the desire for migration—and the nostalgia for the land and the people who will be left behind. The caressing breeze of the summer night tells him to stay, and the inviting song of the migrating birds, whose feathers stuff his pillow, tempt him to leave. The struggle results in some of the most engaging moments in Sepehri's poetic career:

Where are my shoes?
Who was it that called "Suhrab"?
Familiar was the sound as is air with a leaf.
Mother is sleeping,
And Manuchihr, and Parvanih, and perhaps the whole town.
The summer night spreads over every second gentle as an elegy
And a cool breeze sweeps my sleep from the edge of the green blanket.
Migration is in the air,
My pillow is filled with the sound of swallow's wings.
Morning will come,
And the sky will migrate
To this bowl of water
I must leave tonight.[31]

The nocturnal migration is on the surface of the poem and relatively easy to detect. What is not that close to the surface is the prophetic connotation. Using the historical embeddedness of words, Sepehri adds the prophetic association by drawing a parallel between his impending exodus and that of the founder of the Islamic faith, the event that marks the beginning of Islamic history. Choosing the Arabic term *hijrat* to refer to his nightly migration, he evokes the nocturnal flight of the unappreciated prophet, the journey of Muhammad from Mecca to Medina. At the same time, he is aware of unwanted connotations that might accompany the association with institutionalized religion. To avoid undesirable implications, he inserts a brief disclaimer into the poem at a suitable moment. We are told that the poet feels sad as a gray cloud at the sight of the neighbor's young daughter studying *fiqh* (Islamic law), under the rarest elm tree on earth.

These examples indicate Sepehri's ties to the Muslim cultural/religious tradition, which has nurtured him. Indeed, these evocations of traditional Islamic themes and images are so prevalent that one may wonder if his is just another extension of the classical Sufi voice, which has been a familiar voice in Persian poetic discourse from the time of Sanāʾī's (d. 1130). Similarities in theme and terminology may appear to confirm this finding. Closer attention, however, reveals the exchange between Sepehri's mystical worldview and the mainstream Sufi tradition to be complex. Despite his eagerness to reach beyond the wood's surface for "the garden that lived in its memory," Sepehri insisted on linguistic and conceptual refashioning both of the garden and the way that led to it. This comes to sharper focus in categories, Sufi or otherwise, which he redefined fundamentally. I begin with God.

GREENER THAN GOD'S DREAM

Twentieth-century Persian poetry, like its counterparts in other cultures in the region, revisited the fundamentals of the Islamic faith, notable among them the nature and definition of God. Sepehri contributed to a significant degree to this rearticulation of God and remarkably did so by avoiding any direct reference to the issue. Instead, he made sure that few vital poetic moments were celebrated without God's presence. By evoking God in these frequent, simple, and unexpected moments, he caught the reader off guard, leaving them little choice other than feeling God's unimposing yet permeating presence:

> The mountain is near me, behind the maple trees,
>   the oleasters.
> The open desert is visible.
> Stones are out of sight, so are little flowers.
> Distant shadows are visible,
> Shadows like the loneliness of the water,
>   like God's singing.[32]

In *The Expanse of Green* and "The Footsteps of Water," it is hard to avoid God. He is not just in distant shadows but everywhere. A more careful reading of these instances reveals a deliberate strategy in Sepehri's refusal to unravel the enigma of his presence. These elusive references to God underline the futility of theological endeavors to comprehend, through conceptualization, his playful and evolving nature. From these flashes of contact with the divine, which do not piece a full or final picture together, we learn much.[33] God is no longer the distant transcendental supreme ruler of the universe difficult to visualize or interact with. He is like moonlight, capable of spreading on most ordinary things. Not only is he near at hand "amid the flowers" and "beneath the tall pine tree," he accepts visitors as ordinary as our poet on a daily basis.[34] To Sepehri, such visits come as easy as visiting a tree would come to the wind. Yet in the poem "The Message from the Fish," where he carries their message to God, the "incidental" visit to his quarters is given centrality by being announced casually in closing line:

> The wind was blowing to the sycamore tree,
> I was heading for God's quarters.[35]

God in his new garb is in the human habit of singing and his song must be audible to ordinary humans. This audibility can be surmised from the fact that Sepehri seeks the help of the metaphorical *avaz-i khuda* (God's song) to facilitate for his reader the perception of indistinct shadows in the distance. A metaphor needs to be more accessible than what it stands for. Otherwise, it will fail to facilitate the perception of its object.

I will not dwell on whether this God is in need of human activities or whether he simply initiates them to share in our world. We know, however, that he leaves his "footprints" behind to be discovered whenever the goodness and purity of a people instigates a visit.[36] This anthropomorphous God is not alien to human desires and dreams. In the poem *Nishani* (Direction), which maps the way to the "friend's" house, the green alleyway that houses the tall elm tree, with the nest of light built on it, is "greener than God's dreams."[37] The humanity of God displays itself even in the subtle, if not theologically elaborate, description that depicts the moonlight as a condition for his visibility. He is clearly different from the God of the Qur'anic sura *Al-Nur*, who is himself the light of the heavens and the earth:

> It was a full night
> The river flowed from the foot of the firs
>   into the distance
> The valley was inlaid with moonlight, and the mountain was
>   so bright,
> That God was visible.[38]

CLOSE TO THE INCEPTION OF THE EARTH: ARCHETYPAL REPRESENTATION OF HUMAN VIRTUE

Although the human attributes of God in these poems are to be perceived as an indirect endorsement of humanity, Sepehri remains aloof from admiring exemplary paradigmatic individuals such as Hallāj or Jesus. Even in the elegy for Farrokhzad, where Sepehri expresses the most admiration for a specific person, the poem is titled *Dust* (The Friend) to avoid mystification and exaggerated grandeur. In the poem itself, the opening phrase "buzurg bud" (she was grand) is followed immediately with the qualifier "va az ahali-yi imruz bud" (and she was of the people of today) thereby historicizing her and defusing any mythical overtone.[39] Similarly in other poems, ordinary people, if at all visible in the picture, are small, finite, and captive to their habits and petty concerns. At the same time, it is very important to remember that these human shortcomings are described in rather neutral, at times even compassionate, terms. At no point are these poetic documentations of human smallness couched in the bitter and accusing tone stemming from the sense of betrayal harbored in Shamlu's poetry, for example. We are nonetheless reminded that no eyes "gaze at the earth with love," no one "is ecstatic at the sight of a garden," and people do not know "that labdanums are not accidental." In short, "the insight of the fellow townsmen" does not penetrate the "splendor of the oranges":

> The insight of the fellow townsmen, alas!
> Was a line tangent to the circumference
>   of the splendor of the oranges.[40]

The death of these finite beings, predictably, does not bring about visible change to the cosmic order. The "wheat" remains "wholesome," the "waters flow" as always, and the "horses" continue to "drink" them. The constants that compensate for volatile human existence and contribute to the bigger cosmic picture are natural elements, the raindrops that continue to fall, the snow that "piles on the shoulders of silence," and the "spine of the jasmine tree on which time" can "rest."[41]

In a more specific sense, the absence of paradigmatic individuals such as Hallāj or Jesus in Sepehri's worldview is compensated for by archetypal representation of human virtues. Mother's presence is an example. On one level, she is the agent voicing vague philosophical dissatisfactions in the face of the "sadness of the season." On another, her laughter expresses simple joy in playful moments when the pomegranate juice splashes into the poet's eyes and leads to an amusing scene. Even more prominent than the archetypal mother in Sepehri's cosmos is the *parsa* (the archetype of piety). Not only is the *parsa* literate in mysteries of nature, he is inseparable from it with his red robe—an extension of the red-skinned pomegranates—evoking red-robed Buddhist monks. He is wise, for he knows that "the best thing that can happen to one is meeting a pair of eyes wet with the advent of love." And, he is even more mystifying than God (who could be visited in his quarters), for one has to travel the "road of the night until the moon warns to stop" and let one's body be "absorbed completely into the music of the night" before the parsa can be reached.[42]

The most prominent of all such prototypes, in Sepehri's poems, is the archetypal figure of "*dust*" (the friend). Though not expressly defined as holy, the dust has occupied a wide range of honored positions in Persian poetry from medieval to modern times. Classical Sufi poetry, attuned to ambiguity and paradox, has already made the *dust* into a mold for God, the mundane beloved, and a host of other characters. Despite the varying roles, the personalities of the *dust* possess many traits in common, most prominently being the object of longing, which constitutes a propelling force in poetry. In the ghazel opening with "News from you inflamed the sore of separation," Sa'dī demonstrated the versatility and resonance of the image in one short composition. In the second verse of the ghazel, the *dust*—a friend in the general sense—is encouraged to join the company of friends trading material gifts with the gift of a personal visit. In the fourth verse, the friend has transformed into the "fair-faced" beloved showing signs of *bi-wafa'i* (disloyalty). By the closing verse, the figure reemerges dressed fully in a sacred garb. Sa'dī demonstrated the sacred status by preferring the company of the *dust* to "opening one's eyes on paradise daily," a standard allusion to the Sufi preference for union with God instead of earning his rewards.[43] In Sepehri's poetry, the personality of the *dust* is refashioned in certain respects while it shows consistency in others. As expected, the *dust* is elusive. With his/her footprints "imprinted on the poet's eyelids," his/her place of residence is nowhere to be found. Yet hope is not completely lost, for if "the child within climbing the pine tree to catch birds in the nest of light" is located, the mysterious whereabouts of the *dust* may be revealed.[44] In "the Heartbeat of the friend's shadow," a night walk is converted into a nocturnal journey with the wayfarers holding the "moon in their eyes and the night in their sleeves." Their shoes, "made from the material of prophethood," can make them fly just as Muhammad's horse did on his night journey to God. Sepehri's travelers, however, do not head for heavens but sit by a riverside where "the friend's voice" is audible in the lucidity of the night. The time is now right to revive Sepehri's elegy for his contemporary poet and friend Farrokhzad entitled *Dust*. This poem provides the opportunity to examine the ways in which the poet adds to the potential that the archetypal friend embodied.[45]

The elegy for the friend is prefaced by the famous quote from T. S. Eliot "I should be glad of another death," making clear from the start that Farrokhzad's departure is not to be taken as an end to her presence. The poem, then, praises her grandeur with "buzurg bud," moving immediately to the relevance of her work to present-day concerns. Some of the poem's key statements here unravel the friend's rare abilities as "being related to all open horizons" and "understanding the language of the water and the earth." In the following stanza, her qualities of attachment to reality, appreciation for nature, generosity, and kindness are further affirmed. In this poem, Sepehri's poetic vocabulary and syntax follow his refreshing preference for unconventional images and for weaving together a tapestry of concrete and abstract thoughts:

> And her hands
> —Leafing through the lucid air of generosity
> Pushed kindness our way.

Yet no mythical characteristics are attributed to the concurrently real and archetypal friend until the third stanza. Here, Sepehri makes his contribution by expanding the semantic field that until now has defined the characteristics of the *dust*. He adds creativity, artistic talent, and courage for expressing intimate moments— a quality that Farrokhzad had in abundance—to the list of friend's virtues. Note that the word *khalvat,* rendered into "solitude" in the first line, denotes seclusion for worship and meditation as much it does the privacy for lovers' intimacy:

> She took the shape of her solitude
> And interpreted for the mirror
> The most passionate contours of her moments.
> And like rain's repeating songs,
> She was filled with freshness.

After this acknowledgment in complementary terms, of Farrokhzad's ability to explore and express the feminine self, Sepehri turns to her other remarkable achievement. This is Farrokhzad's courage and creativity in reinventing the sacred, and her contribution to the poetic articulation of the desire for the sacred:

> For us, one night
> She articulated the green prostration of love
> With such clarity
> That we touched the affection in the surface of the earth
> And felt refreshed, like the accent of a bucket of water!
>
> And so many times did we see her
> Leaving with so many baskets
> To pick one bunch from the grapes of glad tidings.

Here, the sanctity of the object of Farrokhzad's exploration is signaled through usage of key terms associated with Islamic piety such as *sujud* (prostration) in the "green prostration of love" or *bisharat* (glad tidings) as she anticipated ripening bunches of grapes with her many baskets. Not only does Sepehri's revival of the metaphorical basket of fruits in these closing lines underline the poetic import of Farrokhzad's grapes of glad tidings, it provides the poet with an opportunity for tasting his sacred apples once more. This is an affectionate, yet ritualistic, gesture to mourn the loss of the friend who has walked "to the edge of nothingness beyond the patience of the rays of light" without realizing how lonely it feels to eat an apple, for those left behind.

Just as Sepehri's poetic landscape is sparsely peopled, his own poetic persona remains absent in poems that unfold in real time and space. The well-known autobiographical allusions in the opening sections of "The Footsteps of Water" do not define him beyond a native of Kāshān, a painter, and a Muslim.[46] The poet within prefers anonymity and, perhaps in a sense, feels empowered by this intentional silence. The largely undefined poetic persona finds representation in a rather unexpected mold, the archetypal primitive man. When exploring the self, Sepehri often speaks to the reader through this inner primal being whom he feels he knows intimately despite historical distance. Whether in brief and sporadic statements such as "man bi aghaz-i zamin nazdikam" (I am close to the inception of the earth) or passages as long and focused as the following, he views himself as an extension of this primeval being:

> In this darkness
> I see the extension of my wet arms
> Under the same rain,
>   Which moistened the first prayers of man.
> In this darkness
> I have opened a door to ancient meadows
> To the golden [images] visible on the walls of myths.[47]

In passages such as this, time stands still allowing Sepehri to bypass his contemporary discontents and reach out for a prehistoric past. Interestingly, this past bears no relations to the pre-Islamic historical period that some contemporaries of Sepehri seek to glorify in service of a nationalistic agenda. Not only is Sepehri's primeval being devoid of nationality, he has a distaste for historical narrative, which seeks to captivate him in his historicity. In "The Footsteps of Water," Sepehri parodies historical writing altogether as "books in which the wind does not blow." By contrast, the people and objects of the mythical land of the unwritten past are alive and vibrant. Sepehri's longing for a past uncontaminated by historical findings is rooted in the dissatisfaction with things contemporary. It results in the desire to break away from the present and culminates into a total defiance of time. At a time when political commitment is essential for a viable poetic credential, this deliberate detachment from current social discontent brings harsh criticism on Sepehri's work as a whole. His admirers seek to refute this blemish with equal zeal and dedication.[48] The desire to stay out of political activity, minding the canary as it "ties the yellow thread of its song around a feeling of comfort," is best expressed in *Bi bagh-i ham'safaran* (To the Garden of Fellow Travelers). This poem, quoted partially below, is a nostalgic yearning for sleep under a tree away from the age of "asphalt roads" and "ascent of steel."

> Keep me warm!
> (Once, out in the wilderness in Kāshān, clouds filled the sky.
> There was a downpour and I felt cold.
> Then, sheltered behind a rock, the flame of anemones warmed
> My cold hands.)
>
> In these dark alleys,
> I fear hesitation multiplied by matchsticks.
> I fear the concrete face of our times.
> Come! So, I do not fear the cities in whose dark earth graze bulldozers.
> Open me like a door onto pears rising on trees, in this time of the
>   ascent of steel.
> Let me go to sleep under a tree,
> Away from the night of the friction of metals.
>
> If the finder of the morning mine arrived,
> Call me, and I shall wake with Jasmines
> Rising in the dawn of your hands.[49]

With or without historical paradigmatic Sufi figures, Sepehri kept the doors to the resonant world of the Sufis open. It was an old treasure-house packed with images, themes, and concepts ready to be fitted to his fresh poetic needs and sensibilities. He revived even the seemingly overused narrative structures such as that of a traveler on the allegorical road to self-realization and refashioned it to serve the modern context. In the long poem *Musafir* (The Traveler), lovers walk hand in hand with time exploring "the other side of the day," they sail the *hidayat* (waters of salvation) in *ishraq* (old vessels of illumination) to the realm of *Tajalli-i 'ijab,* where inner wonders are manifested.[50] Using overtly Sufi terminology such as "ishraq," "hidayat," and "tajalli" in the above example is one of Sepehri's strategies to stay connected to the Sufi collective of feelings and ideas at the verbal surface. Yet, this is only the surface. The connection is maintained at the deeper levels by evoking literary characters and borrowing complex narrative structures from the Sufi classics. These structures would resonate in the cultural memories of large numbers of readers regardless of specialization or personal conviction. The poem *Musafir,* for example, makes unambiguous comparisons between Sepehri's traveler and 'Attār's (d. 1220) journeying birds in *Conference of the Birds*.[51] In the latter, a large number of birds travel in search of their legendary king, *simurgh* (phoenix), signifying the truth. As those who are weak for the arduous journey fall by the wayside, the thirty surviving birds (literally *si murgh* in Persian) arrive at the destination and the realization that the king they sought is no other than they themselves. Hardly has any Sufi tale resonated with Persian speaking readers as has 'Attār's linguistic enactment of self-realization. Although Sepehri's borrowing of the traveling pattern would have been sufficient to establish a broad analogy between his *Musafir* and 'Attār's celebrated birds, he provides specific allusions to the classic tale. He sends his modern traveler on a search for the *hudhud* (hoopoe), the wise travel guide and the problem solver in 'Attār's *Conference of the Birds:*

> "Where is the direction of life?
> Where should I turn to reach a hudhud?"
> Listen!
> For all through the journey
> This one question
> Opened and closed the windows of sleep.[52]

Yet the freshness in this twentieth-century search for the hudhud is in the fact that the parameters of the search are expanded. The structure is not just borrowed but modified significantly to accommodate a more inclusive vision. For Sepehri's traveler, the horizons open up to include a much wider range of fellow travelers and experiences. In *Conference of the Birds,* for example, the beautiful Christian girl who steels the heart of the wise sheik of Sam'an gains true legitimacy only after seeing the light and converting to Islam. Our twentieth-century traveler, however, confronts and warmly embraces a different and more diverse group of seekers. Here, Christian monks are given poetic authorization to represent guidance along the way through their silent graceful gestures. Even more, they are integrated into the ordinary population of Lebanese peasants and blind Iraqi children in the same stanza:

And all through the journey, along the road
Pure-hearted Christian monks
Pointed to the silent portrait of Jeremiah, the prophet,
As I recited aloud
My "book of the society"
And a few Lebanese peasants
Sitting under an aging lotus tree
Counted the fruit of their orchards,
   in their minds.

On the roadside, blind Iraqi children
Were looking at the script on the tablet of King Hammurabi.
I skimmed through major daily newspapers of the world.[53]

It is important to remember that in this and similar poems openness to the "other" is counterbalanced with strategies that delineate the orientation of the poem. As a result, the poems do not turn into vague spiritual endorsements of all but remain grounded consistently in one specific mystical worldview: that of Islam. Yet, this loyalty to the Islamic/mystical vantage point is not confining because it entails an expansion of the tradition in daring manners. For one thing, these poetic retellings of the tradition maintain an experiential orientation discouraging literalist law-oriented perspectives on the making and functions of the sacred. For another, regardless of their thematic focus, they preserve a personal space in which the presence of the poet remains central to the occurrence of the inner experience. Readers can enter a mutually beneficial, intimate, and interactive relation with the poet as opposed to remaining in the distant didactic position of passive reception. In this setting, nature is the catalyst, the liaison, and the arena for the human interaction with the sacred. It provides the script, the visual treasure-house of colors and shapes, as well as the sacred temple—the setting—in which the spiritual tale unfolds. In this tale, the role of nature is central, stabilizing, and multifaceted. Unlike Farrokhzad's nature, it does not share the human folly of messiness, mischief, or erotic temptation. Rather, it is the wise teacher that empowers the poetic voice and, at the same time, the rare and enigmatic tale crying out to be told:

An uproar is in the air
I am the lonely recipient of the discourse of the winds
The rivers of the world teach *me*
Their untainted mystery of fading into the sea
Only *me.*
I interpret for the robins, who live
   In the valley of the Ganges.
On the roadside at Sornat, I describe

The Thebaten earrings studded with gnosis
To the unadorned ears of the girls in Varanasi.

Oh the morning song!
Put all your Vedic weight on my shoulders,
   all the weight of your freshness.
I am feverish with desire to speak.
Oh olive trees in the land of Palestine!
Address the fullness of your shades to me!
To this lonely traveler returning from the Sinai
   Restless, still, with the warmth of an exchange with the divine.[54]

The Night Is Articulate, Smooth, and Open

As themes discussed so far testify, Sepehri's re-envisioning of the sacred and scripting it on colorful nature provided endless possibilities for poetic exploration. Instead of a random walk through this landscape, I here narrow the spectrum of ideas to a central and specific Sufi theme, that of the *pir* (spiritual leader). The narrowing of the focus complements the general perspective that I have provided on the broader compositional structures in Sepehri's work. It should supply a close-up of the details in one inch of the canvas, to revive Elkins's metaphor of oil paintings. This is the approach that I have privileged throughout the present volume. I will also use this close-up as the concluding moments to the exploration of Sepehri's poetic sacred making in this chapter.

Aware of the significance of leadership, and in the absence of paradigmatic individuals as guides in blood and flesh, Sepehri sought to redefine the traditional Sufi concept of the pir in order to adopt it. Not surprisingly, to fill the void, he reached out to nature. Nature became the guide, the object of contemplation, the grace giver, and the refuge; everything that a pir would be to the followers.[55] This was a relationship of radical and mutual compromise. Just as the pir needed to undergo poetic reconstruction to fit into modern natural garb, nature as the complex agency that replaced the spiritual guide needed to be redefined and reconstructed. In such dramatic reconstructions, nature was often disembodied of its natural qualities, turning into a "*hichistan*" (place of nothingness) to use Sepehri's own terminology. This carefully vacated and prepared hichistan was then inhabited, and revitalized, with mystical beings or forces.[56] In a philosophical sense, this was not a real nature in that it was not subjected to usual demarcations of time and space. It was engulfed in an unbreakable solitude in which "the shadow of an elm tree" could flow to unknown distances to mingle with eternity. The same was true of the "infinite fruits" that refused to be contained in a basket. By far, the most sweeping transformation of this nature was to strip it off its natural instinctive violence. Let me provide some examples.

Potentially turbulent natural forces such as floods and storms do not find adequate representation in Sepehri's poems, while amiable natural phenomena such as light are evoked frequently, displaying mysterious properties. Light, for example, is endowed with the physical power to move objects in the phrase "az hujum-i rawshana'i shishiha-yi dar takan mikhurd" (the glass windows were shaking with the onrush of light). Highly destructive natural phenomena such as earthquakes are almost entirely absent from the poems. In fact, Sepehri's nature is empowered with such miraculous healing abilities that after reading a few poems the reader would have little difficulty accepting that "wickedness" may indeed dissolve "in the presence of the geraniums" (*dar huzur-i sham'dani'a shaqavat ab khvahad shud*).[57]

Like traditional grand masters, Sepehri's nature is eloquent in self-expression. The night is described as a poetic masterpiece would be: "articulate, smooth and open" (*shab salis ast va yikdast va baz*). The clarity of the poet's own words are compared to that of the green grass just as in the elegy for Farrokhzad, her ability to utilize repetition and resonance had been an echo of the freshness of "rain's repeating songs." To bring nature's eloquence home, Sepehri does what every good poet would do. Instead of praising or describing it, he turns *The Expanse of Green* and "The Footsteps of Water" into a podium from which natural phenomena continue to speak each in their individual style. I have already quoted the "fresh accent" of the "buckets of water" and the songs of migration performed by "swallow feathers" in pillowcases. The ensemble has many more players. Tree branches, for example, are not particularly sophisticated, just carefree and loud. But flowers make up for the shortcoming by blooming into epitomes of self-expression. Indeed, we should ideally perceive our mouths as the flower house of our mind (*dahan gulkhanih-i fikr ast*).[58]

It is small wonder that Sepehri's beautiful, wise, articulate, and spiritually alluring nature possesses a powerful magnetic field that draws everyone to it, another quality common to charismatic pirs.[59] This urge to unite with nature, to lose oneself in the inaccessible unutterable distance in Sepehri's poetry, comes close to the Sufi desire for annihilation in God. In "The Call to Start" we read:

> I must leave tonight
> I must pick the suitcase—
>   That is only as large as the shirt of my solitude—
> And leave for the horizons on which are visible
> Trees of mythical dimension,
> In the direction of that nameless expanse that always calls unto me.
> Again someone called: "Suhrab!"
> Where are my shoes?[60]

Sepehri's attraction to this "nameless expanse" is not that of a rationally probing thinker aiming to unravel and confront mysteries of nature. It is the perplexity of a mystic only too happy to remain perplexed. As God is in many mystical traditions, this nature is at once close at hand ("The mountain is near me: behind the maples and sorb trees") and completely remote ("Listen: the furthest bird in the world is singing").[61] It has a godlike ability to absorb and assimilate through an elaborate scheme. It begins the process of alluring the travelers by planting in their hearts "something like a thicket of light," or sending through the air messages from "the blooming flowers on the furthest bush on earth." The journeyers remain hopeful that somewhere along the road they will be embraced by what might be understood as the journey's destination:

> Listen! The distant road calls your footsteps,
> Your eyes are not ornaments for the dark.
> Shake [the sleep] off your eyelids! Put your shoes on! and come!
> And come to the point where the feather of the moon warns your
>   feet to stop,
> Where time sits on a lump of earth with you,
> And the music of the night absorbs your body, like a song,
>   to itself.[62]

Yet there is a palpable difference in Sepehri's urge for self-annihilation in nature that sets it apart from the elusive mystical dissolution in nothingness. In a way the end he seeks is closer to finding, or rather building, an ideal abode, perhaps comparable to the Platonic ideal city, a temple for the worship of the "form of the good." While a Sufi who achieves the mystical annihilation *fana'* is uninterested and unable to describe his/her mingling with the sacred, Sepehri knows with clarity what this place would be like. And although distant in its perfect qualities, in many ways the place is close to where we all live.

The city Sepehri yearns for is best described in the poem *Pusht-i darya'ha* (Behind the Seas). In a delightful mingling of verbal and natural splendor, the poet's search for the city becomes an allegory for the road that poetry can pave to the "friend's house." As he redefines the mystical annihilation into union with nature, nature expands to embrace the temple, the guide, and the destination at once. This city is not to be found but built with the infinity, magnificence, and wisdom of nature used as building blocks. Nature is, therefore, not an end in itself as God is in Sufis' mystical journey. It is the channel through which the human intellect may access true wisdom. The ideal city one can find/build behind the seas had its windows open to *tajalli* (manifestations). In it time has a different scale, and age is not a measure of maturity, for in that city the arm of any ten-year-old is a "branch of wisdom." There, the earth hears the music of human feelings, and the sound of the wings of mythical birds can be heard in the wind.[63]

The transforming exchange, taking place through this alchemical poetic give and take, leads to a "naturalization" of religion as much as it sanctifies nature.

Farrokhzad's ultimate immaculate conception transformed human sexuality and the sacred by merging them. Sepehri's merger brings the sacred down to earth, by turning nature into its temple and a location for construction of new sacred-making paradigms. When "the tiles in the mosque assault the idea of prostration," it is time to put muezzins on cypress trees and let the flowing moonlight speak for God.[64]

With the spontaneity that is the hallmark of his work, and that assumes no pretension to fulfilling paradigmatic roles, Sepehri injects the dying divine with "natural" blood. It is important to realize that this is not a nature borrowed wholesale but one carefully re-envisioned to suit the operation. In so doing, the poet mimics the person who, in *Ta nabz-i khis-i subh* (Till the Drenched Pulse of the Morning), arrives to extend Sepehri's arms "as far as the muscles of heaven." The divine light of religions emanates from the shirt buttons of this stranger whose voice is refreshed with the "watery attributes of the rivers" and who can "weave windows from the dry fodder of ancient verses." The poem concludes Sepehri's master collection *The Expanse of Green,* where the enlivened divine continues a meaningful existence. In the meantime, our poet and his stranger friend put their desk out in the open and abandon the scriptures to the "sanctity of the rain."[65]

6

> ─ ⊷ ◈ ⊶ ○ ⊷ ◈ ⊶ ─

"Hurry, Nazarene, Hurry!"
True Prophets Do Not Turn Back nor Do They Die

A discussion of political commitment and the place of poetry in the ideal of progress and social change brings the present monograph to its concluding stages.[1] The relevance of this topic to the poetic act of sacred making may not be apparent in the first instant. Indeed, the two are often perceived to be of opposing nature. The impulse to socially reform while engaging modernity and the need for the presence of a divine force fall "naturally" in opposite poles. The first denotes rationality and agency, the second submission and passivity. It is therefore easier to classify the poetic output in twentieth-century Iran, with its numerous political upheavals that engaged the imagination of the major poets, as a predominantly "secular" activity. The classification seems logical, particularly when dealing with writings prior to the 1979 revolution, at which point religion became the official ideology of the state.[2] I have dealt earlier with the problematic nature of outmoded postenlightenment categories such as the secular and their inadequacy to shed light on the complex behavior of modern Persian poetry. I have already quoted numerous examples from the writings of politically committed influential poets who engaged in poetic sacred making decades before the 1979 domination of state-sponsored religion. Furthermore, the assumption that all modern Persian poetry prior to the 1979 revolution was devoid of the impulse to locate, re-envision, make, and revere the sacred leaves the revolution itself inexplicable (unless we subscribe to the theory of a schizophrenic divide separating the "secular" intellectuals and the "religious" masses).[3] I hope to have demonstrated, through the poets quoted so far, that this simplified two-colored picture does not hold. In its place, I have offered a different outlook, one that acknowledges the intellectuals/writers of twentieth-century Iran to be sharing much of the religious/spiritual impulse that fueled the revolution. At the same time, I am hoping to have documented the diversity, dynamism, and evolving nature that characterize their approaches to the sacred. This diversity and dynamism, in turn, reflect the multivalence of the process of sacred making in general in twentieth-century Iran.

The discussion cannot be complete without a closer look at the verbal political activism that made its mark on modern Persian poetry. I hope this chapter will make some general judgments possible, for example, that poetic commitment/ activism did not replace the need for the presence of the sacred and its intervention in human condition. Once again, we are looking at another master painting with all its dazzling details. The main purpose is not to determine the dominant subject matter or explain the main purpose of the painting. It is to recover something of the story that is told in "the thickness of oil," the details at work in every inch on the canvas. I quote a few remarkable figures with formative influence on twentieth-century Persian poetry who used their poetic medium to mobilize masses or bring about political change, among other things. This leads to examination of excerpts from the writings of such figures as Siyavash Kasra'i (1927–) and Hamid Mosaddiq (d. 2001), who, despite the significance of their poetic contributions, are near anonymous to English readers. Much of this chapter, however, will be woven around the poetry of Ahmad Shamlu (1925–2000), the modern Persian poet par excellence, the epitome of political activism, and the self-confessed iconoclast with a conscious will to challenge religiously sanctioned authority over the faithful masses.[4] The choice of Shamlu allows the survey of poetry presented in this monograph to conclude on a high note. His poems are superb examples of poetic energy and artistry, providing fine details that I discuss to shed light on the topic of this chapter as well as modern Persian poetry in general. The choice is not meant to single out Shamlu as the sole formative force in the development of the genre or to underestimate the contribution of other contemporary figures. Rather, his poetry is the culmination in the evolution of the paradigm.

I would like to open the discussion with a rather provocative observation: the concept of a politically committed poetry is a tautology. Good poetry has no choice but remaining political, and a living/evolving poet cannot be other than committed. Examples are many; I opt for an unlikely candidate. Sa'dī's (d. 1292) mystical reflection that "to an intelligent observer" every leaf on a green tree is a "page in the book of divine gnosis" was as much a political statement as it was an ethical instruction.[5] While for us the statement may remain a simple personal expression of God's pervasive presence, Sa'dī was speaking in a milieu in which political and religious power concentrated in a selected few who drove their authority from an increasingly narrowing canon of pious acts and thoughts. As a committed Muslim, a free thinker, and a master poet interested in opening up the horizons of personal encounter with beauty and with the sacred, Sa'dī disliked the conceptual limits that these political conditions sought to impose on his world. Besides whatever moves he might have made to confront these politically limiting conditions directly, he took his main action in the poetic domain where his decrees could not be easily challenged. He appropriated the theologically sanctioned attributes of God, did away with the scholastic prerequisites for perceiving them, and spread them on tree leaves for every ordinary observer to touch, even redefine. Medieval Persian poetry has more politically poignant statements to be sure, but I have quoted an example from Saʿdī to show that variations on such statements surface even in the works of a figure understood to be the pillar of the moral and political establishment.[6]

The poets of twentieth-century Iran were no exception. Either they were poets of consequence or they were not. If in the latter category, they failed to move beyond the moment that encompassed their immediate concerns, and their presence (political or otherwise) remained brief and precarious. If, however, they fit in the former category, their contributions were relevant, noteworthy, and necessarily political. The works of such poets, as we have already seen, were embraced enthusiastically by a massive lay as well as elite readership. Had they ignored their own evolving social roles, the changing conditions of their country, or the extreme inequities of the world at large, their poetic messages would have failed to acquire the significance that they did. A cursory look at the preceding chapters easily corroborates this assessment.

"IF I SIT IDLE, WHO WILL RISE?" POETRY OF ACTIVISM, OR POLITICS AT THE SURFACE OF POETRY

If the political nature of writing is understood in the broad structural sense described above, the continuous and formative role of politics in writing is not open to question. From this perspective, political engagement is at the heart of an evolving perception of the self and the society. Not surprisingly, this level of political engagement is crucial for the vitality of literary—and other varieties of artistic—expression. In twentieth-century Iran, the onset of modernity and the resulting social upheavals pushed the debate on political consciousness to the center of artistic and intellectual debate. By mid–twentieth century, political activism was not just a plus but a constitutive element in the activity of writing, which was itself viewed as a central tool for social reform.[7]

Political activism captured the attention of modern Iranian poets in a more particular sense: as an ultimate goal in life. Literature foregrounds specific concerns or layers of meaning from among the vast number of issues it broaches. Thematization is among the literary strategies that make the foregrounding of selected concerns possible. While poetry speaks of far more themes and concepts than its central subject matter, it always privileges some as its main subject. One dominant theme in the poetry of twentieth-century Iran was "to be or not to be political." This thematic political emphasis, or politics at the surface of poetry, found varying manifestations. It often advocated political commitment in the limited and immediate sense of mass mobilization and uprising. Prevalence of this poetry of activism led to the evolution of the thematic genre that was to serve as the gun in the hands of advocates for social change. Furthermore, it promoted unconditional preference for poetry that fueled such activism and expressed contempt for all other literary creation as irrelevant. This commitment as a "presuppositional engagement" with social causes and revolutionary ends, as

Hamid Dabashi calls it, was directly related to the social position of the literati in recent Iranian history. In other words, a meaningful study of the dimensions of this commitment should go beyond a literary study of texts and trace the formation of the intelligentsia as a "self-conscious social group in modern Iranian history."[8] Such an inquiry will shed light on the larger attitudinal patterns toward politics and ideological leanings that in Dabashi's mind underlie the "troublesome problem" of commitment in the poetry of the time. While sociological factors are of utmost significance, as Dabashi rightly observes, "the fact remains that some principles of aesthetics, doctrines of beauty and truth, must tyrannically rule our creative imagination if not our habitual civility."[9] In this chapter, I address the literary manifestations of these "doctrines of beauty and truth" as central to the creativity of committed poets in this period.

Perhaps the strongest advocacy for "poetry of activism," and its most dramatic expression, appeared with the publication of *Shi'ri ki zindagist* (Poetry That Is Life), Shamlu's manifesto of modern Persian poetry.[10] Yet, there were more popularly embraced examples of poetry that thematized, or allegorized, political activism. Hamid Mosaddiq's long poem *Abi, khakistari, siyah* (Blue, Gray, Black), first published in 1969, for instance, had reached its eighth edition by 1978.[11] Premodern Persian court poetry had already molded the beloved and the patron into one for centuries. Mosaddiq's poem uses a similar technique of playing on ambiguity. Against a lyrical backdrop combining praise for the beloved with pleas for her attention, it voices the main message of the poem: the appeal to the masses for uprising. The following short, simple, and effective stanza from the poem has gained unprecedented popular recognition:

> If I rise
> If you rise
> All shall rise.
> If I sit idle
> If you sit idle
>   Who will rise?
> Who will face the enemy?
> Who will engage the enemy in battle?[12]

While in *Abi, khakistari, siyah* Mosaddiq salvaged certain poetic qualities such as lyricism or attention to the lucidity of the images, the political message was clearly privileged. In the polished and resonant style of such poets as Siyavash Kasra'i, this activist poetry moved beyond encouragement for armed struggle and provided fine examples of theme and artistry. In his exquisite modern epic *Arash-i kaman'gir*, Kasra'i retells the story of Arash, the mythical Iranian archer. Arash settled the territorial dispute between the ancient Iranians and their Turanian adversaries by putting his life in the arrow that determined the border separating the war-torn countries. In Kasra'i's recreation, Arash is not just a soldier defending the Iranian territorial integrity. He embodies the lofty ideals of the pre-Islamic Zoroastrian worldview devoted to eternal struggle between forces of light and darkness:

> He kneeled to pray [at the foot of the mountain]
> Opening his arms toward the peak:
> Rise! O sun! The staple of my hope!
> Rise! O fruit of heavens!
> You are a spring gushing forth
> I am weakened with thirst.
> Rise! Pour over me! Quench the thirst of my soul!
>
> Now that I am about to meet a bitter end,
> With all my heart fighting against the vicious ruler of darkness,
> Anoint me with your waves of light!
> Give me your beauty, my golden flower! Give me your scent![13]

Despite sanctioning the heroic suicide of Arash, who according to the myth lends the arrow his own life to help it fly deeper into the enemy's territory, Kasra'i does not overemphasize self-sacrifice or trivialize life. Instead of mourning the loss of Arash, the poem succeeds in celebrating the sanctity of life, and the vibrant beauty of the nature that embodies this life. The old storyteller in the poem, 'Amu Nowruz, who has begun the tale of Arash with "I had told you [before] life is beautiful," provides ample evidence for his claim:

> The open sky, the golden sun
> Gardens filled with flowers,
> Vast plains that defy doors and fences.
>
> A lone flower sticking its head out of snow to bloom,
> The gentle flow of the fish dancing in crystal waters,
> The scent of the earth moist with rain
> Fields of wheat sleeping, drenched in moonlight,
> To come, to go, to run
> To fall in love
> To share in the sorrow of others
> And to dance shoulder to shoulder with people in happy times.[14]

Only if the survival, peace, and harmony of this exquisite chorus of life are at risk are human beings justified in putting their own lives in danger to save the collectivity. Thus Arash clarifies in his prayer:

> My heart abhors death
> For death is devilish and carnivorous.
> But when the soul of life is darkened with sad things

When the time has come for good to confront evil
Meeting one's death is all right
It is the only thing worthy of a liberated soul.[15]

The poem keeps the ideal of political activism at the forefront of the panorama that it presents of life. More specifically, the socialist flavor of the activism is underlined on many occasions, not least by making Arash a member of the masses. A true representative of the working classes, the archer hero articulates his devotion to the glory of Iran in socialist terms, which are at times uncharacteristically learned for a simple worker. Thus Arash addresses the enemy:

I am Arash, a free soul, a soldier
With my last arrow
I am ready for your bitter ordeal.
My ancestry is not important
I am a son of true hardship and toil.[16]

Later in the same monologue, our hero holds the heart of the people in his "fist" and leans against the hopes of the "silent masses" (*mardumi khamush*) for success in his battle against darkness. The words *kar* (labor), *paykar* (armed struggle), and *khalq* (the masses) are terms with strong and clear socialist overtones. Furthermore, the image of Arash, addressing the enemy with closed fists, leaves no doubt as to the inevitability of the ensuing confrontation. Neither is there any ambiguity concerning the identity of the oppressed represented in the poem by Arash or the enemy allegorized into the rival powers threatening the borders of ancient Iran.

Despite the objective of mobilizing the masses to fight social injustice, Kasra'i succeeded in presenting his readers with a poem, which will last beyond these immediate concerns. Ultimately, the poem points in the direction of life and touches the force that life has "in its gaze and its smile" *bi-niru'i kih darad zindagi dar chishm u dar labkhand.* It is this force that tears the mask off the face of death and empowers Arash—and by extension us—with its majesty and vitality. Thus Arash seeks help not from a particular leader but from this lasting life force:

O proud, silent summits!
Who touch the awe-inspiring thunder with your forehead!
Who watch the dreamy vistas of the night!
Who let the golden day—arriving with its silvery feet at dawn—
Stand on your shoulders!
Who give refuge to burning clouds!
Raise my hope!
Like the flag of early morning breeze you hold above your head!
Nurse my pride!
Like the pride of the leopards you shelter in your midst.[17]

In *Arash-i kaman'gir,* Kasra'i gave a fine example of transcending petty politics while remaining politically engaged, put the garb of a mythical hero on the working classes, and gave twentieth-century Persian poetry a beautiful epic of its own.

LITERARY DEVELOPMENT AND THE IDEOLOGY OF REPRESENTATION

Kasra'i's attempt was a subtle example of an overt ideological functionalism widespread among twentieth-century Iranian writers. Thematically political works gained such centrality that the paradigm has been identified as an episodic developmental pattern in the history of writing in Iran.[18] Kamran Talattof, whom I have quoted with reference to his description of writing in twentieth-century Iran as a "secular" activity earlier, advances the theory of episodic development in modern Persian literature in his *The Politics of Writing in Iran.* I dealt with the problematic nature of the concept "secular" earlier.[19] Talattof considers "ideological paradigms" as the dominant factor in the development of "form, characterization, and figurative language of literary texts." According to him, ideological features, which themselves change with social and political change, are responsible for what he describes as "literary shifts" occurring in "episodic fashion" and leading to the formation of "literary movements." He enumerates the main episodic literary movements of twentieth-century Iran as Persianism, committed literature, Islamic literature, and feminist literary movement. Talattof's observation of the determinant role of state ideology and political opposition in the formation of literary movements is astute. So is his documentation of the impact that the political milieu has on a wide number of elements ranging from author/reader relationships to the particular directions in which canonized words and metaphors develop. His "episodic model," however, shows troubling flaws when it advances sweeping theoretical observations on the development of Persian literature. "Persian literary history," he writes, "is not an integrated continuum but a series of distinct episodes distinguishable by their ideology of representation." The limited nature of what Talattof views as episodes becomes even more apparent as he assigns short and restricted time periods to each episode.[20] According to this model, for example, we are to consider the episode of committed literature gaining dominance in the 1950s and "promptly declining" after the 1979 revolution. It is not therefore clear where to place the poetry written by Shamlu after the 1979 revolution, to use one example. Shamlu clearly does not belong to the episode Islamic literature beginning with the onrush of the revolution; neither has he renounced his well-established political commitment.[21] There are other, equally problematic, instances in application of Talattof's episodic model. Where would the pre-1979 writings of Shafi'i-Kadkani be placed? He wrote some of the most effective of his revolutionary poetry, permeated by Islamic spiritual paradigms, in years prior to what according to the episodic model constitutes the beginning of the episode Islamic literature. To make matters harder, Shafi'i-Kadkani devoted some of his spiritually inspired literature to influential leftist figures.

Talattof himself quotes Kadkani's poetry, and rightly so, as commemorating the aborted leftist armed struggle at Siyahkal.[22]

There is no need for further examples to demonstrate the continuity, indeed the overlap, between identifiable "episodes" in Persian or any other literary history. Whatever their "ideology of representation," such episodes will have to remain interconnected with one another as well as with their various pasts to maintain the flow of viable and resonant poetic building blocks. Even departing from tradition entails reliance on existing resonant elements throughout the process in which the new elements gain currency. The present work, among those of many others, has contributed to understanding of the depth and the significance of the individual way in which every work of art is rooted in the broader tradition from which it springs.[23] There is no denial of distinguishable episodes, movements, or whatever one may choose to call the pattern, that emerge in the history of any literature. Viewing such episodes as disconnected with one another and with earlier existing patterns from which they were generated however poses a major limit on understanding the development of such patterns. Finally, in order to appreciate the presence and significance of this continuity, there is no need for viewing Persian literary history as a seamless or "integrated" continuum. Change and breaking away from generic prototypes is a most constant dialogue between any evolving tradition and the parent tradition that nourishes it.[24]

In the latter decades of the twentieth century, as the dust of the revolution settled, critics began to point to the limited nature of the vision that advanced the poetry of activism as the sole viable conduit for engaged writing. Some went further to consider such ideological commitment as a serious handicap for the more encompassing vision vital to the evolution of engaged poetry. In his lucid essays on Iranian culture, Shahrukh Meskub critiqued the development of this narrowness of vision and its consequence for twentieth-century Persian literature:

> From the time of the first congress of Iranian writers (1325/1946)—and fundamentally to the present—the Iranian political ideology is limited to that of the Tudeh party, which divides the world into the oppressor and the oppressed, the socialist and the imperialist camp, the good and the evil. It assumes the emancipation of the workers and the defeat of the capitalist ruling class following deadly unavoidable confrontations in a near [historically speaking] future. This division of existence into light and darkness, and the unavoidable confrontation of the two culminating in the uprising of the masses, spilled from ideology into literature. Not only did it become the philosophical and emotional resting place for some writers, but became a testimony to literature's *haqqaniyat* (true nature). In this manner, through serving the masses and their goals, literature justified its very existence.[25]

Fortunately, in his criticism of the activist/reductionist approach to literature, Meskub transcended the dismissive or one-sided ideological disputes that were the hallmark of the angry "intellectual" exchanges between the supporters and opponents of the 1979 revolution. Rather, he sought to expose the limits that any reductionist ideological approach would impose on poetry and other forms of writing. In a passage that criticized Shamlu's *Shi'ri ki zindagist,* Meskub lamented the fact that in its poorly fitting garb as a mere political tool, poetry will fail to be anything other than a gun to be used in battle, the gallows for hanging the oppressor, or at best the *ahrum* (lever) with which to remove the hurdles from the path of the masses. The major harm in assigning poetry this functional role, as far as Meskub was concerned, was in blinding it to the fundamental subjective questions such as those of time, love and death, and other larger philosophical matters that have always been the preoccupation of Persian poetry. "Where do we come from and why are we here," "the plight of a conscious humanity captive to the blind forces of nature," and basically "the injustices that we endure not because of social inequalities but because of being in the world" were among the questions that Meskub named.[26] In a related passage that described *mediocrity* as one of the consequences of this narrowness of purpose for literature, Meskub lashed out at Samad Bihrangi, the author of *Mahi-i siyah-i kuchulu* (The Little Black Fish) and the most acclaimed Iranian writer of children's literature in the twentieth century. Bihrangi's little black fish became the metaphorical prototype of the politically aware and won its creator widespread international recognition. This unique combination of political awareness and international renown, plus the suspicious circumstance of Bihrangi's death, afforded the author a heroic status enriched with artistic creativity, courage to confront the system, and martyrdom. As a result, next to Shria'atis and Ale Ahmads of his generation, Bihrangi remained immune to criticism for decades. Meskub is to be commended for the courage to be the first to allow his critical probes to penetrate the heroes' shield. Illustrating the "mediocrity that resulted from limiting literature to party politics," Meskub used the example of Bihrangi's famed short story *Ulduz va kalagh'ha* (Ulduz and the Crows). In the story that documents the miseries of the poor and motherless Ulduz, a crow teaches her to protect herself by returning the blows of her oppressors. Meskub's greatest objection, however, concerned the introduction to the story in which Bihrangi extends his views of the irreconcilable divisions between the communities of the oppressor and the oppressed to his young readership declaring "these children are not permitted to read my stories: children who are brought to school by a servant, children who are driven to school in expensive personal vehicles."[27]

Looking beyond Functionalism and Party Politics: The Mirror That Reflected Ida's Beauty

Meskub provided an engaging, balanced, and justifiably critical reading of Shamlu's stance toward traditional Persian poetry. To back his argument, he presented close reading of certain sections from *Shiʾri ki zindagist*. Where Shamlu declared the "poet of the past" to be captive in "the snare of the beloved's ridiculous curls," Meskub asked the pertinent question no one had asked thus far: "who were these poets of the past?" The point of the query was simple: Saʿdī, Rūmī, and Hāfez are simply not reducible to captives in such imaginary snares, whereas many of the lower-ranking poets had not been significant players in the history of Persian poetry anyway. In other words, Shamlu had reduced the "poet of the past" to a hollow, exaggerated, and indefensible straw man in order to be able to safely destroy him. Meskub, who was careful to endorse the need for critical evaluation of Persian poetry, remained unequivocal in his dissatisfaction with "ranting and ravings" of the Shamlu kind. Such vague yet noisy expressions of anger, Meskub told his readers, did not clarify anything nor did they help anyone.[28] Meskub was, once more, pioneering courageous and perceptive criticism toward a figure as elevated and idealized as Shamlu. Here too, his criticism remained moderate and well substantiated.

What Meskub failed to acknowledge was that Shamlu himself transcended the narrow political agenda he seemed to outline for modern Persian poetry in the poem in question. While, in *Shiʾri ki zindagist,* Shamlu sought a poetry that would work as a weapon in the hands of the oppressed, his own poetry was infinitely more versatile. To reduce Shamlu's poetry to a political tool, or to a means for the articulation of leftist ideology, was as grave a reductionism as was Shamlu's portrayal of all "the poets of the past" as captives in the snare of the beloved's curl. Indeed what had afforded Shamlu the elevated poetic status he occupied was that the gun he had fashioned for struggle turned as easily, in lyrical moments, into the mirror that reflected Ida's beauty.[29] These candid expressions of lyricism had the tenacity to coexist with the political goals without losing their subjective and intensely personal nature. And, as I demonstrate in tracing the footsteps of the sacred in Shamlu's poetry, this same mirror transformed into the temple from which prophetic figures rose. These were prophets who personified an oppositional and constantly evolving sacred. The rise of the prophets is all the more remarkable as it coincided with the poet's unceasing struggle against the passivity of unquestioned faith. Indeed, evolution and redefinition are the key features of what emerged as Shamlu's personal encounters with the sacred. What I will present in this chapter as Shamlu's poetics of sacred making are the metaphorical pulsations of a conflicted worshiping heart that renewed and renamed its devotion in beats alternating between acceptance and complete denial. It is not in the harmonious environment of reverence and approval but in the energy generating from struggle, conflict, and collision that this evolving sacred lived on and underwent transformation. Other poets have borrowed the mantle of the prophets from time to time; what is distinct here is the prophetic mission that Shamlu set for himself: "altering the world" through the miracle of poetry.[30]

Focusing on Shamlu's politically enlivened poetics of sacred making, in this chapter I move beyond the poet's personal achievements. In the process, I attempt to make a number of points. First, I demonstrate that meaningful poetry fit for survival draws its energy from sources more diverse than ideological motivation and political activism. Even when politically motivated, this poetry addresses a broader range of human experiences with a vision inclusive of the past, focused on the present, and pointing in the direction of the future. Continuity, and tolerance for seemingly outmoded elements, is therefore a feature of his poetry despite its strong impulse for renewal. While change in the dominant taste that determines the subject matter of poetry is to be expected with time, literary development in the full sense can hardly be viewed as episodic. Any episode torn from the continuous literary current that nourishes it with strength and vitality from the body of tradition rooted in the past will be devoid of long-term resonance. Poetry that fails to make this connection will not survive beyond the life expectancy of the immediate political concerns motivating its genesis. It is fair to say that Shamlu did not attain his poetic status and his normative role in modern Persian poetry due to the overt political functionalism of the kind displayed in *Shi'ri ki zindagist.* Neither can his triumph in "altering the world" be viewed as a sole result of his skill in breaking out of dying traditions. He earned his unique position mostly due to the ability to remain rooted in the vital areas of the tradition while working anxiously and skillfully to revise and refashion the same tradition. These vital areas are not easily apparent, narrowly defined, or exclusive. They include every theme and style that proved significant and relevant even if it involved expression of religious devotion, or complex strategies of sacred making, which appeared to be anathema to the poet.

I begin by exploring Shamlu's comfortable adoption of images and concepts that owe their potency to their traditionally sacred nature or to their proximity to the sacred. I demonstrate that these are not rare instances. Rather, this ardent critic of religion in twentieth-century Persian poetry had a habit of collecting fragments from the shattered sacred and piecing them together in freshly encoded poetic messages. I then focus on the poet's prophetology. Here Shamlu's personal identification with the prophets he champions is notable. Out of affinities and conflicts between the revolutionary and prophetic sides of the poet emerge pieces of a self-portrait with considerable confidence, serenity, and content. Aware of his elevated status, Shamlu still struggled for justice, but no longer by fashioning guns to place in the hands of the proletariat. "The tired poet" (Bamdad-i khastih) passing through the *Astanih,* the threshold that led him to what came after death, and looking back at a long and stormy poetic career, was "shadmanih u shakir" (happy and grateful). He celebrated having been born in the "glorious human form" as he "danced" his way through the threshold and out of life.[31] Shamlu's triumphant exit through the threshold of beyond was not a political victory brought about by the fruition of a leftist—or any other—revolution. This was a triumph rooted in the knowledge that his poetry had penetrated the thin surface of immediate concerns, of ideological affinities, and of political functionalism. He had moved beyond these pressing but passing urgencies and stepped onto the infinitely broader and more enduring plains of human struggle for self-exploration and self-expression. The readings of Shamlu in this chapter do not provide glimpses of his evolution and survival alone. They testify to the resilience of an evolving poetic tradition. These examples document significant moments in the history of the evolution of Persian poetry as it survives—even thrives—under Shamlu's ruthless creative strikes aimed at reshaping and renewing the tradition.

THE MUTINY OF MY CREATION IS KNOWN TO THE DEVIL NOT TO GOD

Most probably, Shamlu did not consider Saʿdī's spreading of divine gnosis on tree leaves to be a notable political move.[32] There were many instances in Shamlu's life in which political commitment and the impulse to revolutionize required a more acute, oppositional, and activist nature. Meskub's model of the world divided into the oppressor and oppressed, inspired by the Tudih party's political ideology, may not be spacious enough to house all of Shamlu's political concerns. But it is not a complete misreading either. After all, as far as Shamlu was concerned, even "speaking of the trees" was itself "more or less a crime" where exposing the crimes of the oppressor had to be the poet's foremost priority. Under such conditions, speaking of the trees was—in truth—a silence that masked what needed to be exposed.[33] Saʿdī, as far as Shamlu was concerned, was guilty of the "crime" of speaking merely of the beauty of the trees. He was a skilful versifier bereft of any social commitment or impact altogether. In an interview in the early 1990s, Shamlu responded to "What do you think of Saʿdī?" with:

> I have no thoughts about Saʿdī. That is the easiest answer I can give. Saʿdī just *is*, has occupied a place for himself. That is all. One of our problems as a people, like anyone who is drowning, is that instead of finding a fundamental solution, we just reach out to hold onto broken branches and pieces of straw [*khar u khashak*] floating on the surface of the water. Our culture is the [the culture of] illogical gropings of a drowning person. We speak of "Saʿdī's brilliant prose," but do not for one instant ask ourselves "What is the function of this brilliant prose?" We do not ask where and for whom a brilliant piece of writing should become useful. Is this the case that a person with ability to write brilliantly has the right to say anything he wants? Do I not have the right not to be receptive to his work? Fine, he has some writing in the Persian classical fashion, phenomenal in its miraculous linguistic capacity [for artistic expression?]. But what does this miracle have for me? Women in Saʿdī's work, homosexuality in Saʿdī's work,

ethics in Saʿdī's work, social issues in Saʿdī's work, which of these solve any of my problems?[34]

These comments are surprising not just in their denial of the occurrence of social criticism in Saʿdī's *Bustan* and *Gulistan,* but in refusing to acknowledge qualities such as lyricism or humor, which Saʿdī possessed in abundance. After all, these are qualities that distinguish Shamlu's own work from political slogans produced by many of his "committed" contemporaries. Shamlu's exaggerated expectation that poetry should function primarily as a tool for social change is present in his approving remarks about the poetry of another classical figure, Hāfez (d. 1388?). Apparently, the attraction of Hāfez was not in the sophistication of his lyricism, the philosophical depth, or the intricacies of the ghazels. Rather it was in the tenacity of the poet to fight and expose the deceit and decadence of the corrupted age in which he lived:

> For me the most interesting aspect of Hāfez is his readiness for confrontation and struggle. He is a man who, in one of the most duplicitous periods of the history of our country when playing the *khanqah* game, hypocrisy, and deceiving the masses is at its height . . . stands up alone to the sheiks of these khanqahs and exposes them. These are circumstances in which murderers such as Amir Muzaffar and his son Shah Shuja' use these "pious" games to legitimize their rule, when khanqahs and royal courts are allies.[35]

Shamlu's angry and sweeping generalizations make better sense when placed in the broader context of his fear of stagnation. As a poet facing modernity and change, he was acutely aware of the need for poetic renewal and creativity. In chapter four, I pointed to the resonance of this topic throughout Farrokhzad's poetic carrier as well.[36] After all, one had to be able to cut the umbilical cord with the past to be born fully into the new era. To exaggerate the shortcomings of the tradition was one way to assert the newly earned independence. Shamlu subscribed to a particularly simplistic perception of traditional Persian poetry. This "peerless treasure," he once stated, would leave you with only a handful of writers "whose words have been recycled by the rest" if you sift through it properly.[37] Nor was this condemnation of the past vague or general. Shamlu often articulated specific justifications for rejecting each traditional mode of thinking and the formal genre that was associated with it. About ghazel, for example, he issued the following verdict:

> The ghazel is not the poetry of our time. This is my first verdict and the last. . . . language goes forward, and expands itself, hand in hand with time. But the ghazel does not do so. In a ghazel nothing moves faster than a caravan. A car cannot enter the limited space [*mahdudah*] of a ghazel. In that realm, the latest means of transportation is a camel litter [*kajavah*].[38]

I Was, Then I Became!

Encoded into poetry, the exaggerated impatience with stagnation transformed into a powerful plea for dynamism that kept its persuasive edge throughout his poetic career. In his last collection, *Hadith-i bi-gharari-i Mahan*, Shamlu renewed the plea for "being" as a perpetual "becoming" in a poem in praise of a young woman he had known throughout her childhood. The poem opened in an uncharacteristically serene ambience passing through loud thunders and unfettered downpours to listen to the gentle flow of the inner songs, springs rooted in the quiet sea within.[39] Soon, the readers were rewarded with an example of the spring in the poet's own voice reminiscing about his first memories of this strong and persuasive young person. Describing her childish autonomous talent, which the poet had desired to shape, gave him the opportunity to think of perpetual becoming:

> Then, again, I said to myself:
> "*Being* is one thing and *becoming* another . . .
> The one who *became,* once
> Will not fail to become again.
>
> She will walk with wide strides, singing on the road
> With golden rules of her own
> Lodged deep in the vastness of her confident thoughts."[40]

The young woman, the personification of perpetual becoming, had by the end of the poem transformed into a full tree, its branches spread across the horizon and its shade conquering the earth. As far as Shamlu was concerned, nothing short of this open-ended narrative of change was worth living. Indeed, this was the mission of humanity.

I here argue that the exaggerated aversion to religion that the supposedly secular Shamlu expressed is rooted in the same fear of stagnation. Despite his many public denouncements of faith, I would argue, he was desperately hopeful for a potential all-powerful sacred presence who would vitalize life, enhance beauty, and support the human struggle for justice. Shamlu would acknowledge, revere, even seek such a sacred with all its traditional trappings if one condition alone was fulfilled: preserving the space in which "to be" is "to become." If that condition was fulfilled, the impulse to partake of the sacred was not an ossifying one. It was as empowering as the sky embracing reverently the soul of a martyr:

> I was.
> Then I became.
> Not in the manner that a bud becomes a flower
> Roots turn into green shoots

> Or seeds grow to be the forest.
> But in the fashion
> That a simple man
>   —turned martyr—
> Is revered by the sky.[41]

As I show in specific examples in the present chapter, however, Shamlu found traditional modes of celebrating the sacred as paralyzing as he had found their traditional counterparts in composing poetry. That he did not surrender to the latter tradition is well established. What I argue here is that he did not simply do away with the notion of the sacred. Rather, he devoted a tremendous amount of poetic energy to remaking that sacred, just as he had done to encoding fresh poetic messages.

His poetic strategies of sacred making ranged from broader and more standard ones to those that were distinctly his. I start with a metaphorical example that scrutinized the process of coming to life with love, or becoming, using the imagery and structure of resurrection. The move was discrete but powerful, perhaps the most indirect manner of opening the space to summon the sacred. This was one of many borrowed sacred rhythms and structures that Shamlu used to enhance resonance while avoiding direct allusions. The poem was entitled *Rastakhiz* (Resurrection). Step by step, it pieced together a symbolic eschatological process culminating in the "true" resurrection that is love:

> I was the dead body of all birds,
> Birds that sing
>   And those who don't,
> I was the carcass of the most beautiful beasts
>   on earth and in water,
> The corpse of all humans,
>   good and bad.
> I was there, in the past, silent
> Devoid of mystery, laughter, desire.
> Tenderly,
> In a time unexpected
> You dreamt me.
> Then you woke from your sleep
>   And so did I.[42]

In the short poem *Milad* (Birth), love unveiled itself through another sacred structure: that of the sun rising in the east. In a world intoxicated with this manifestation of light, humanity was born. Again, although there were no direct allusions to a Sufi contemplation of creation, the borrowed structure and terminology that permeated the poem left no doubt as to the sanctity of the space in which the birth had taken place.[43]

In its institutionalized manifestation, however, surrender to the sacred was far from birth or resurrection. Rather, it was the opposite of it. In its new habitat, misunderstood and misused, the sacred was the evil spell that turned life into a short pause between the primordial sin and hellfire. In the poem *'Ashiqanah* (In Love), composed days after "Resurrection," the sun had transformed into a curse, the breeze was a foul temptation, and the moonlight nothing but the blasphemy that had polluted the world. Shamlu punctuated this poem with a personal plea summoning the voice of love to break the deadly silence.[44]

Despite the grave disappointment and anger directed at unchecked religious authority and its punitive style, the above poem was not a critique of religion. Rather it made use of such accessible and resonant concepts as *ma'siyat* (sin), *'uqubat* (punishment), and *kufr* (infidelity) in order to portray the bleakness of the social conditions. In such poetically encoded social commentaries, Shamlu often mocked and revered different representations of the sacred at the same time. In *Akhir-i bazi* (End of the Game), lovers were *sarshikastah* (ashamed), alleyways devoid of the sound of footsteps, and wherever the despot had set foot plants refused to grow. In the same poem, just as the soldiers of the despot were presented as *bi-'itiqad* (without faith), Shamlu used the concept of *taqva* (piety), associated closely with Islamic piety, to describe the misunderstood and violated nature of earth and water. In a yet more vividly contrasting image, the closing stanza of the same poem juxtaposed religiously charged imagery that fulfilled contradictory roles. As the tyrant was promised "the curse of Hell," mourning mothers appeared with their *sajjadih* (prayer rugs). Curved in prostration and covered in black, these worshiping figures formed a gigantic inkblot, the full stop that visually signaled the end of the poem. The longer narrative, the reign of injustice, was also to come to an end when these suffering worshipers finally rose from their prostrations.[45]

TEACHING BEAUTY IN THE CEMETERY OF GODS

This is a good time to remember that Shamlu's use of the sacred impulse to empower the poetic idiom was not limited to specific subject matters. In *Surud-i panjum*, the fifth love song dedicated to his wife Ida, he described her as the "heart that, in this cemetery of gods, taught beauty as if teaching a religion."[46] This statement was, perhaps, more of a self-image than the poet had cared to admit. Acknowledged or not, the greatest of anxieties animating Shamlu's poetic voice was that of abandoning the sacred to the injustices of power brokers who had fashioned it into a yardstick. This was a double disappointment the second tier of which focused on the mediocrity of the masses who tolerated the injustice in the name of God. The abusive relation infuriated Shamlu. What, to his mind, needed to be rescued was not just the masses but God as well:

They smell your mouth lest you might have uttered the word love
They smell your heart
These are bizarre times my darling!
And love . . . they tie to the lamppost on the roadside
   and flog
Hide love in a safe place![47]

Poems and songs were being burned. Smiles were "surgically removed" from the lips; even "canaries" were in danger of "being scorched" sitting on flowers, which were set ablaze in these bizarre times! As the triumphant devil was busy celebrating his dark victory, Shamlu closed the poem with "Hide God in a safe place!"[48]

In the poet's perception, *khuda* (God) of the old days as the embodiment of decency was defeated and victimized. Although mourning this symbolic loss of decency, Shamlu was not anxious to revive the old deity. What has escaped the critics' attention is that pieces of this shattered sacred were deliberately and consistently spread across Shamlu's poetic landscape. In other words, this markedly "secular" poet of our times, as this chapter demonstrates, was at the same time the most God conscious of his generation. The ongoing saga of love and hate with God continued to unfold in his poetry and animate his creative impulse. Life-changing conversations with this deity shaped the vocabulary, structure, and rhythm of living as well as that of writing poetry. There was restlessness and fluctuation in relating to this sacred, which itself changed with time. Not surprisingly, as the poet went through stages of his evolution, so did the ever-present deity. The complexities of this search for a meaningful sacred were not lost on Shamlu himself. In the poem *Safar* (Journey), which opens, and is punctuated, with "where is my place of worship," the poet embarks on a sea journey led by the prophet Noah in search of a mosque. Passing through a dead sea framed with a low gray horizon and covered with corpses, they arrive at a stormy sea interspersed with rocks that pierce through the surface and endanger the ship. The two seas allegorize the revolutionary uprising of a society that has been paralyzed under the weight of undemocratic rule. The journey ends in a serene and clear sea that rivals the sky with its moonlike silvery fish. With the poet's arrival in his final destination, an island enveloped in "eternal solitude," the reader is expected to have a vision of the peace and fulfillment that comes with social emancipation. This is the place of worship that our poet has sought throughout the journey and defined as *masjid-i man,* meaning "my mosque" or more literally "my place of prostration." In the poem, as he steps on this island of self-fulfillment, the journeyer prostrates himself to revere the sanctity of the island. There could have hardly been a more emphatic way to entwine social change and inner attainment. The poem also underlines the difficulty of the journey and the bewilderment in locating the island itself. In another sense, it allegorizes the open-ended struggle that is Shamlu's life and career.[49]

Summoning the Good God(s)

The kind and vulnerable God went through considerable poetic shape-shifting to fulfill a variety of roles. When a comrade fell in armed struggle, for example, God took the shape of his hands to underscore the value of taking action. Unfortunately for the poet, as well as for the needy and the oppressed, the deity shared their vulnerabilities. Worse still, it simply fled the scene when humans remained silent in the face of injustice.[50] In "The Poem from the Edge of Solitude," the poet comes across a number of worshiping women in black (this time arousing disgust in him). The women—presumably crying in ritual Shi'i mourning—listen to a preacher's message from a "killer and despotic God." As the evil god shows teeth and claws from the distance of the preacher's words, the poet summons his "kind and slaveless" deity. This is a god neither *jabr'kar* (tyrannical) nor *khauf'angiz* (frightening). Alas, he is exiled to the same realm of *inziva'i bi-umid* (hopeless solitude) to which the poet has been confined.[51]

The uneven distribution of power between the good and bad deities was replicated systematically across Shamlu's broader poetic landscape. As helpless sympathetic gods did little to improve the plight of humanity in its unending struggle against injustice, evil gods continued to serve despotic and corrupted forces on earth. *Hava-yi tazih,* first published in 1964, the collection that established Shamlu's undisputed position in modern Persian poetry, was infested with the curse, wrath, and malpractice of evil gods. These were either "alien gods" (*khudayan-i biganih*) who did not provide refuge for the needy or they were such despicable creatures whose "eternal curse" was more desirable than their paradise.[52] What Shamlu did in the face of the tyranny of the corrupted sacred at first seemed like an insignificant act of despair:

> I struck the anvil of my head
> With my heavy hands
> And moaned liked a God in chains.
> My loud cries spread like a storming herd of grasshoppers
>   Destroying the harvest of my happiness.[53]

There was, however, more to this cry of despair than it appeared in the first instance. The human moaning "like a God in chains" was not putting up an empty imitation of gods. S/he was destined to fill the cosmic vacuum left by fleeing good gods. In a gradual process that would be hard to chronologically document but numerous examples of which are found in his poetry, the moaning human continued to develop in godlike qualities to become *insan,* one of Shamlu's re-creations of the sacred. Insan was "God of all gods," "related to all gods," "the fountainhead of all seas," "a world onto itself," "a miracle," and at the same time "the devil that challenged and defeated God."[54] In short, the world was neither beautiful nor just until insan appeared "on the scene." As s/he thought about this *'adl-i dast'nayaftih* (unfulfilled justice), beauty was created (*ziba'i dar vujud amad*).[55] This insan was more developed, domesticated, victimized, and certainly more self-aware than the primitive man with whom Sepehri associated. Moreover, his/her presence was acknowledged more prominently, and his/her pains were discussed affectionately and in great detail. At times, such as in "The Ghazel of the Last Solitude," the plight of this suffering warrior for justice is recounted with such sympathy and admiration that one wonders as to who should be held responsible for the injustice.[56]

The story of the autonomy and glory of insan could, from one perspective, be seen as a continued celebration of humanism that had always been present in Persian literary consciousness. Khayyám, Hāfez, and many of their counterparts had concerned themselves with the fate of insan before the modern period. Shamlu's insan, however, demonstrated a paradoxical (though interesting) behavior worthy of special attention. While s/he appeared to challenge the power of God, this representative of sanctified humanity never demonstrated full autonomy. As the reader prepared to celebrate the uncontested reign of insan, something prevented insan from taking the final step of freeing himself completely from the old sacred. Still, the old gods—these supposedly defeated forces—continued to be subjected to long angry monologues. "Why so much anger against an outmoded imaginary being?" one might rightly ask. In Khayyám-like outbursts of discontent with creation, Shamlu often closed his praise for human struggle blaming gods for their unwillingness or inability to intervene. In "The Nocturnal Song for the Alleyways," he created a colorful epic of mass uprising in which his self-flagellation for not having joined the masses earlier punctuated the poem. As the poem drew to an end, Shamlu struggled to convince the reader that he had changed. He now wrote for "the prostitutes," "the bare-feet," "the diseased," and "the homeless." But most of all, he wrote "for those who no longer nursed any hopes in heavens."[57] If such passing sarcasm was not enough to get back at gods who had disappointed "the barefeet," he picked bigger fights. In *Ida dar ayinih,* otherwise celebrated for masterful examples of lyricism, Shamlu created a dark parody of lovemaking as a means of human instinctive reproduction. In a poem entitled "To a Skull," he put on the mantle of Hamlet and mocked the skull for its "philosophical" laughter at the folly that had come to be called life! The "true" story was simple, "the graveyards were hungry" and "the young trees had to be fed." This "simple" story, however, arose in our poet the regular angry feeling of being shortchanged. In the closing stanza, he directed the anger against God by mocking angel Israfil's "clumsy trumpet." On the supposed day of judgment, we were told, he would not move for the sound of the trumpet was too "unpleasant" to resurrect him.[58]

"Hurry, Nazarene! Hurry!"

Like most exaggerated poetic bipolarities, insan destined to be God and the dethroned khuda had more in common than their antagonistic relationship revealed at first. Each possessed strengths in areas that the other lacked. In a way, the two were each other's mirror images. God had a distanced and aloof disposition that kept him protected and at the same time alien to human condition. Insan, on the other hand, was vulnerable in the face of death, pain, and oppression, a condition that made him/her an easy target. God had an inflated self-image because he had been blindly obeyed from time immemorial. Insan, despite being the true miracle, had little confidence and self-appreciation. It made perfect sense for them to come together in the space in which an interface between khuda and insan could empower them both.

The site where the two seas came together could not be constructed with wholly new building blocks. Sacred making, as I have documented in the earlier chapters, depends on objects, processes, people, or concepts that are already resonant with large populations. As Shamlu accessed the fountainheads of human sacred heritage to recultivate the imagined expanse, time and again the same poetic answer emerged from the image he pieced together: the portrait of a prophet. Divine messengers were the historically vibrant constructs in whom sacred power and human action successfully met. They had many more virtues suitable for his poetic purposes. They were as susceptible to pain and oppression as were other humans. They made mistakes despite their sanctified positions. Above all, they represented a broad and colorful variety of personalities, styles, and temperaments. Through a consistent process of sacralization, aided with artful poetic reconstruction, insan was infused with the sacred impetus that gods no longer deserved to possess. A combination of borrowing and invention led to poetic birth of full-bloomed yet fresh prophets who assumed central roles in Shamlu's poetry. Obviously, the process did not entail linear and orderly stages of replacing the old disintegrating deity with the newly installed. Rather, in a commingling of the old and the new, as the remains of the subverted God continued to surface in many poems, and the vulnerable earthly insan made standard appearances, humans began to put on the mantle of the prophets and evolve into world-changing figures:

> The poem that is the life of insan
> Ends in a bloodied red rhyme
> Like Jesus crucified on the eternity of history.
>
> Insans, chained together, at the ankle
> Who write their history with the rhythm of their heartbeats,
> Are the world-conqueror apostles of a religion.[59]

Not all prophets, or their apostles, were such makers of history. Some, like Job, simply failed and lost their holiness through passivity and compliance.[60] Others remained unsuccessful, even after they had triumphed through long endurance. Some among them had braved torture and oppression:

Our holy scripture is the book of love and beauty
So the nightingales of kisses may sing on cercis trees
We wish the wretched blissful
The captive free
And the forlorn filled with hope
So the human divine lineage
And his eternal reign on earth is restored.

Alas, others following in the line had betrayed these values allowing the scriptures to be reduced to an empty praise of earlier martyrs.[61] The triumphs and failures of individual prophets, however, was not the most important justification for their existence. It was their transforming presence that made them indispensable. With the appearance of each prophet came the opportunity for stretching existing paradigms and redefining old norms. Even concepts such as failure and triumph themselves came to be understood in new lights. Insan could die and be completely defeated, but insan-turned-prophet borrowed the Abrahamic endurance of walking through flames and fashioning his own God. In the seminal poem "The Song of Abraham in Fire," which gave its title to the collection in which it appeared, the poet sang:

I was not a petty and compliant slave
My road to paradise did not pass through the cattle pasture of full
    surrender
I deserved a different God
One worthy of a creature
    —his existence not centered around begging the daily bread—
And a different God
I fashioned.[62]

This sanctified insan, this antiprophetic prophet empowered with the essence of a renewed sacred, possessed the strength not to "turn back" in defeat or "die." In its paradigmatic passage through the Jesus stage, insan acquired the immortality offered to Christ on the cross.

Although one of many prophets adopted by the poet, Jesus was the most prominent among them. Others prophets such as Moses, Abraham, and Noah did take center stage from time to time.[63] The crucified Jesus and the moment of his crucifixion, however, formed a continuous source of sacred energy surging frequently to revitalize Shamlu's poetic landscape. I pointed earlier in "The Death of the Nazarene" to the poet's retelling of the crucifixion into a tale of political terror and oppression. Here, instead of surveying Shamlu's prophetology as a whole, I continue to focus on the versatility and significance of the revived Jesus as a source of sacred making in Shamlu's poetry.

For Shamlu's Jesus, the road from crucifixion to immortality was neither short nor simple. Much poetic reconstruction was lavished on the details of the event. The poem *Mard-i maslub* (The Crucified Man) is a most interesting example. Once again, Shamlu did not call the prophet by his name 'Isa to avoid unwanted connotations.[64] Furthermore, frequent reference to "the crucified man" in the poem privileged crucifixion over and above other events in the life of the prophet. In contrast to "Death of the Nazarene," in which the injustice of the authorities and the ignorance of the crowds had been magnified, here the full focus was on the enormous physical pain that overpowered the body of "the crucified man." The poem itself was divided into segments echoing the disjoined thoughts of the prophet mirroring his wounded body. The thoughts went through his head as he regained momentary consciousness, and his body hanged from the cross "heavy as the earth" tearing the "live wounds on his palms." Thus the crucified prophet cried:

> Lighten my burden father!
> Help me pass through this threshold of pain!
> Immortality—offended and belittled—
> Running restless between mountains and seas
> In the boundless expanse of his being, cried:
> "Do not moan in vain!
> I will devour you to make you mine
> Endure the pain!"[65]

The poem was more than a glorification of endurance achieved through pain. Fresh nuances and complications were introduced into the narrative of crucifixion including a new conspiratorial exchange. As the prophet gave in to pain in the hope of embracing eternity, pain and immortality held hands and celebrated their victory through his destruction. Here, Shamlu left his most original mark on the plot by reading the mind of the suffering prophet who moments before his death doubted having earned any glory at all. The image of his head bent in pain and sorrow formed the iconic foundation on which an entire religion was built. Still, immortality shared the pain of the prophet to the point that it spread its black veil on the mourning followers kneeling down in silence. The story had been turned against itself subverting its most conventional message: the ascent of Jesus to heavens. Yet, the crucified man had triumphed. He had triumphed in his sincere pain and loneliness and, above all, in his last-minute courage to face the "truth" of his own vulnerability. If he did not possess godly powers to transport him to the safety of heavens, he had instead his human weakness, which he wore like a crown on his wounded forehead. So important was the downfall of this earthly prophet that the earth trembled, the storm rose in rebellion, and the sun hid his face.[66]

The triumph of the dedicated and sincere prophet—despite his misunderstood death—was not a new or passing theme. As early as 1960, in one of his longest self-portrayals, Shamlu had compared his own perseverance in building the edifice of his poetry to that of Jesus. He shouldered the burden of his own words, we were told, but not like those who betrayed their brothers and sisters to serve their executioners. Rather, he carried the weight of these poetic building blocks, although they formed his prison, as the son of Mary had carried his own cross. To dispel any doubts we may harbor about the sacralizing purpose of the comparison, he closed the poem by describing himself as "a word, blowing within the majestic storm of history."[67] Shamlu recognized, and deeply revered, the sacred as well as the poetic reservoir he had discovered in the concurrently vulnerable and triumphant Jesus. He exerted authorial discretion in recontextualizing the prophetic narrative directing its sacred energy into carefully selected junctures in ancient or modern history. Shamlu's boldness in rearticulating the tale of Jesus is none other than revolutionary in its freshness as well as in the social ideals it pursued. When placing him in the modern context, Shamlu stripped the prophet of patience, endurance, and surrender. To become an advocate for social change, modern Jesus was empowered and invigorated with action and agency:

> Here I am
> —having pulled the nails out of my palms with teeth—
> Standing on fallen cross
> As tall as a loud cry![68]

Jesus is only one of Shamlu's re-created prophets. The full range of divine messengers utilized in his poetry brings together a spectrum of colorful and adventurous explorations that deserve a separate study. The main achievement in these poetic articulations of the past is not limited to borrowing the prophets' sanctity and resonance. The process of importing this sanctity into the contemporary space and grafting it on the poet's personal vision is equally impressive.

"I Am Your Name! Do Not Misunderstand My Meaning": Toward Reconciliation

As Shamlu went through years of maturation and growth, his multifaceted poetry began to display a sense of peace and contentment unprecedented for his fiery temperament. This was not because he now had a more optimistic take on the social conditions that he had been fighting to improve, or because he had abandoned the desire to change the world. Rather, he seemed to have found the bridge that connected the seemingly irreconcilable. Good and evil, oppressor and oppressed, heaven and earth no longer appeared total aliens to one another. The prophets had been a major source of sacred making in his poetry and the site in which insan and khuda had met in peace to evolve together. In his early years, whenever he had reached for a direct dialogue with the sacred par excellence, the source of all life, doubt and anger had transformed the "conversation" into a statement of denial and accusation. It was time for less anger and more gratitude, for peace and respect to find their way into the dialogue with heavens.

Shamlu made one of his major attempts at reconciliation with the sacred, the force of regeneration at the heart of life, in a poem composed in 1985 and named *Ashti* (Reconciliation).[69] The poem opened with insan's grievance spoken directly to God. You created the oceans vast and deep, said s/he, and the mountains gloriously tall and strong, yet neither had any self-awareness. But I, continued insan, was created to be nothing but "a mote devoid of glory," begging for my survival, fearful of your wrath. You created me ashamed, bewildered, and finite. How magnificent can your divine glory be, if I am the best of all that you have created? Up to this point the poem had displayed no difference from dozens of previous angry dialogues. Here, however, something totally unprecedented took place, something of the nature of a breakthrough. God, who had so far existed only in the hollow acts of worship performed by unquestioning believers, spoke with a voice of his own. Do not misread the creation, he warned insan, you are not the "floating darkness" of the oceans or the "absolute rigidity" of the mountains. You have partaken of the wine of *farzanigi* (wisdom). All existence finds meaning in your presence. In this seminal poem in which a new face of the sacred was unveiled, Shamlu introduced a resonant Qur'anic note into the exchange. To be sure, the allusion was given a Shamlucan subversive twist. Still, it maintained its Qur'anic significance. In an account of the creation of Adam in the second chapter of the Qur'an, God had taught him "the names" of things. Shamlu's God closed the dialogue with a phrase that reversed the process: "I am your name," God said. "Do not misunderstand my meaning!"[70]

In the above exchange Shamlu's perception of the sacred took a significant turn. It demonstrated an equally prominent development in his portrayal of insan. In the struggles to change undesirable social conditions, in the battles with forces beyond his control, and in attempts to make sense of what lay beyond, insan had developed into a fuller being. Yes, he still trembled at the thought of his total dependence on the world that surrounded him. But he was older, quieter, humbler, less certain of his judgments, and more at peace with the sacred. He had come a long way.

This peace, humility, and expansion of the horizons of insan found its most eloquent expression in the poem *Dar astanih* (At the Threshold), one of Shamlu's master works, published in 1997.[71] The poem captured a moment that contained a short glance at the past and a long look at what lay beyond. You arrive at a small door, he told his readers, which opens when the time is right, and you pass through. Shamlu encoded this simple moment into a deep and moving encounter with death. As language was sculpted into pun after pun to add layers of meaning, the poem, in its fullness, defies translation. For example, one had to be *frutan* (humble), literally "small figured," to pass through the threshold. The process of final judgment was to be attributed to no judge other than time, so the word *davari* (judgment) found echo in the word *advar* (time cycles), which flanked it. As each human soul fell like a drop into the dark ocean beyond, words were repeated to echo the rippling effect. These are just a few details in a poem that deserves a full independent reading. I here present a brief reading focused on the central concern of the present work, the sacred.

Dancing through the Threshold of Compulsion

Of activities controlled by rules and regulations, dancing is one that maintains its liberating quality. Rhythm can infuse with ecstasy the very structure of control. Shamlu borrowed the metaphor to enliven his passing through *astanih-yi ijbar* (the threshold of compulsion) with personal rhythm:

> Farewell!
> Farewell (says Bamdad, the poet)
> I pass dancing through the threshold of compulsion
> Happy and thankful.[72]

In what follows, I argue that Shamlu choreographed on sacred tunes—traditional and otherwise—the "dance" that was to take him to the other side of compulsion *shadmanih u shakir* (happy and thankful). He introduced the first sacred note, through the resonant Sufi trope of the mirror within, even before the door opened. "You can be a well-polished mirror," he said, so you look within and see that you are groomed properly to enter. Though the presence of standard players such as the spirits and the saints was emphatically denied, a nostalgic plea for judgment rang through the poem and envisioned the ultimate judge wearing the robe of time:

> But there sits a judge on the other side of the door
> —not in the ominous mantel that the judges wear—
> His nature made with intelligence and fairness
> His appearance in the shape of time.
>
> Your memory will, for ever, be judged
> In the passage of time.

The following stanza, dealing with the evolution of life, traced the journey of insan from objectified existence to agency of perception and finally to becoming the agent observer. This perception and awareness brought meaning to the world that was unaware of its own existence. Although there were no direct quotes, in Shamlu's stages of human development rang a celebrated passage from the *Masnavi* of Rūmī.[73]

When, due to the same awareness, insan was finally born in the form of responsibility (*tajassud-i vazifih*), his abilities were vast and impressive among them, the ability to love and to be loved, to hear, to see, to speak, and to laugh. Here Shamlu inserted a resonant sacred note, this time borrowed directly from the Qur'an. According to verse seventy-two from the chapter *Ahzab* in the Qur'an, insan had carried the divine trust that the heavens and the earth had failed to carry. Hāfez had later echoed the Qur'anic assertion adding his own twist to the Qur'anic one. Shamlu now included among the dozen characteristics that insan had "*tavan-i jalil-i bi-dush'burdan-i bar-i amanat*" (the magnificent ability to shoulder the weight of the *trust*).[74]

What followed in the poem was a plaintive and personal plea for opening the human horizons with freedom and movement. This poet of liberty and social struggle, as he has often been called, remained loyal to the ideal of freedom even in his farewell statement:

> I walked through the occasion that was my life
> We walked through the occasion that was our lives
> Silenced
> Hands tied behind the back
> And we saw the world
> Through the narrow eyes
>   of the crack in the wall of wickedness.
> Here it is, now, the small door
> And the waiting doorman's signals.[75]

Now that it was all coming to an end, standing at the threshold, he was neither restless nor angry. His poetry had celebrated the growth and dignity of insan for over half a century. He had not been hindered by sanctity of tradition or fear of controversy. Indeed, he had thrived on being unpredictable and controversial. While devoting much of his creative energy to political activism and social change, he had given modern Persian poetry some of its most lyrical and passionate examples. He had been as unpredictable when it came to the poetic process of sacred making. Denouncing the conventional God and rebelling against unquestioning conformation, he had peopled his landscape with prophets who were retelling their tales in his idiom. Twentieth-century Persian poetry had produced the second Omar Khayyám, one who had made the sacred spacious enough to have room for his cries of uncertainty and discontent. This was cause for celebration and Shamlu knew that. So "the tired Bamdad" ended the "short and tiring journey" dancing through the threshold of compulsion on a warm and humble note of gratitude:

> It was unique and lacked nothing
> I am humbly grateful.[76]

Epilogue
An Infinite Basket for Infinite Fruits—Methodological Conclusions

It would be appropriate to end with a Sepehrian metaphor, infinite fruits and the kind of basket needed to carry them home from the market. The past chapters have uncovered sacred elements in unforeseen configurations thriving in their poetic environment. It may be said that the metaphor of fruit and basket introduce a note of objectification and something of the old duality of content and form into a discussion that has been about a dynamic and mutually enriching relation between poetry and the sacred. I should hasten to add that this is no ordinary fruit basket but one in which the borders between the container and the contained are crossed frequently. This monograph is a testimony to the unlimited possibilities of color and taste in ripening fruits of the sacred and an indication of the equally infinite nature and function of the basket itself. To catch a mere glimpse of the rich possibilities and the changes, however, Sepehri's word of advice is in order once more:

> *chishm'ha ra bayad shust,*
> *Jur-i digar bayad did*
> [Eyes need to be washed
> For the manner to see has to change].[1]

And so, to "wash the eyes" and to be on the lookout for new paradigms is the first methodological conclusion arising from this study of modern Persian poetry in search of the new faces of the sacred. These faces once appeared behind the multi-layered and ornamented veils of Qur'anic allusions and through colorful parables in biographies of intoxicated friends of God. They now appear in the Qur'anic rhythm of celebrating the uniqueness of a leaf under a twentieth-century willow tree or in the wounded palm of the poet/prophet who pulls the nail out of his hands with his teeth to descend the cross and lead a revolution for social change.

The new "manner to see" reveals the old themes losing currency in a most gradual fashion as they witness the jelling of the freshly arrived. While they finally fade into the background and leave the stage to the new, there is nothing episodic, disconnected, or fully novel in the paradigm shift. Continuity of stabilizing and resonant elements is a key feature of this changing scene, as is tolerance for seem-ingly outmoded components. Ironically, leaning against the old for support is a dominant characteristic of the forward-looking process of renewal. When Far-rokhzad unites with the spring in an erotic human union with nature, she echoes Shirin's bathing scene, although she has appropriated the male gaze—a preroga-tive of Khusraw in the classical version—and made it hers.[2] The sexually potent feminine that gradually emerges in her work is then—in her later collection *Tavalludi digar* (Another Birth)—able to make a cradle out of her love to mother a new Jesus. It is fascinating that in order to mother Jesus she does not have to silence the erotic but rather sacralize and celebrate its liveliness and vigor. Again, Qur'anic/biblical echoes of immaculate birth keep her connected to the past even as she travels in search of the sacred to "the fragrant core of a fertilized egg."[3] And so, here is a second observation of methodological significance: the outmoded is not omitted. It is very much present as the backdrop effecting the resonance and resolution of every image.

The intertextual nature of the evolution of the sacred comes to the fore read-ily with the present study. The evidence is plentiful, ranging from the allusions mentioned above to direct thematization, as is the case for example with the revival of Hallāj by Shafi'i-Kadkani to be a main protagonist once more. From a chronological perspective as well, the process of sacred making spreads across the twentieth century—which is the focus of the present study—prior to and follow-ing the 1979 Islamic Revolution. The linguistic embeddedness of the process of reimagining the sacred, together with its strong intertextual resonance across time and space, urges us to remain mindful of a third methodological issue: freeing our imagination from rigid and limiting categories such as "religious" and/or "secu-lar." If all the nuances of interaction with the sacred, and the attempts to reshape it explored in the present volume, were to be qualified as secular, then secular would have to be defined in many different—and often conflicting—terms. The category is clearly inadequate. It serves the limited purpose of excluding a small range of writings, which adopt a literalist conventional approach to worship and devotion. At the same time it fails to differentiate or explain the wide variety of thoughts and practices that remain under its rubric because all they have in com-mon is that they fall outside the conventional limits. If we remain loyal to "secu-lar" as a category of analysis, a wealth of shades and nuances unrecognized by the conventional norms of sacred making is lost on us completely.[4]

Realizing the superficiality—and limited use—of categories such as "secular" or "religious" suggests a fourth methodological conclusion: the necessity for open-ing up the study of making and celebrating the sacred to disciplines other than scriptural analysis. While the study of the scriptures will always remain significant in so far as it provides a very specific vantage point, the present volume alone docu-ments the range of possibilities that open before us the instant we reach out to new disciplinary domains. Literature, and in the present study poetry, offer especially important and nuanced perspectives.

The many insights gained from the poets in this volume support Richard Rorty's suggestion that in freeing oneself of old traditions, poetry is a great ally to hermeneutics. Whether it is Shafi'i-Kadkani's retelling of the prophetic nocturnal journey or Sepehri's conversion of a minaret into a cypress tree, our poets confirm his view that poetry has a strong tendency to "create and appreciate new ways of acting and speaking." The present work is replete with examples of the willingness of poetry to explore unfamiliar territory in search of the sacred by reinterpreting our "familiar surroundings" in exciting "unfamiliar terms" of new inventions.[5] It demonstrates that twentieth-century Persian writers took the tradition through a colorful process of inventing and rearticulating the desire for the sacred as they encoded their fresh poetic messages. The possibilities that poetry opened before them had everything to do with their success in these inventions.

One clear advantage of using literature to better understand concepts such as the sacred is that in literature the linguistic embeddedness of the construct, which carries its fine connections to a multitude of personal and communal matters in the culture, is foregrounded. The awareness of the linguistic complexities of the construct, and the manner in which the poet articulates it, provides a rare opportunity for attention to fine nuances. For example, Sepehri and Farrokhzad both use natural elements as building blocks to piece together the sacred, which becomes their place of refuge from stagnation, the harshness that has come with modern life, or slavish submission to technology. Their poems, however, reveal two completely different views of nature to us. Sepehri's nature is remote, pure, and venerable. The temple that Sepehri makes with pieces from this nature is equally holy and remote. It is a utopia dreaming of which mesmerizes and allures the reader. Farrokhzad's nature, on the other hand, is the garden in which she plants her hands for swallows to lay their eggs "in the hollow of her ink-stained fingers." The temple she builds with pieces from this nature is a sanctuary for life, a place in which she and the trees go through the same seasons of drought. It is also a place in which she can travel to the fragrant core of a fertilized egg or conceive by the moon. This nature is messy, human, and within reach. So is the pulsating sacred that guards this sanctuary for life. This brief comparison illustrates the need for the last methodological modification, which I just suggested. Scriptural studies may be the most obvious and direct road to unveiling faces of the sacred, but unless we take the untrodden roads of literary (and other disciplinary) studies, many more faces of the sacred will remain veiled.

As always, making proper use of poetry requires familiarity with its generic norms and conventions. To decode the puzzles pieced together in these poems and to capture a glimpse of the sacred as it is shaped and reshaped is as perilous as it is delightful. For if in this world of make-believe things were always what they seemed, poetry would have ceased to be the transforming magic that it is. Appearances, therefore, are and are not most important! Let us take Shamlu's example. He spends most of his poetic career fighting to bring about the awareness and will for social change. So great is his desire to instigate in the reader the self-will for liberating the society and liberalizing the mind that he is ready to convert his poetic resilience into guns in the hands of freedom fighters and gallows to hang those unwilling to face change. Yet Shamlu does not attain his poetic status due to the overt political functionalism of the kind displayed in *Shi'ri ki zindagist,* or because of his increasing frustration with the fading tradition, which he accuses of inertia and lack of originality. He earns the recognition for his rare ability to remain rooted in vital areas of the tradition while having the courage and skill to revise and refashion the same tradition without mercy. Aside from pruning the old, and despite the anxiety to reshape poetry into a useful tool for social reform, Shamlu will go down in history as having given twentieth-century Iran some of its finest examples of love lyrics ever produced in Persian language. The mirror that finds and reflects in Ida's lips *zirafat-i shi'r* (the intricacy of poetry) is a testimony to the achievements of a poet who did not sacrifice his heart to join the masses in their struggle.[6]

In chapters 1 to 3 of the present work, I provide a more general overview of issues. I use these chapters as a kind of open landscape if you like, in which to lay out many examples from East and West, as well as premodern and modern, and provide the larger context necessary for making sense of the specific points that I discuss in the three chapters that follow. As the writing of the book progressed, however, it became increasingly clear that I needed to move from these generals toward more specificity so as to focus the ideas and provide more tangible examples. This is the main reason why I chose specific poets to be the focus of chapters 4 to 6. I hope these chapters are understood as more than tributes to these individual poets, although I have intended them to be in part a tribute as well. There is no question that the current critical writing in English would benefit from a more intimate familiarity with the tremendously rich poetic legacy left to us by Farrokhzad, Sepehri, and Shamlu. Yet, personal achievements aside, the works of these poets have become culminations in the complex and gradual processes of paradigm shift that can be best understood through specific examples. These chapters, therefore, do not just celebrate the significance of the works of these individuals but also the paradigmatic and representative aspects of their contributions.

The current study is not a historical survey. It does not seek to provide a full overview of the development of trends and ideas in modern Persian poetry, much less in modern Persian literature. Historical surveys can of course remain thematically focused but they would be obliged to provide a more comprehensive range of the trends prominent in the periods they cover. I have chosen instead to focus on the plurality of the poetic expressions of the sacred and to demonstrate the misconceived nature of attempts in this regard that remain limited to conventional themes and disciplinary methodologies. As a result, a wide range of traditional approaches to the veneration and/or poetic celebration of the sacred in twentieth-century Iran are not included in the present study. Noteworthy among these are the writings of the poets who came to prominence after the 1979 revolution. Most such poets devote their talents to new poetic explorations of what they perceive as the hitherto unacknowledged revolutionary messages of the Qur'anic and hadith literature.[7]

While not a comprehensive documentation of the poetic achievements in twentieth-century Iran, this work, I hope, nonetheless unveils a fresh, nuanced, and multifaceted face of many Iranian intellectuals/poets. These are figures often not adequately represented in the current literary critical writing in English. For example, I hope to have shown that the intricacies of Sepehri's poetic creativity is indicative of a figure more robust than the passive nature mystic often presented as not doing much more than meditating in his ivory tower. Side by side with the gentleness of his nature-loving tendencies, he possessed the desire and the will to tame nature and to reshape key mystical concepts. Roaming around a re-envisioned nature, he then encoded his fresh mystical message with poetic precision. Similarly, I hope to have uncovered the sacred-loving and prophet-oriented dimensions of Shamlu's confrontational and God-challenging poetic instinct. At the same time, I hope to have brought out in my readings of his poems the Khayyámian doubts and hesitations that are the hallmark of his engagement with the sacred. From this perspective, Shamlu's anger transforms into a deeply inquisitive mode of interaction seeking insight through direct challenge and confrontation. In Farrokhzad's case, her courage and frankness in owning her sexuality has already been admired and talked about by critics.[8] I hope to have added a new perspective by offering a fresh way of understanding this dimension of her poetic contribution. Among other things, I have looked at the specific manners in which she has translated the potency of her feminine sexuality into the site for the rebirth of the displaced sacred, the safe haven to which the "dove of faith" can return.

In placing the focus of the last three chapters of the present work on the writings of these individual poets, I have pursued another specific methodological objective. I have attempted to foreground the human agency and underline the concurrent historicity as well as subjectivity in the art of poetic sacred making. True, social and historical conditions have everything to do with the ways in which human beings perceive—and express their perception of—the sacred. At the same time, their individuality and human agency cannot be excluded from the discussion when it comes to specific ways in which they choose to engage the sacrosanct presence. I hope to have demonstrated, by focusing on these three prominent poets, that while the social and political contexts in which they wrote are highly significant, their personal contributions should not be underestimated. There-fore, while keeping us aware of the emergence of new paradigms, I have main-tained an equally strong focus on the poets as important players who bring their individual tastes and talents to bear on the intricacy of the poetic messages they encode. Farrokhzad's sensitivity to the nuances of gender and sexuality in the human interaction with the sacred is a good example. Clearly, conditions of modernity are the important catalyst in empowering her to articulate her femi-nine desire for living fully and building a sanctuary for life. At the same time, it is her highly personal style of reaching out and mingling with vital forces in this sanctuary that expands the process beyond providing a safe haven for the "dove of faith." At the peak of this transforming process, Farrokhzad's body becomes the sanctuary in which the sacred and the erotic meet to empower each other. Indeed, she enables us to rethink Veikok Anttonen's notion of set-apartness, which he has presented as one of the three defining characteristic of the sacred in his sur-vey.[9] In Farrokhzad's poetic articulation of the sacred, the features of life-giving and growth, which are also acknowledged by Anttonen, remain central, while set-apartness is downplayed to the point of elimination. Clearly, Farrokhzad's own gender—and personal cosmological positioning of her womanhood—have much to do with her ability to experience the kind of close encounter that she has with the sacred and that she shares with us. Her tremendous poetic achievement is a mix of sociohistorical conditions and a subjective readiness for courageous per-sonal self-exploration.

It is neither possible nor desirable to sum up in this epilogue every implica-tion that the present study of poetic sacred making might have for new ways of re-envisioning the sacred. I hope the implications are many, and that future stud-ies will start where these chapters end while adding new perspectives and further refining the methodological approach. I would like to end the epilogue, and with it the book, by pointing to three specific observations as direct and significant outcomes of this study. These concluding observations pertain to my perception of the nature of the sacred and are offered as additions to the defining features outlined in Veikok Anttonen's survey of the sacred. I have discussed his summary of these defining features in the second chapter and also earlier in this epilogue.

First, my exploration of poetic sacred making in twentieth-century Iran, brought together in the present volume, suggests the addition of a fourth defin-ing characteristic for the concept of the sacred. This is the inherent *tendency for expansion.* Whether it is in its most traditional Qur'anic manifestation as the "light of the heavens and the earth," the liberating acts of Shamlu's prophets, or Sepehri's "call to start," and "the expanse of green," the sacred is perceived and presented as an expansive force that defies any demand for interpretation. While this expansive nature brings an elusive quality to the concept and makes it diffi-cult to define, it is not identical with the concept of *transcendence.* What makes it different from transcendence is the strong tendency it has toward physicality and the interface with daily matters. In Sepehri's landscape, where shadows of elm trees expand and flow to eternity, cows graze in the nearby pasture. Similarly, the infinite fruits that overflow his basket, and wear the robe of Buddhist monks, stay on the lunch table. In both these cases, the expansive sacred maintains its tangible physical dimension. At the same time, the expansiveness serves a clear ontological purpose by perpetuating itself through inviting and encouraging possibilities of rearticulation. A comparison can help illustrate the difference between the well-established notion of the transcendence of the sacred and the tendency for expansion I am suggesting here. A good example of the transcendence of the sacred in Persian poetry is ʿAttār's legendary bird simurgh. In *Conference of the Birds* a group of birds come together and travel in search of their legendary king simurgh. The simurgh keeps expanding in the experience of the birds that look for him, and at the same time keeps the birds searching by appearing to them in a different guise every instant. The readers of the tale too have, for centuries, expanded their perceptions of the truth that the simurgh represents. It is safe to say, on the basis of our literary evidence, that the rearticulated sacred retains this expansive tendency and defies finality. At the same time, ʿAttār's simurgh lacks the physicality that enables the "shadow of the elm tree" or the "basket of fruit" to stay close to a grazing cow or sit on the lunch table and be a part of everyday life.

Merging and mingling is a fifth characteristic that these poems add to Anttonen's defining characteristics of the sacred. Things of this world are not restless to overflow, to mingle with everything within their reach, and to transform them. They do not necessarily have a great impact on one another or on us. But the beauty of Sepehri's sacralized nature pulls us to the nameless unknown, and the shadow of his elm tree flows to eternity. The moon by which Farrokhzad can conceive a new Jesus spreads to merge with the trees that shed their bark in the sleepy garden. The thirst for mingling is equally great at the receiving end:

> Now windows see themselves opened
> to pleasant scattered perfumes again
> trees in the sleeping garden all shed their bark again
> and the earth's myriad of pores
> suck down the atoms of the moon.[10]

It is ironic, and fascinating, that the sacred in most belief systems is perceived to be simple and pure, yet its poetic articulations express its sanctity in terms of numerous merging and mingling. Further exploration of this paradoxical coexistence of simplicity and plurality of the sacred may reveal it to be another manifestation of the linguistic embeddedness of the construct. Perhaps the question should not be posed in terms of a possible paradoxical coexistence between simplicity and plurality of the sacred. Rather, it should be directed at the poetic aspects of the processes of sacred making and the reasons why these processes rely for sacralization of the mundane on merging and mingling. The emergent sacred is always a result of such merging. Human sexuality and the sacred, nature and the sacred, and revolutionary warrior and the sacred are among the more distinct instances of the newly sacralized that I have discussed in the last three chapters. In all these mergers, the sacred quality expands and infuses its mundane companion, who subsequently acquires his/her own independent sacred identity. Obviously, the third and fourth characteristics of the sacred, the expansive nature and tendency to merge and mingle, are interrelated.

Finally, the findings of the present study make another point clear. The human tendency to institutionalize acts of sacred making and bring them under tight control is perhaps the result of an acute awareness that, as these poetic examples indicate, the process by nature defies control and remains perpetual. Indeed, encounter with social change, which appears to displace the notion of the sacred, is itself a most productive catalyst in starting a new phase of sacred making. True, it usually ignites the need, and therefore the processes of redefinition and re-presentation of the sacred, which disturb a number of believers to begin with. However, almost always a vast majority of sacred-lovers appear to welcome the opportunity to open the horizons and allow the expansive tendencies inherent in the construct to come to play. The ways the expansion and redefinition play out exactly has to be understood case by case in their cultural embeddedness and full historicity. While time and space have much to do with these fine processes, the perpetual acts of construction and reconstruction of the sacred rely heavily on human agency, and on being acted out in ritualistic communal settings. These acts are often fully, or partially, linguistic.

We come to terms with social change only when our very personal sacred sanctions the change. Emboldened by the change, we utter the sacred in new and changing terms. The revitalized sacred then consoles us in its new habitat and through its newly acquired language. We listen, learn to come to terms with more change, and rearticulate our sacred once more. Perhaps Shamlu had a similar eternity in mind when he said to Ida:

> I place a mirror facing your mirror
> That is how I expand you to eternity.[11]

Notes

CHAPTER 1

1. "Imaginative struggle with language" was coined by Robert Detweiler as an alternative to application of "uncompromising categories" to make sense of what he described as "the infinite complexity and subtlety of language." See his *Story, Sign, and Self: Phenomenology and Structuralism as Literary Critical Methods* (Philadelphia: Fortress Press, 1978), 3.

2. This pressure is particularly high on scholars of Islam. They have to demonstrate emotional freedom from belief as well as opposition to violence. In her discerning essay on the post–September 11 Western project to "rescue" Afghan women, Lila Abu-Lughod observes that writing about Islam and Muslim women requires a particularly high level of denouncing the harm done by Islamic movements around the world for the writer not to be accused of being an apologist for the religion. "There never seems to be a parallel demand for those who study secular humanism and its projects, despite the terrible violences that have been associated with it over the last couple of centuries, from world wars to colonialism, from genocides to slavery." "Do Muslim Women Really Need Saving? Anthropological Reflections on Cultural Relativism and its Others," *American Anthropologist* 104, no. 3 (2002): 388.

3. Robert Detweiler, "Vexing the Text: The Politics of Literary-Religious Interpretation," *Christianity and Literature* 41, no. 1 (1995): 66.

4. From the long poem "The Footsteps of Water." Suhrab Sepehri, *Hasht kitab* (Tehran: Kitab'khanah-'i Tahuri, 1358/1979), 272–73.

5. Timothy Fitzgerald, *The Ideology of Religious Studies* (New York: Oxford University Press, 2000), x, 3–4.

6. Greg Salyer, "Reading with Abandon, Writing to Play: The Work of Robert Detweiler," *Religious Studies Review* 28, no. 3 (July 2002): 209.

7. Ibid., 210.

8. James Elkins, *What Painting Is: How to Think about Oil Painting, Using the Language of Alchemy* (New York: Routledge, 2000), 5.

9. The categories "religious" and "spiritual" are as contested as God or the Sacred. Since defining the religious or spiritual impulse in twentieth-century Persian poetry is the overall aim of the present discussion, I have decided to keep the spirit of search alive by avoiding rigid definitions as far as possible. In the following chapter, I provide a broad working definition for the Sacred. I use *spiritual* to denote a less structured and more individualized species of "religious."

10. This is not to underestimate the valuable contributions of a handful of critics such as Ahmad Karimi-Hakkak, *Recasting Persian Poetry: Scenarios of Poetic Modernity in Iran* (Salt Lake City: University of Utah Press, 1995).

11. For an account of this revolution, see Ervand Abrahamian, *Iran between Two Revolutions* (Princeton, N.J.: Princeton University Press, 1982). For an analytical reading, see Nikki Keddie, *Roots of Revolution: An Interpretive History of Modern Iran* (New Haven: Yale University Press, 1981). I expand on this topic in chapter 3.

12. Karimi-Hakkak, *Recasting Persian Poetry,* 58–59.

13. Keddie, *Roots of Revolution,* 183. Keddie's categorization is contested by the presence of figures such as Ali in works such as Roy Mottahedeh's *The Mantle of the Prophet* (New York: Pantheon Books, 1985). Furthermore, figures such as Ali Shari'ati, who exerted formative influence in the 1979 Iranian revolution, were rooted in both the elitist intellectual and the religious tradition. See Abdulaziz Sachedina, "Ali Shar'iati: Ideologue of the Iranian Revolution," in *Voices of Resurgent Islam,* ed. John L. Esposito (New York: Oxford University Press, 1983), 191–214.

14. To give one example, it is considered normal for a collection of Shamlu's poetry to be distributed in ten thousand copies and reach a seventh or eighth edition in a decade.

15. Continuity is a major theme emerging in Karimi-Hakkak's pioneering study of Iranian literary modernity discussed earlier. See *Recasting Persian Poetry,* chapters 1 and 2.

16. Ninian Smart, *Religion and the Western Mind* (Albany: State University of New York Press, 1987), 8.

17. Mohammad Tavakoli-Targhi, "Refashioning Iran: Language and Culture during the Constitutional Revolution," *Iranian Studies* 23, no. 1–4 (1991): 77–101.

18. Fatemeh Keshavarz, "The Call to Prayer from the Cypress Tree: Modernity and Redefining the Spiritual in Persian Poetry," *Religion and Literature* 29, no. 1 (Spring 1997): 17–42.

19. Rudolf J. Siebert, *The Critical Theory of Religion: The Frankfurt School* (Berlin: Mouton, 1985), 28–32. I do not focus here on the work of the skeptics because this book focuses on artwork affected by emotions resulting from acknowledgment of the religious/spiritual phenomenon. In his discussion of Habermas's criticism of instrumental rationality, Rudolf Siebert refers to Professor R. Ulrich's pain-aggression study on rats. During these experiments, which were conducted from 1964 to 1974 in the psychology department of Western Michigan University at Kalamazoo, rats exposed to six hundred volts of electricity demonstrated extremely aggressive behavior under severe pain. Professor Ulrich later stopped the experiment stating that the acquired data did not add to common knowledge and its only value was in its "scientific certainty."

20. Hartmut Scheible, "Max Horkheimer's frühe und späte Aufzeichnungen," *Frankfurter Hefte* 33, no. 6 (June 1978): 50–54.

21. Robert Penn Warren made these comments in a 1976 interview with Bill Moyers. Quoted in Robert S. Koppelman, *Robert Penn Warren's Modernist Spirituality* (Columbia: University of Missouri Press, 1995), 3.

22. Forugh Farrokhzad, *Harf'ha'i ba,* radio interview by Hasan Hunarmandi. Ahmad Shamlu, *Hava-yi tazah* (Tehran: Intisharat-i zamanih, 1372/1994), 89.

23. Antonio R. Damasio, *Descartes' Error* (New York: G. P. Putnam, 1994), xv–xvi. Joseph LeDoux's study *The Emotional Brain: The Mysterious Underpinnings of Emotional Life* (New York: Simon and Schuster, 1996) is quoted extensively in William E. Connolly's thoughtful essay "Refashioning the Secular," in *What's Left of Theory? New York on the Politics of Literary Theory,* ed. Judith Butler, John Gillory, and Kendall Thomas (New York: Routledge, 2000), 164.

24. Antonio R. Damasio is M. W. Van Allen Professor of Neurology and head of the Department of Neurology at the University of Iowa College of Medicine in Iowa City. He is internationally recognized for his research on neurology of vision, memory, and language and also for his contributions to the elucidation of Alzheimer's diseases. The center that he and his wife have created at Iowa is acknowledged as the leading facility for the investigation of neurological disorders of mind and behavior.

25. Obviously, Sigmund Freud referred to this kind of anxiety rather than a paralyzing incurable disease when he described religion as a "collective anxiety neurosis." He did, however, search for the roots of this anxiety predominantly in the dynamics of infantile repression. *The Future of an Illusion,* trans. W. D. Robson-Scott (New York: Liveright, 1949), 14.

26. Kamran Talattof's *The Politics of Writing in Iran: A History of Modern Persian Literature* (Syracuse, N.Y.: Syracuse University Press, 2000) is a good example of ignoring the impact of religion. While I do not wish to reduce Talattof's contribution to a single issue, it is remarkable that he describes writing in twentieth-century Iran as a "secular" act.

27. Smart, *Religion and the Western Mind,* 8.

28. Thomas S. Kuhn, *The Structure of Scientific Revolution* (Chicago: University of Chicago Press, 1970).

29. Ibid.

30. This view is expressed by J. Samuel Preus in *Explaining Religion: Criticism and Theory from Bodin to Freud* (New Haven: Yale University Press, 1987), xi. For a definition of the preparadigmatic state, see Kuhn, *The Structure of Scientific Revolution,* 175–78. For a discussion of Hans-Georg Gadamer's view of human experience, see Georgia Warnke, *Gadamer: Hermeneutics, Tradition, and Reason* (Stanford, Calif.: Stanford University Press, 1987), 26.

31. Preus, *Explaining Religion,* 161.

32. Emile Durkheim, *The Elementary Forms of Religious Life,* trans. J. W. Swain (New York: Free Press, 1965), 87.

33. Freud, *The Future of an Illusion,* 14, 74.

34. Ibid., 9–11, 24, 26, 34.

35. Ibid., 27, 43.

36. Ibid., 51–55.

37. Nasir al-Din Sahibzamani, *Khatt-i sivvum: Dar barah-yi shakhsiyyat, sukhanan, va andishah-yi Shams-i Tabrizi* (Tehran: Ata'i 1374/1996), 5.

38. Faridun Sipahsalar, *Risalah dar ahval-i Maulana Jalal al-Din,* ed. Said Nafisi (Tehran: Kitabkhanah-yi Iqbal, 1325/1947), 123.

39. For an analysis of Shams's personality, see Sahibzamani, *Khatt-i sivvum,* 113–21; for the concluding remarks on the *insan-i kamil,* see 626.

40. For a study of Rūmī's lyrics, see Fatemeh Keshavarz, *Reading Mystical Lyric: The Case of Jalal al-Din Rumi* (Columbia: University of South Carolina Press, 1988).

41. Elkins, *What Painting Is,* 5.

42. Ahmad Shamlu, *Hava-yi tazah* (Tehran: Intisharat-i Zamanih, 1372/1994). For a discussion of mysticism, see chapter 5.

43. Warnke, *Gadamer,* 3, 19, 21.

44. The essay "Refashioning the Secular" appears in a critical volume on the state of theoretical thinking in the postmodern age called *What's Left of Theory?* 156–91.

45. From the long poem "The Footsteps of Water," Sepehri, *Hasht kitab,* 272–73.

46. From the poem "The Night of Good Solitude," ibid., 372.

47. Forugh Farrokhzad, *Guzina-yi ash'ar* (Tehran: Intisharat-i Murvarid, 1372/1993), 219.

48. Connolly, "Refashioning the Secular," 160–61, 169–72.

49. Ibid., 165–66.

50. Louis Massignon, *The Passion of al-Hallāj: Mystic and Martyr of Islam,* trans. Herbert Mason, 4 vols. (Princeton, N.J.: Princeton University Press, 1982).

51. Muhammad Riza Shafi'i-Kadkani, *Dar khucha bagh'ha-yi Nishabur* (Tehran: Intisharat-i Tus, 1350/1971), 46.

52. Ahmad Shamlu, *Barguzidah-yi ash'ar-i Ahmad-i Shamlu* (Tehran: Intisharat-i Katibah, 1336/1957), 183–86. *Marg-i Nasiri* [The Death of the Nazarene] inspired the title of chapter 6 and will be discussed there in detail.

53. Shamlu, *Lawh* [The Tablet], in *An Anthology of Modern Persian Poetry,* trans. Ahmad Karimi-Hakkak (Boulder, Colo.: Westview, 1978), 56, 58–59.

54. Forugh Farrokhzad, *Tavalludi digar,* 98.

55. Sepehri, *Hasht kitab,* 373–76.

56. Ibid.

57. Connolly, "Refashioning the Secular," 164, 161, 177, 180.

58. Anouar Majid, *Unveiling Traditions: Postcolonial Islam in Polycentric World* (Durham, N.C.: Duke University Press, 2000), 35.

59. Timothy J. Reiss, *The Meaning of Literature* (Ithaca, N.Y.: Cornell University Press, 1992), 2. Compare Reiss's interesting parallel in seventeenth-century England of the development of the purpose of poetry as the embodiment of "plain demonstrative justice" side by side with the "inception of stable civil society" (87).

60. Warnke, *Gadamer,* 47–48, 69.

61. Ibid., 62.

62. For a study of literary applications of the Gadamerian approach to art, see Joel Weinsheimer, *Philosophical Hermeneutics and Literary Theory* (New Haven: Yale University Press, 1991).

CHAPTER 2

1. Omar Khayyám, *Taranah-ha-yi Khayyam,* ed. Sādeq Hedāyat (Tehran: Parastu, 1353/1974), 103.

2. *Kuzih'gar-i dahr* [the master potter] of creation is a term Khayyám uses often to refer to God (ibid., 83).

3. See p. 20, above.

4. Mircea Eliade, *The Sacred and the Profane: The Nature of Religion,* trans. Willard R. Trask (1959; repr., San Diego: Harvest Books, 1987).

5. Veikok Anttonen, "Sacred," in *Guide to the Study of Religion,* ed. Willi Braun and Russell T. McCutcheon (London: Cassel, 2000), 271; for extensive quotes from Richard Comstock see 273.

6. Claude Lévi-Strauss, *The Savage Mind* (Chicago: Chicago University Press, 1966), quoted in Anttonen, "Sacred," 276.

7. Anttonen, "Sacred," 278.

8. For a discussion of the secular and a reference to Fitzgerald, see p. 7, above.

9. Timothy Fitzgerald, *The Ideology of Religious Studies* (New York: Oxford University Press, 2000), 10.

10. ˈAnttonen, "Sacred," 272–78.

11. Premodern Persian poets and philosophers commented on the interconnected nature of the poetic and prophetic since Ibn Sīnā (d. 1037). He believed in the notion of "continuous intellectual emanation" through "poetic logic." Peter Heath, *Allegory and Philosophy in Avicenna (Ibn Sīnā) with Translation of the Book of the Prophet Muhammad's Ascent to Heaven* (Philadelphia: University of Pennsylvania Press, 1992), 150–51.

12. Abū ol-Qāsem Firdawsī, *Shāh-nāmeh*, ed. Jules Mohl (Tehran: Amuzish-i Inqilab-i Islami, 1370/1991), 3.

13. Ibid., 4, 6.

14. Ibid., 19–20.

15. Ibid., 40–54.

16. Abū ʿAbdollāh Jaʿfar ebn Mohammad Rūdakī, *Divan-i* Rudaki, ed. Manuchihr Danish'pazhuh (Tehran: Intisharat-i Tus, 1374/1995), 31.

17. Ibid., 33.

18. Ibid., 20.

19. ʿAbd al-Vasiʿ Jabali, *Divan*, ed. Zabihullah Safa (Tehran: Amir Kabir, 1361/1982), 558, 523.

20. Muhammad ibn ʿAbd al-Malik Muʿizzi, *Kuliyyat-i Divan*, ed. Nasir Hayyiri (Tehran: Nashr-i Marzban, 1362/1983), 692, 697–99.

21. Ibid., 705.

22. As demonstrated later in this section, this continuum has already been envisioned in the Sufi writings by this time and in the genre of rubaʿi even earlier.

23. Jan Rypka's assessment of the situation is fairly typical. See *History of Iranian Literature*, trans. P. van Popta-Hope, ed. Karl Jahn (Dordrecht: D. Reidel, 1968), 191–93.

24. For Najm al-Din Razi's remark, see *Mirsad al-ʿibad min al-mabdaʾ ila al-maʿad* (Tehran: Intisharat-i Sanaʾi, 1353/1974), 18. Earlier this century A. J. Arberry sifted through numerous "complete collections" to identify 250 quatrains as authentic (see Rypka, *History of Iranian Literature*, 192).

25. Khayyám, *Taranah-ha-yi Khayyam*, 70.

26. Ibid., 74.

27. Ibid., 80, 69.

28. Ibid., 71.

29. Ibid., 89.

30. Ibid., 69.

31. Ibid., 98.

32. Ibid., 58, 63.

33. Rypka, *History of Iranian Literature*, 96, 143–44, 234.

34. Abu Saʿid's life and thought are documented by Jamal al-Din Abu Rawh Lutf Allah Ibn Abi Saʿid, one of Abu Saʿid's great-grandchildren. A critical edition of the text was published by Muhammad Riza Shafiʿi-Kadkani, a poet discussed for his own writing in the next chapter. See *Halat va sukhanan-i Abu Saʿid Abu al-Khayr* (Tehran: Intisharat-i Agah, 1366/1997).

35. Mohammad Shams al-Dīn Hāfez, *Divan-i Hafiz: Qazvini-Ghani,* ed. Muhammad Qazvini (Tehran: Intesharat-i Iqbal, 1365/1986), 34.

36. Abu Saʿid Abu al-Khayr, *Sukhanan-i manzum-i Abu Saʿid Abu al-Khayr,* ed. Saʿid Nafisi (Tehran: Sanaʾi, 1373/1994), 11.

37. Ibid., 7.

38. Ibid., 88.

39. Ibid., 9.

40. Ibid., 74.

41. Ibid., 27.

42. Ibid., 23.

43. Ibid., 9.

44. Ibid., 6.

45. Ibid., 13.

46. Annemarie Schimmel, "The Genius of Shiraz: Saʿdi and Hafez," in *Persian Literature,* ed. by Ihsan Yarshater (Albany: State University of New York Press, 1988), 214–25. I have critiqued the metaphor for evoking rigidity; see Fatemeh Keshavarz, *Reading Mystical Lyric: The Case of Jalal al-Din Rumi* (Columbia: University of South Carolina Press, 1998), 138–39.

47. Keshavarz, *Reading Mystical Lyric,* 97.

48. From a ghazel of Rūmī, quoted in ibid., 91.

49. Fakhr al-Dīn ʿIrāqī, *Kulliyat-i Divan,* ed. Saʿid Nafisi (Tehran: Intisharat-i Javidan, n.d.), 21–24.

50. The *Masnavi* of Rūmī is a notable exception in that its didactic themes are interspersed with lyric moments.

51. For Rūmī's innovations in the genre of ghazel, see Keshavarz, *Reading Mystical Lyric,* 138–60.

52. ʿIrāqī, *Kulliyat,* 95.

53. "*Fa idha sawwaytuhu wa nafakhtu fihi min ruhi fa qaʾu lahu sajidin.*" Qurʾan 15:29.

54. ʿIrāqī, *Kulliyat,* 110.

55. Ibid., 195.

56. Ibid., 225.

57. Ibid.

58. For a balanced and interesting study of Sanāʾī's work, see J. T. P. DuBrujen, *Of Piety and Poetry: The Interaction of Religion and Literature in the Life and Work of Hakim Sanaʾi of Ghaznah* (Leiden: E. J. Brill, 1983). For an in-depth topical analysis of Sanāʾī's writings, see two valuable contributions by Muhammad Riza Shafiʿi-Kadkani, *Taziaynahʾha-yi suluk* (Tehran: Nashr-i Agah, 1376/1997) and *Dar iqlim-i raushanaʾi: Tafsir-i chand ghazal az Hakim Sanaʾi-i Ghaznavi* (Tehran: Nashr-i Agah, 1373/1994). For the ghazel quoted above, see Shafiʿi-Kadkani, *Dar iqlim-i raushanaʾi,* 143.

59. Saʿdī, *Kulliyat-i Saʿdī,* ed. Muhammad ʿAli Furughi (Tehran: Amir Kabir, 1366/1987), 411. The second hemistich in the first verse may be read to mean "The bird in the air [He] fed with the fish in the sea."

60. Ibid.

61. Ibid., 427.

62. Ibid., 787.

63. Ibid., 445.

64. Ibid., 426, 428, 446.

65. Ibid., 469. The verb *didar* from the root *didan* [to see] in Farsi denotes mutual pleasure in the encounter of two parties.

66. Ibid., 448.

67. Rypka, *History of Iranian Literature*, 263. For Dawlat Shah's descriptions of Hāfez, see *Tadhkirat al-shuʿarā* (Tehran: Kulalah-i Khavar, 1366/1987), 227–31.

68. Hāfez, *Tadhkirat al-shuʿarā*, 89.

69. Ibid., 88, 66.

70. Ibid., 44.

71. Ibid., 57.

72. Ibid., 115.

73. Ibid., 124–25.

74. Hafez, *Dīvan*, 288.

75. Ahmad Hatif Isfahani, *Divan-i Hatif-i Isfahani*, ed. Vahid Dastgirdi (Tehran: Intisharat-i Nigah, 1375/1996), 47–51. For reference to trinity see 49.

76. An example of this is the panegyric poem by the contemporary ghazel writer Rahi Muʿayiri for the eighth Shiite Imam ʿAli ibn Musa al-Riza. "Three Contemporary Poems Honoring Imam Riza," trans. Fatemeh Keshavarz, in *Windows on the House of Islam: Muslim Sources on Spirituality and Religious Life*, ed. John Renard (Berkeley: University of California Press, 1998), 98–102.

Chapter 3

1. These transformative events were the Constitutional Revolution of 1906 and the Islamic Revolution of 1979. For a full account of these revolutions, see Ervand Abrahamian, *Iran between Two Revolutions* (Princeton, N.J.: Princeton University Press, 1982) and Nikki Keddie, *Roots of Revolution: An Interpretive History of Modern Iran* (New Haven: Yale University Press, 1981).

2. Ahmad Karimi-Hakkak, *Recasting Persian Poetry: Scenarios of Poetic Modernity in Iran* (Salt Lake City: University of Utah Press, 1995), 58–59.

3. For a comprehensive and analytical study of the development of the Shiite doctrine with attention to social and cultural change, see Said Amir Arjomand, *The Shadow of God and the Hidden Imam: Religion, Political Order, and Social Change in Shiite Iran from the Beginning to 1890* (Chicago: University of Chicago Press, 1984).

4. Keddie, *Roots of Revolution,* 183.

5. Roy Mottahedeh, *The Mantle of the Prophet* (New York: Pantheon Books, 1985).

6. For a brief lucid account of Shari'ati's contribution to intellectual reform in twentieth-century Iran, see Abdulaziz Sachedina, "Ali Sharʿiati: Ideologue of the Iranian Revolution," in *Voices of Resurgent Islam,* ed. John L. Esposito (New York: Oxford University Press, 1983), 191–214.

7. Mohammad Tavakoli-Targhi, "Refashioning Iran: Language and Culture during the Constitutional Revolution," *Iranian Studies* 23, no. 1–4 (1991): 77–101.

8. Mirza Aqa Khan Kirmani, *Ayinah-yi Sikandari* (Tehran: n.p., 1324/1906), 118.

9. ʿAli ibn Julagh Farrukhi, *Divan-i Hakim Farrukhi-i Sistani* (Tehran: Vizarat-i Ittilaʿat va Jahan'gardi, 1355/1976), 381.

10. For an overview of the literary movement known as bazgasht, see William Hanaway, *Bazgasht-i Adabi,* in *Encyclopaedia Iranica* (London: Routledge and Kegan Paul, 1982–), 4:58–60.

11. Kirmani, *Ayinah-yi Sikandari,* 17, 14.

12. Nima Yushij, *Barguzidah-'i asar-i Nima Yushij,* ed. Sirus Tahbaz (Tehran: Intisharat-i Buzurgmihr, 1369/1980), 18. As Hakkak demonstrates successfully, the process of change in Persian poetry was instigated before Nima and involved an array of individuals and traditions. Nima's vocal opposition to formal restrictions earned him the title. He is the culmination of a long process of reform rather than the solé innovator (Hakkak, *Recasting Persian Poetry,* 3–4).

13. Nima, *Barguzidah-'i asar-i Nima Yushij,* 22, 27.

14. Ibid., 30–31.

15. Forugh Farrokhzad, *Bride of Acacias: Selected Poems of Forugh Farrokhzad,* trans. Jascha Kessler with Amin Banani (New York: Caravan Books, 1982), 47–48. For the original Farsi see, Farrokhzad, *Divan-i ash'ar* (Tehran: Intisharat-i Murvarid, 1374/1995), 346–47.

16. Forugh-i Farrokhzad, radio interview by Hasan Hunarmandi.

17. Farrokhzad, *Bride of Acacias,* 109. I have, here, suggested a different reading of the first line, "*madar tamam-i zindigiash sajjadah-'ist gustardah dar astan-i vahshat-i duzakh.*" Kessler and Banani suggest the following reading: "All her life, mother has been a prayer rug spread at the gate of hell's terrors."

18. Nadir Nadirpur, *Barguzidah-yi ash'ar,* 1326–1349 (Tehran: Kitab'ha-yi Jibi, 1349/1970), 80–81.

19. Ibid., 40. The small city of Qom in central Iran, known worldwide after the 1979 revolution, is one of the most influential centers of Shiite learning in the world.

20. Georgia Warnke summarizes Gadamer's view on the authority of tradition in *Gadamer: Hermeneutics, Tradition, and Reason* (Stanford, Calif.: Stanford University Press, 1987), 155.

21. Ibid., 151.

22. The translation is Hakkak's. *An Anthology of Modern Persian Poetry,* trans. Ahmad Karimi-Hakkak (Boulder, Colo.: Westview, 1978), 56.

23. For an extensive discussion of Sa'dī see Shamlu's interview in the special edition devoted to Shamlu in *Zamanah* 1, no. 1 (1991): 7–42. Hallāj was the ninth- or tenth-century Persian mystic who, caught in the political turmoil in the 'Abbāsid Baghdad, was eventually killed for expressing oneness with deity. For an account of his life see Louis Massignon, *The Passion of al-Hallāj: Mystic and Martyr of Islam,* trans. Herbert Mason, 4 vols. (Princeton, N.J.: Princeton University Press, 1982). For a lucid updated summary, see Carl Ernst, *Words of Ecstasy in Sufism* (Albany: State University of New York Press, 1985).

24. If nothing else, popular movies such as *King of Kings, Ben Hur,* and *The Ten Commandments* had romanticized biblical themes with the masses.

25. Farrokhzad, *Divan-i ash'ar,* 361.

26. Ibid., 362.

27. Ibid., 364. Here, Farrokhzad plays on the round shape of the letter *fa'* in the word *farda* [tomorrow], which children tend to exaggerate when they first learn to write.

28. Suhrab Sepehri, *Hasht kitab*, 373.

29. Ibid., 374–75.

30. Ibid., 375.

31. The often-quoted verse by Saʿdī is *"Barg-i dirakhtan-i sabz dar nazar-i hushyar / Har varqi daftarist maʿrifat-i kirdigar"* [To the intelligent observer, every green leaf is a book filled with knowledge of God].

32. Martin comments on the similarity of this poem to the "early visionary Meccan surahs," though he does not seem to be aware of the tradition of borrowing the scriptural rhythm in the poetry of the period discussed here. See Suhrab Sepehri, *The Expanse of Green: Poems of Shorab-i Sepehri*, trans. David L. Martin (UNESCO Kalimat, 1988), 186.

33. Muhammad Riza Shafiʿi-Kadkani, *Dar kucha bagh'ha-yi Nishabur* (Tehran: Intisharat-i Tus, 1357/1979), 9–12.

34. Ibid., 7.

35. For a brief account of Hallāj's and ʿAyn al-Qudat's lives, see "Hallaj" and "ʿAyn al-Qudat," *Encyclopaedia of Islam*, new ed. (Leiden: E. J. Brill, 1991), 1.

36. Shafiʿi-Kadkani, *Dar khucha bagh'ha-yi Nishabur*, 10.

37. Ibid.

38. Ibid.

39. James Elkins, *What Painting Is: How to Think about Oil Painting, Using the Language of Alchemy* (New York: Routledge, 2000), 96.

40. Of classical Persian poets, Khāqānī (b. 1121) used the Jesus imagery most extensively. The index to his *Divan* lists over 120 occurrences of the name ʿIsa alone; see Afzal al-Dīn Khāqānī *Divan-i Khaqani Shirvani*, ed. Ziya al-Din Sajjadi (Tehran: Intisharat-i Zavvar, 1357/1978), 1074.

41. Sorour Soroudi, "On Jesus's Image in Modern Persian Poetry," *Muslim World* 69, no. 4 (October 1979): 221–22.

42. Ahmad Shamlu, *Barguzidah-i ashʿar-i Ahmad Shamlu* (Tehran: Intisharat-i Katibah, 1336/1957), 183–86.

43. It is more common to use "Nasiri" in the combination "ʿIsa-yi Nasiri," which Shamlu does not use because he is trying to avoid the component "ʿIsa."

44. The edition of *Az in Avesta* used for this study is the tenth printing published by Intisharat-i Murvarid in 1996 in Tehran. The influence that the poet sustained on a broad readership in over three decades is typical of almost all the major poets quoted in the present work.

45. Ibid., 129.

46. Ibid., 220.

47. See "Zoroaster" and "Zoroastrianism," in *The Oxford Dictionary of World Religions*, ed. John Bowker (Oxford: Oxford University Press, 1997).

48. Akhavan, *Az in Avesta*, 109.

49. Mazdak was the leader of a revolutionary religious movement in Sāsānid Iran during the reign of Qubad. He caught the attention of Iranian reformist poets as a pre-Islamic expression of Iranian identity. His sympathy for the masses, and persecution by the ruling regime, gave him additional political attraction. See "Mazdak," *Encyclopaedia of Islam*, new ed., vol. 6 (Leiden: E. J. Brill, 1991).

50. Akhavan, *Az in Avesta*, 79.

51. Ibid., 80.

52. Farid al-Din Muhammad ʿAttar, *Muslim Saints and Mystics: Episodes from the Tadhkirat al-awliyaʾ* (Memorial of the Saints), trans. A. J. Arberry (London: Routledge and Kegan Paul, 1966), 100–123.

53. Ibid., 105–6. For a complete translation of Bayazid's *Miʿrajnamah,* see chapter 7 in *Early Islamic Mysticism: Sufi, Qurʾan, Miʿraj, Poetic and Theological Writings,* trans. and ed. Michael A. Sells (New York: Paulist Press, 1996), 212–51.

54. Muhammad Riza Shafiʿi-Kadkani, *Az budan va surudan* (Tehran: Intisharat-i Tus, 1357/1978), 20–31. One can, of course, consider the Prophet's *Miʿraj* as Shafiʿi-Kadkani's main source of inspiration except that the Qurʾanic allusion to it is brief: "Glory to Him who by night took His servant journeying from the sacred mosque to the distant mosque, *al-Aqsa,* whose precincts We have blessed, in order to show him Our revelations. He is the One who hears and sees all," Qurʾan 17:1. For the term *miʿraj* in the Qurʾan, see *Readings in the Qurʾan,* trans. Kenneth Cragg (Brighton: Sussex Academic Press, 1988), 350.

55. Shafiʿi-Kadkani, *Az budan va surudan,* 21.

56. Ibid., 31.

57. For information about al-Hallāj, see references listed in note 23.

58. Shafiʿi-Kadkani, *Dar kucha baghʾha-yi Nishabur,* 46–49. Earlier in this chapter, I referred to the poem *Dibachah* in this collection, which echoed Qurʾanic rhythm (9).

CHAPTER 4

1. From the radio interview of Forough Farrokhzad by Iraj Gurgin published as *Harf ʾhaʾi ba Furugh Farrokhzad* (Tehran: Intisharat-i Murvarid, 1356/1977), 48.

2. Mary Douglas has provided interesting insight into the matter; see *Purity and Danger: An Analysis of the Concept of Pollution and Taboo* (London: Ark Paperbacks, 1989).

3. Ahmad Karimi-Hakkak, *Recasting Persian Poetry: Scenarios of Poetic Modernity in Iran* (Salt Lake City: University of Utah Press, 1995).

4. In a chapter titled "Unveiling the Other," Farzaneh Milani has discussed in detail Farrokhzad's pioneering contribution to describing male sexuality; see *Veils and Words: The Emerging Voices of Iranian Women Writers* (Syracuse, N.Y.: Syracuse University Press, 1992), 127–52.

5. Ahmad Shamlu, *Hava-yi tazah* (Tehran: Intisharat-i Nigah, 1372/1993), 82.

6. Forugh Farrokhzad, *Bride of Acacias: Selected Poems of Forugh Farrokhzad,* trans. Jascha Kessler with Amin Banani (New York: Caravan Books, 1982), 47.

7. Ibid.

8. Ibid.

9. Ibid., 48.

10. Ibid.

11. Ibid., 34–35.

12. Ibid., 34.

13. Ibid., 35.

14. From Puran Farrokhzad's 1971 interview with the national daily paper *Kayhan* on February 8.

15. *Harf ʾhaʾi ba Furugh.*

16. Ibid., 28.

17. The extended image appears in the seminal poem that gave its title to Farrokhzad's last collection, *Tavalludi digar;* see Bihruz Jalali ed., *Forugh Farrokhzad: Javdanah zistan, dar awj mandan* (Tehran: Intisharat-i Murvarid, 1375/1986), 227.

18. Daniel Yusof's discussion of the role of ordinary souls in sacred making is interesting in "Redirection of the Sacred: The Intricacies of Islamic Meaning," *American Journal of Islamic Social Sciences* 18, no. 2 (Spring 2001): 110.

19. Veikok Anttonen, "Sacred," in *Guide to the Study of Religion,* ed. Willi Braun and Russell T. McCutcheon (London: Cassel, 2000), 280–81.

20. Ibid.

21. Farrokhzad, *Divan-i ash'ar,* 449.

22. Lotte Trakka, "Other Worlds—Symbolism, Dialogue, and Gender in Karelian Oral Poetry," in *Songs beyond the Kalevala: Transformations of Oral Poetry,* ed. Anna-Leena Siikala and Sinikka Vakimo, vol. 2 (Helsinki: Finish Literature Society, 1994), 250–98.

23. Farrokhzad, *Tavalludi digar,* in *Divan-i ash'ar,* 419. The expression *Jazirah-yi sargardan* [wandering island] occurs in the long posthumous poem "Let Us Believe in the Oncoming Season of Cold" (429). For a complete, and impressive, translation, see Farrokhzad, *Bride of Acacias,* 95–102.

24. See page 66, above.

25. Kessler and Banani translated under the title "Sinning." Farrokhzad, *Bride of Acacias,* 127.

26. Michael Hillmann attributes the controversy surrounding the poem to the fact that it portrays a woman (Farrokhzad) as the agent or "lover" while the man is the recipient or "beloved." *A Lonely Woman: Forugh Farrokhzad and Her Poetry* (Washington, D.C.: Mage and Three Continents Press, 1987), 78.

27. For the poem *Pasukh* in the original Farsi, see Farrokhzad, *Divan-i ash'ar,* 220.

28. Ibid., 221.

29. Farrokhzad, *Bride of Acacias,* 18.

30. Ibid., 19.

31. Ibid.

32. Farrokhzad, *Divan-i ash'ar,* 194–95.

33. Farrokhzad, *Bride of Acacias,* 49–50.

34. Kessler and Banani translate the second line in this excerpt as "As though my heart flowed on the other side of *love*" with no explanation about the change in the text (ibid., 49).

35. Ibid., 50.

36. Ibid.

37. The quotation is from an interview concerning the documentary she made about the lepers colony in Tabriz, *Furugh-i Farrokhzad,* 238–48. Her documentary won the first prize in the Oberhausen Film Festival in 1964. The cited comment was a reaction to wide speculations that she might opt for the medium of cinema at the cost of abandoning poetry. For discussions of her documentary, see 229–66.

38. For an extensive discussion of the motivations for poetic creation with Sa'id and Sirus Tahbaz, see *Furugh-i Farrokhzad,* 202.

39. Farrokhzad, *Divan-i ash'ar,* 357–60; for English translation, see Farrokhzad, *Bride of Acacias,* 54–56.

40. Farrokhzad, *Bride of Acacias,* 55.

41. Ibid., 56.

42. Farrokhzad, *Divan-i ashʿar,* 387–98; for English translation, see Farrokhzad, *Bride of Acacias,* 74–80.

43. Farrokhzad, *Bride of Acacias,* 78.

44. Farrokhzad, *Divan-i ashʿar,* 354; for English translation , see Farrokhzad, *Bride of Acacias,* 52; for a discussion of "Earthly scriptures," see pp. 66–69, above.

45. Farrokhzad, *Divan-i ashʿar,* 341; for English translation, see Farrokhzad, *Bride of Acacias,* 45.

46. Farrokhzad, *Divan-i ashʿar,* 373–74. My translation. Except when indicated, chapters are from Banani and Kessler, *Bride of Acacias.*

47. Ibid., 374.

48. Ibid.

49. Ibid., 323–26; for English translation, see Farrokhzad, *Bride of Acacias,* 32–33.

50. Farrokhzad, *Bride of Acacias,* 33.

51. From the poem *Didar dar shab.* Farrokhzad, *Divan-i ashʿar,* 376; for English translation, see Farrokhzad, *Bride of Acacias,* 65.

52. From the long poem *An ruzha* [Those Days]. Farrokhzad, *Divan-i ashʿar,* 290; for English translation, see Farrokhzad, *Bride of Acacias,* 13.

53. Farrokhzad, *Divan-i ashʿar,* 308; for English translation, see Farrokhzad, *Bride of Acacias,* 24.

54. Farrokhzad, *Divan-i ashʿar,* 415. My translation.

55. Ibid., 314; for English translation, see Farrokhzad, *Bride of Acacias,* 27.

56. Farrokhzad, *Divan-i ashʿar,* 315. My translation.

57. *Divarʾha-yi marz* [The Frontier Walls] (along with two others, *Gul-i surkh* [The Red Rose] and *Juftʾha* [Couples]) is missing from the editions of *Tavalludi digar* published in Iran after the 1979 revolution, including the *Divan-i ashʿar,* edited by Behruz Jalali (Intisharat-i Murvarid, 1995), which I have used in the present study. There are no references to these censured pieces or any explanation for the omission. The editions appear complete to readers unfamiliar with the contents. For English translation, see Farrokhzad, *Bride of Acacias,* 40–42.

58. Ibid., 41.

59. Ibid., 40.

60. Ibid.

61. Ibid., 41.

62. Ibid.

63. Ibid.

CHAPTER 5

1. For a comprehensive account of classical Islamic mysticism and its divisions, see Abu Bakr al-Kalabadhi, *The Doctrine of the Sufis,* trans. A. J. Arberry (Cambridge: Cambridge University Press, 1935).

2. Richard King, *Orientalism and Religion: Post-colonial Theory, India and the Mystic East* (London: Routledge, 1999), 7.

3. See chapter 1.

4. Jonathan Z. Smith, *Imagining Religion: From Babylon to Jonestown* (Chicago: University of Chicago Press, 1982), xi.

5. King, *Orientalism and Religion*, 8.

6. Even in the absence of organized Sufi orders, of which there are still quite a few operating in present-day Iran, it is common for small communities to form around individual leading figures, such as a *pir* [spiritual leader] or sheikh.

7. King devotes an entire chapter to what he calls "The Politics of Privatization," *Orientalism and Religion*, 161–86.

8. *"Dar banaris sar-i har kuchih chiraghi abadi raushan bud"* [In Varanasi each alley was lit with an eternal light], *Sida-yi pa-yi ab* [The Footsteps of Water], in Suhrab Sepehri, *Hasht kitab* (Tehran: Kitab'khanah-'i Tahuri, 1358/1979), 285.

9. Ibid., 274, 285.

10. King, *Orientalism and Religion*, 9.

11. Ahmad Karimi-Hakkak, *Recasting Persian Poetry: Scenarios of Poetic Modernity in Iran* (Salt Lake City: University of Utah Press, 1995), 18.

12. Both ʿAttār and Rūmī were influential literary figures. For a brief biographical discussion and evaluation of their poetic output, see Jan Rypka, *History of Iranian Literature*, trans. P. van Popta-Hope (Dordrecht: D. Reidel, 1968), 237–42.

13. See Alasdair MacIntyre's chapter on tradition and translation in *Whose Justice? Which Rationality* (Notre Dame, Ind.: University of Notre Dame Press, 1988), 371–88.

14. See pp. 82 and 88, above.

15. For the poem that brings "kindness," "apples," and "faith" together, see Sepehri, *Hast Kitab*, 350. Though the complexity of Sepehri's work is acknowledged, critics have often described him as "escapist," "individualistic," and "feminine." See Afshin Kuchikzad, *Hayahu-yi bisyar barayi hich*, in *Raz-i Gul-i Surkh*, ed. Sahar Maʾsumi (Tehran: Bih Nigar, 1375/1996), 225.

16. One such study is Kamiyar ʿAbidi's *Az musahibat-i aftab: Taʾammulat va justujuʾhaʾi dar shiʿr-i Suhrab-i Sipihri* (Tehran: Nashr-i Salis, 1375/1996). The book devotes a substantial section to Sepehri's paintings and the critiques of them. It also provides the most comprehensive bibliography on the poet to date.

17. Sepehri's other collections published prior to those used in this chapter are *Marg-i rang* [The Death of Colors] (1951), *Zindigi-yi Khvabʾha* [The Life of Dreams] (1952), and *Avar-i Aftab* [The Debris of the Sun] and *Sharq-i Anduh* [The East of Melancholy] (both 1961).

18. Sepehri, *Hasht kitab*, 369–70.

19. *"Le petit prince, qui me posit beaucoup de questions, ne semblait jamais entendre les miennes."* Antoine de Saint-Exupéry, *Le Petit Prince* (San Diego: Harcourt Brace, 1979), 11.

20. The quotations are from the poems *Sida-yi didar* [The Sound of Encounter], *Vahih'i dar lahzih* [An Oasis in the Moment], *Niday-i aghaz* [The Call to Start], and *Dar Dar Gulistanih* [In Gulistanih] in the collection Sepehri, *Hasht kitab*, 370, 361, 393, 351.

21. Ibid., 349.

22. Ibid., 350.

23. Ibid., 350–51.

24. David Martin, the translator of *Hajm-i sabz* into English describes Sepehri as a nature mystic poet who "broke from the Sufi poetical tradition" by writing in the free verse style and "by not addressing the Divine as his beloved." *The Expanse of Green: Poems of Sohrab Sepehy,* trans. David L. Martin (n.p.: UNESCO / Kalimat Press, 1988), vii.

25. *Vaha'i dar lahzah,* "An Oasis in the Moment" and *Paygham-i mahi'ha* [Message from the Fish] in Sepehri, *Hasht kitab,* 361, 357.

26. *Raushani, man, gul, ab* [Light, Me, Flower, Water], *Az ruy-i pilk-i shab* [On the Eyelid of the Night], in Sepehri, *Hasht kitab,* 336, 334.

27. Ibid., 338–39.

28. Ibid., 339.

29. Ibid., 336.

30. Ibid., 356–57, 390–93.

31. Ibid., 391–92.

32. From the poem "Nostalgia," Sepehri, *Hasht kitab,* 353.

33. For examples of flashes of the divine in Sepehri's work, see *Hasht kitab,* 334, 347, 353, 356–57, 359.

34. Ibid., 272.

35. Ibid., 357.

36. Ibid., 347.

37. Ibid., 359.

38. Ibid., 333–34.

39. Ibid., 398.

40. Ibid., 391, 384, 370.

41. Ibid., 387.

42. Ibid., 343–44, 370, 372.

43. The ghazel opens with "*Khabarat kharab'tar kard jirahat-i juda'i.*" Sa'dī, *Kulliyat-i Sa'dī,* ed. Muhammad 'Ali Furughi (Tehran: Amir Kabir, 1366/1981), 599.

44. Sepehri, *Hasht kitab,* 382, 358–59.

45. Ibid., 366–68, 398–401. For Muhammad's night journey to God, see "Mi'radj," *Encyclopaedia of Islam,* new ed. (Leiden: E. J. Brill, 1991), 7:97–100. For the poem *Dust* [The Friend], see Sepehri, *Hasht kitab,* 398. Sepehri's search for the *dust* became the inspiration for a film by prominent contemporary Iranian director and screenwriter Abbas Kiarostami in 1996 called *Where Is the Friend's Home.* The film, now considered a classic, earned Kiarostami Locarno's Bronze Leopard.

46. Sepehri, *Hasht kitab,* 267.

47. Ibid., 389.

48. Shahrukh Miskub's essay *Qissih-'i Suhrab va nushdaru* is one such eloquent response to the accusation that, in Miskub's words, "Sepehri is reclining in his ivory tower protecting the 'crystal of his solitude' against possible cracks. In short he detests politics and is disinterested in social life." *Chand guftar dar fargang-i Iran* (Tehran: Zindihrud, 1371/1992), 198. Miskub's essay goes beyond Sepehri and provides a lucid critique of the social condition that ties contemporary Persian literature to immediate political concerns keeping it from finding a broader more universal vantage point (201).

49. For "books in which wind does not blow," see Sepehri, *Hasht Kitab,* 294. For "To the Garden of Fellow Travelers," see 394.

50. Sepehri, *Musafir* [The Traveler], in *Hasht kitab,* 309.

51. For a study of the journey of the birds, see Fatemeh Keshavarz, "Flight of the Birds: The Poetic Animating the Spiritual in ʿAttār's *Mantiq al-tayr,*" in *Intimations of Immortality,* ed. Leonard Lewisohn (London: Institute of Ismaili Studies, forthcoming).

52. Sepehri, *Musafir* [The Traveler], in *Hasht kitab,* 311–12.

53. Ibid., 316. For the law code of King Hammurabi of Babylon (ca. 1728–1686 B.C.E.), the fourth out of the seven ancient Near Eastern law codes, see J. R. Porter, ed., *The Illustrated Guide to the Bible* (New York: Oxford University Press, 1995), 63.

54. Sepehri, *Musafir* [The Traveler], in *Hasht kitab,* 320–21.

55. For a definition of this key mystical concept, s.v. "Pir," in *Encyclopaedia of Islam,* 8:306–7.

56. Sepehri, *Hasht kitab,* 360–61.

57. Ibid., 361, 369–70, 370–80.

58. Ibid., 371, 374, 399, 372, 400, 383.

59. Sufi hagiographies have many examples of people being drawn to major Sufi figures. Farid al-Din Muhammad ʿAttar's "Memorials of the Friends of God" describes the arrival of the Sufi master Bayazid in Bastam and the crowd who went out to receive him. *Tadhkirat al-awliyaʾ,* ed. Muhammad Istiʾlami (Tehran: Intisharat-i Zavvar, 1377/1998), 164.

60. Sepehri, *Hasht kitab,* 392–93.

61. From the poems "Exile" and "The Night of Good Solitude." Ibid., 353, 371.

62. Ibid., 372.

63. Ibid., 362–65.

64. Ibid., 283.

65. Ibid., 406.

Chapter 6

1. The title to this chapter makes use of two of Ahmad Shamlu's poems. The first quote is from the poem "The Death of the Nazarene," which magnifies the last few moments of the crucifixion of Jesus. The other two allude to the poet himself in the phrase "I shall not turn back, nor shall I die" in the poem *Harf-i akhir* [The Last Word], the angriest of Shamlu's manifestos declaring victory for modern Persian poetry. Ahmad Shamlu, *Hava-yi tazih* (Tehran: Intisharat-i Nigah, 1372/1993), 310.

2. Kamran Talattof's *The Politics of Writing in Iran: A History of Modern Persian Literature* (Syracuse, N.Y.: Syracuse University Press, 2000) defines "modern Persian literature" that emerged during the late nineteenth and early twentieth centuries as a "secular activity" (3). Talattof's outlook is the latest echo of a generally held view even when it is not stated as directly. A more detailed discussion of his views follow in this chapter.

3. Nikki R. Keddie, *Roots of Revolution: An Interpretive History of Modern Iran* (New Haven: Yale University Press, 1981), 183.

4. Shamlu's work has caught the attention of Iranian literary critics more than any writer in this century. Extensive monographs such as *Safar dar mih: Taʾammuli dar shiʿr-i Ahmad-i Shamlu* (Tehran: Intisharat-i Zimistan, 1374/1995) by Taghi Pournamdarian and *Ahmad-i Shamlu: Shiʿr-i Shamlu az aghaz ta imruz* (Tehran: Intisharat-i Nigah, 1376/1998) by Muhammad Hughughi are two such examples.

5. The line by Saʿdī is "*Barg-i dirakhtan-i sabz dar nazar-i hushyar / Har varqi daftarist maʿrifat-i kirdigar.*" Saʿdī, *Kulliyat-i Shaykh Saʿdī,* ed. Muhammad ʿAli Forughi (Tehran: ʿIlmi, n.d.), 519.

6. Interestingly enough, Shamlu himself views Saʿdī as a mere master of verbalization with no interest in improving the social conditions in which he lives. See the interview with Shamlu in *Zamanah* 1, no. 1 (1991): 17–18.

7. For an extended and perceptive discussion of the political component in artistic expression see Terry Eagleton, *Ideology of the Aesthetic* (Malden, Mass.: Blackwell, 1990). Eagleton also looks at what politics gains by taking art seriously. He argues for the significance of the discourses of reason, truth, freedom, and subjectivity expressed through arts. According to him, if politics does not take these with utmost seriousness it will not be resilient enough to "oppose the arrogance of power" (415).

8. Hamid Dabashi, "Poetics of Politics: Commitment in Modern Persian Literature," *Iranian Studies* 18, no. 2–4 (Spring–Autumn 1985): 149.

9. Ibid., 179.

10. For a discussion of *Shiʿri ki zindagist* [Poetry That Is Life], see pp. 142–43, below.

11. Hamid Mosaddiq, *Du manzumih* (Tehran: Amir Kabir, 1357/1978), 9.

12. Ibid., 32.

13. Siyavash Kasraʾi, *Az khun-i Siyavash: Muntakhab-i sizdah daftar-i shiʿr* (Tehran: Initisharat-i Sukhan, 1379/2000), 80–81.

14. Ibid., 68–69.

15. Ibid., 79–80.

16. Ibid., 76.

17. Ibid., 81.

18. "Revolutionary Literature: The Committed Literary Movement in the Decades before the 1979 Revolution," in Talattof, *The Politics of Writing in Iran,* 66.

19. Please see the section "Refashioning the Secular" in chapter 1 of the present work, p. 20, above.

20. Talattof, *The Politics of Writing in Iran,* 3, 6–7.

21. Ahmad Shamlu's major postrevolutionary poems appear in many collections, including *Taranah'ha-yi kuchik-i ghurbat, Madayih-i bi-salih, Dar astanah,* and *Hadith-i bi-gharari-yi Mahan,* which are quoted later in this chapter.

22. "*An ashiqan-i sharzih ki ba shab nazistand / raftand u shahr-i khufih nadanist kistand*" [The bold lovers who did not tolerate the oppression of the night / departed before the sleeping town understood who they were]. The ghazel beginning with this verse was popularly believed to have been dedicated to Khusraw Gulisurkhi, the leftist activist executed during the shah's regime. See Shafiʿi-Kadkani, *Az budan u surudan* (Tehran: Intisharat-i Tus, 1357/1979), 9. Shafiʿi-Kadkani's commemoration of Siyahkal is quoted in Talattof's *The Politics of Writing in Iran,* 89.

23. For a comprehensive tracing of the roots of modernity in twentieth-century Persian literature, see Ahmad Karimi-Hakkak, *Recasting Persian Poetry: Scenarios of Poetic Modernity in Iran* (Salt Lake City: University of Utah Press, 1995).

24. For a superb study of continuity and interaction between generic forms, see Alastair Fowler, *Kinds of Literature: An Introduction to the Theory of Genres and Modes* (Cambridge, Mass.: Harvard University Press, 1982).

25. Shahrukh Meskub, *Chand guftar dar farhang-i Iran* (Tehran: Zindahrud, 1371/ 1992), 159–60. Meskub's discontent with reduction of literature to an ideological tool has parallels in criticism of religious thought. Most notably, it is echoed by Abdul Karim Sorush in a monograph devoted wholly to the rescue of faith from reduction to a mere tool serving the Iranian revolutionary ideology: *Farbih'tar as idiology* (Tehran: Mu'assisih-yi Farhangi-i Sirat, 1373/1994).

26. Meskub, *Chand guftar dar farhang-i Iran*, 173–74.

27. Ibid., 167. For *Ulduz va kalagh'ha*, see Samad Bihrangi, *Qissah'ha-yi Bihrang* (Tabriz: Intisharat-i Bihrangi, 1377/1998), 11–78.

28. Meskub, *Chand guftar dar farhang-i Iran*, 172–73.

29. Ida, Shamlu's wife in his second marriage, was a major source of poetic inspiration. The collection *Ida dar ayinih* [Ida in the Mirror] quoted in this chapter was dedicated to her.

30. Shamlu finished a public address in Sweden with "Poets seek to alter the world"; see *Ahmad Shamlou: Master Poet of Liberty*, a documentary on Shamlu's life and work directed by Moslem Mansouri and produced by Bahman Maghsoudlou in 1998 and distributed by International Film and Video Center.

31. *Bamdad* [dawn] is Shamlu's pen name. The quotes are from the poem *Dar astanih* in one of Shamlu's last collections taking its title from the same poem (Tehran: Intisharat-i Nigah, 1376/1998), 17.

32. Sa'dī, *Kulliyat-i Haykh Sa'dī*, 519.

33. Quoted in Niyaz Ya'qubshahi, *Ashiqanih'ha: guzidah'i surudah'ha-yi sha'iran-i imruz-i Iran* (Tehran: Hirmand, 1377/1999), 81.

34. Shamlu, interview, *Zamaneh* 1, no. 1 (1991): 17–18

35. Ibid., 8–9.

36. See pp. 99–106, above.

37. Shamlu quoted in Niyaz Ya'qub'shahi, *'Ashiqanah'h: Guzidah-yi surudah'ha-yi sha'iran-i imruz-i Iran* (Tehran: Hirmand, 1377/1998), 82.

38. Ibid., 81. Shamlu did not acknowledge the twentieth-century ghazel writers such as Hushang Ibtihaj or Simin Bihbahani, who have revitalized the genre successfully. Unfortunately, the scope of the present study does not permit a more detailed discussion of the topic.

39. Ahmad Shamlu, *Hadith-i bi-gharari-i Mahan* (Tehran: Intisharat-i Mazyar, 1379/2000), 25.

40. Ibid., 26. The poem is prefaced with "introducing Nida Abkari."

41. Ahmad Shamlu, *Abraham dar abash* (Tehran: Intisharat-i Nigah, 1373/1994), 34. In the last line, the sacred will find a stronger presence if the terms "*namaz burdan*" and "*asman*" are given their fuller spiritual weight in a rendering such as "is worshiped by the heavens."

42. Ahmad Shamlu, *Taranah'ha-yi kuchik-i gurbat* (Tehran: Intisharat-i zamanah, 1379/1990), 50.

43. Shamlu, *Dar astanih,* 35.

44. Ibid., 54–56.

45. Ibid., 26–28.

46. Ahmad Shamlu, *Ida dar ayinih* (Tehran: Intisharat-i Nil, 1357/1978), 71.

47. From the poem *Dar in bunbast* [In This Dead End]; see Shamlu, *Taranah'ha-yi kuchik,* 34.

48. Ibid., 36.

49. Ahmad Shamlu, *Qugnus dar baran* (Tehran: Intisharat-i Nigah, 1372), 9–18.

50. The story of the comrade who fell fighting is a reference to the death of Ahmad Zaybarum in the poem "The Birth of the One Who Died Lovingly," Ahmad Shamlu, *Ibrahim dar atash* (Tehran Intisharat-i Zamanih, 1372/1993), 57. The silence of humanity in the face of injustice and its relation to God's presence is best articulated in "*Sukut-i adami fuqdan jahan va khudast*" in the poem "Isharati," dedicated to the painter Iran Darrudi (53).

51. Ahmad Shamlu, *Hava-yi tazih,* 8th ed. (Tehran: Intisharat-i Zamanah, 1372/1993), 324.

52. See poems "The Poem from the Edge of Solitude" and "Lonely," in Shamlu, *Hava-yi tazih,* 325, 329. For other examples in the same collection to gods' unhelpful or undesirable acts, see 214, 218, 285, 287, 307.

53. Ibid., 307.

54. See poems "Another," "I Am Not Alone," "Fountainhead," "Of Your Uncles," and "The Ghazel of the Last Solitude." Ibid., 199, 201, 206, 222, 281.

55. Shamlu, *Dar astanih,* 38.

56. Shamlu, *Hava-yi tazih,* 276–86.

57. Ibid., 248.

58. Shamlu, *Ida dar ayinih,* 80–82.

59. Ahmad Shamlu, *Qat'namih* (Tehran: Intisharat-i Murvarid, 1363/1984), 81–82.

60. Shamlu, *Ibrahim dar atash,* 15.

61. From the poem *Tikrar* [Repetition], see *Ida dar ayihih,* 45–48.

62. Shamlu, *Ibrahim dar atash,* 34–35.

63. For a reading of the poem "Tablet," in which Moses tries to enliven the ossified ritual of worship through new commandments, see Fatemeh Keshavarz, "The Call to Prayer from a Cypress Tree: Modernity and Redefining the Spiritual in Persian Poetry," *Religion and Literature* 29, no. 1 (Spring 1997): 23, 25.

64. Shamlu refrained from referring to Jesus as 'Isa to avoid similar connotations in the poem *Marg-i Nasiri* [Death of the Nazarene], which I discussed earlier, see Ahmad Shamlu, *Barguzidah-i ash'ar-i Ahmad Shamlu* (Tehran: Intisharat-i Katibah, 1336/1957), 183–86.

65. Ahmad Shamlu, *Madayih-i bi-salih* (Tehran: Intisharat-i Zamanih, 1379/2000), 109.

66. Ibid., 114.

67. From the poem *Ta shikufih-yi surkh-i yik pirahan* [Till the Red Blossom of a Shirt]; see Ahmad Shamlu, *Lahzih'ha va hamishih* (Tehran: Intisharat-i Nil, 1357/1978), 29.

68. Shamlu, *Madayih-i bi-salih,* 106.

69. Shamlu, *Hadith-i bi-gharari-yi Mahan,* 21–24.

70. Ibid., 24. The Qur'anic verse is the thirty-first in the sura *Al-Baqara* [The Cow].

71. *Dar astanih* [At the Threshold] gave its name to the collection; see Shamlu, *Dar astanih,* 17–24.

72. Ibid., 20.

73. "*Az jamadi murdam u nami shudam.*" Jalāl ad-Dīn Rūmī, *Masnavi,* ed. and trans. Reynold A. Nicholson, 8 vols. (London: Luzac, 1925–40), 3:3901

74. Qur'an 33:72. The verse from Hāfez reads "*Asiman bar-i amanat natavanist kashid / Qur'ah-yi fal bi-nam-i man-i divanah zadand*" [The heavens could not tolerate the burden of the "trust" / the game of chance selected a mad one like me], Hafiz, *Divan-i Khvajah Shams al-Din Muhammad Hafiz-i Shirazi,* Qudsi edn. (Tehran: Intisharat-i Pirastih, 1373/1994), 141.

75. Shamlu, *Dar astanih,* 23.

76. Ibid., 24.

EPILOGUE

1. Suhrab Sepehri, *Sida-yi pa-yi ab* [The Footsteps of Water], in *Hasht kitab* (Tehran: Kitab'khanah-'i Tahuri, 1358/1979), 291.

2. *Khusraw u Shirin* is a celebrated medieval romantic epic; see Fatemeh Keshavarz, "Taming of the Unruly King: Shirin as Lover and Educator in Nizami's *Khusraw u Shirin,*" in *Women in Iran from the Rise of Islam to 1800,* ed. Guiti Nashat and Lois Beck (Urbana: University of Illinois Press, forthcoming).

3. See pp. 107–9, above.

4. "Secular" is not the only such noncategory. Pascal Boyer reminds us that the terms *animistic* or *tribal* religion are often used by anthropologists to describe a vast range of practices worldwide that do not fit in the categories of "great religions" or "established denominations." Boyer goes on to say that these terms mean virtually nothing. "They just stand for the stuff we cannot put in any other category; we might as well call these people's religions miscellaneous." *Religion Explained: The Evolutionary Origins of Religious Thought* (New York: Basic Books, 2001), 6.

5. Georgia Warnke, *Gadamer. Hermeneutics, Tradition, and Reason* (Stanford, Calif.: Stanford University Press, 1987), 151.

6. The image is from *Ida dar ayinih,* one of Shamlu's major collections (Tehran: Intisharat-i Nil, 1357/1978), 99.

7. Amin Qaysari and 'Ali Musavi Garmarudi are among the poets who came to prominence after the 1979 revolution. "Revolution and Literature: The Rise of the Islamic Literary Movement after the 1979 Revolution," in Kamran Talattof, *The Politics of Writing in Iran: A History of Modern Persian Literature* (Syracuse, N.Y.: Syracuse University Press, 2000), 108–34.

8. A fine example among these works is Farzaneh Milani's *Veils and Words: The Emerging Voices of Iranian Women Writers* (Syracuse, N.Y.: Syracuse University Press, 1992).

9. In his comprehensive survey of the "Sacred," Veikok Anttonen suggested three defining features: set-apartness, life-giving quality, and involving rituals. *Guide to the Study of Religion,* ed. Willi Braun and Russell T. McCutcheon (London: Cassel, 2000), 271.

10. From the poem "Frontier Walls," Forugh Farrokhzad, *Bride of Acacias: Selected Poems of Forugh Farrokhzad,* trans. Jascha Kessler with Amin Banani (New York: Caravan Books, 1982), 40.

11. Shamlu, *Bagh-i Ayinih,* [The Garden of Mirrors] (Tehran: Intisharat-i Murvarid, 1376/1997), 126.

Index